Amala's Blade™

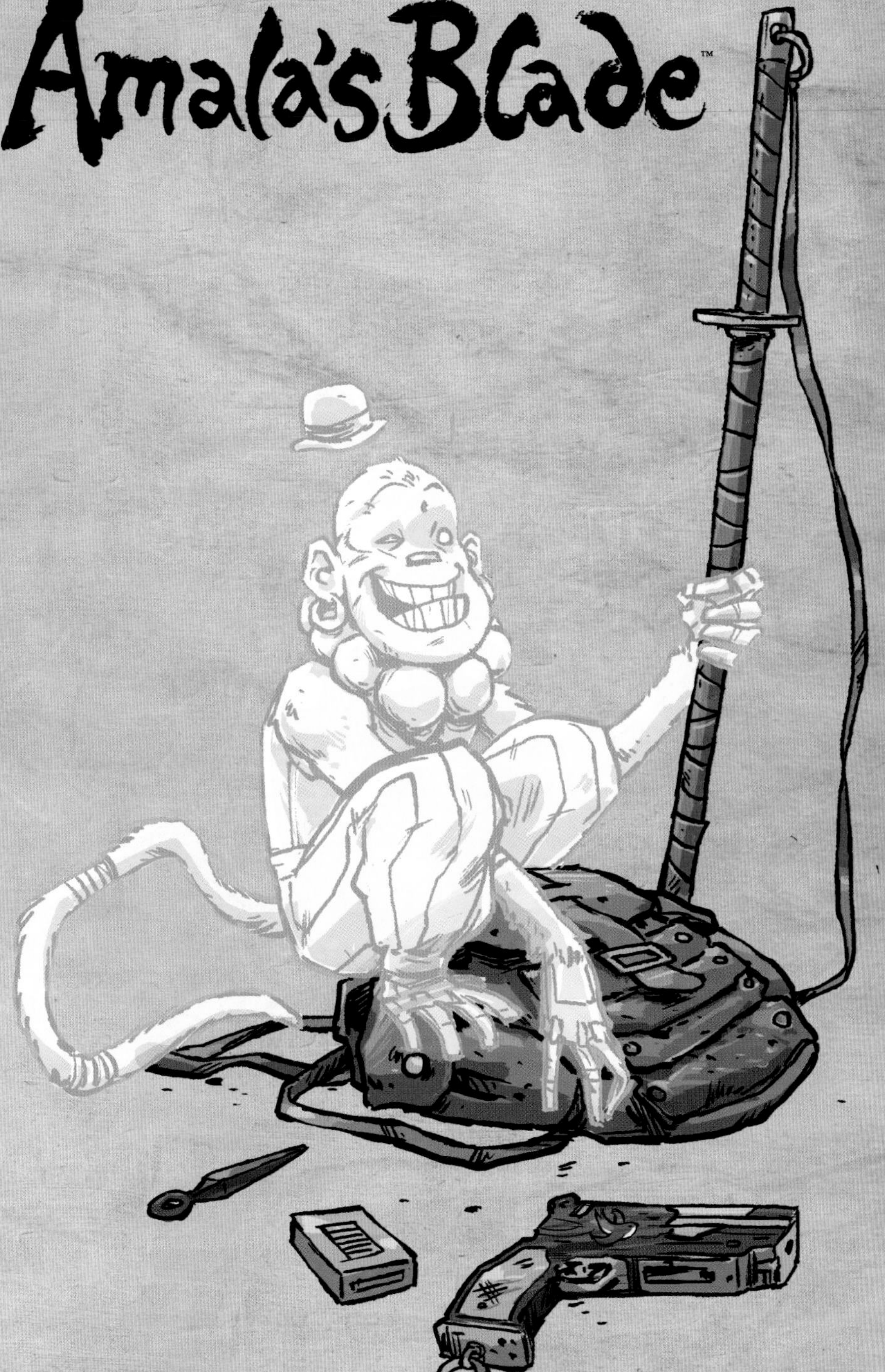

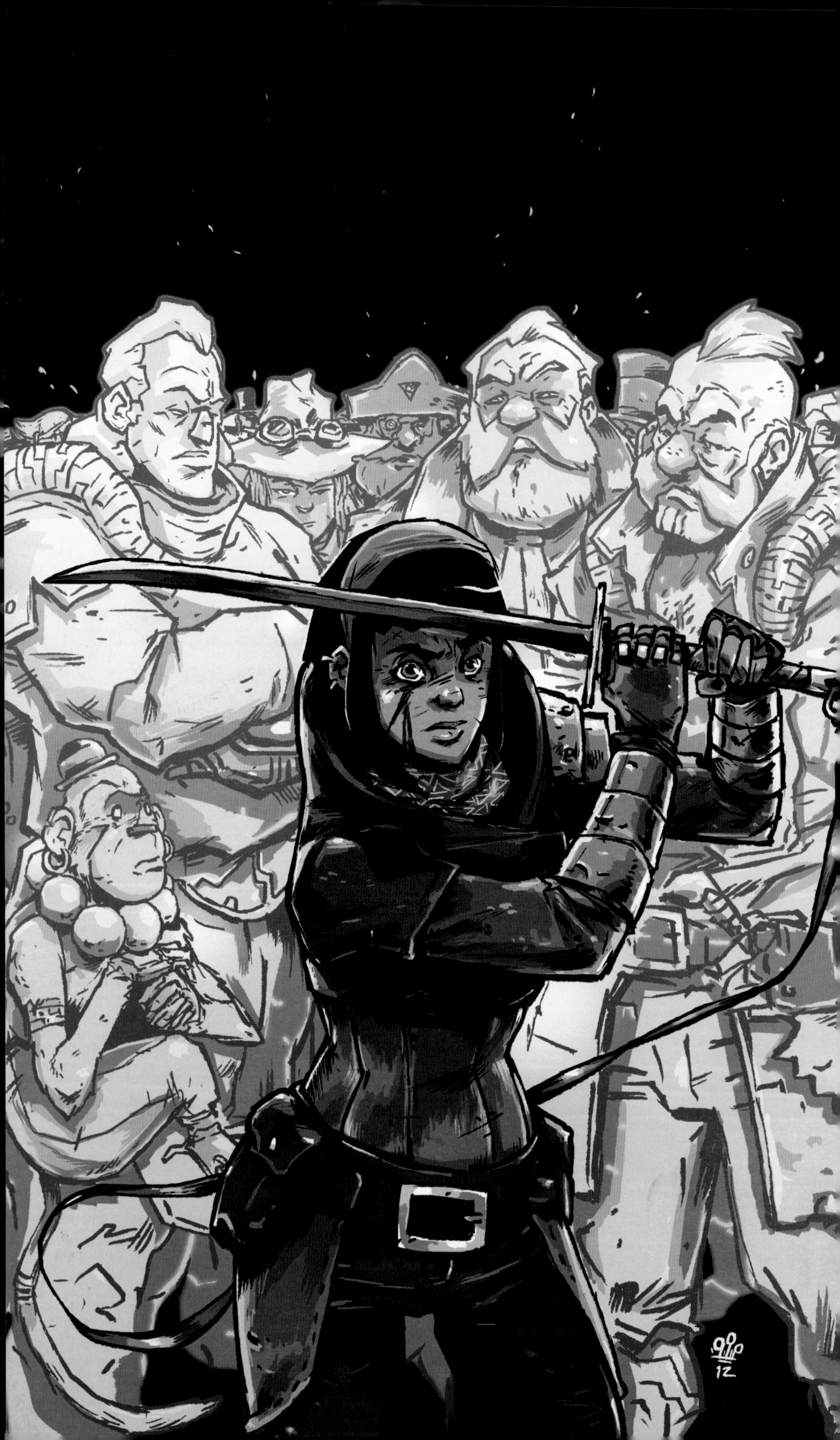

SPIRITS OF NAAMARON

story and lettering
STEVE HORTON

art and coloring
MICHAEL DIALYNAS

DARK HORSE BOOKS

publisher
MIKE RICHARDSON

editor
CHRIS WARNER

assistant editor
SHANTEL LaROCQUE

production
CHRISTIANNE GOUDREAU

designer
JUSTIN COUCH

special thanks to
GUY DAVIS and **DAVE STEWART**

DARK HORSE BOOKS
a division of Dark Horse Comics, Inc.
10956 SE Main Street
Milwaukie, OR 97222

DarkHorse.com

To find a comics shop in your area,
call the Comic Shop Locator Service
toll-free at 1-888-266-4226.

International Licensing: (503) 905-2377

First edition: January 2014
ISBN 978-1-61655-332-6
10 9 8 7 6 5 4 3 2 1
Printed in China.

AMALA'S BLADE: SPIRITS OF NAAMARON

This volume collects issues zero through four of the Dark Horse comic-book series *Amala's Blade*.

Mike Richardson President and Publisher · *Neil Hankerson* Executive Vice President · *Tom Weddle* Chief Financial Officer · *Randy Stradley* Vice President of Publishing · *Michael Martens* Vice President of Book Trade Sales · *Anita Nelson* Vice President of Business Affairs · *Scott Allie* Editor in Chief · *Matt Parkinson* Vice President of Marketing · *David Scroggy* Vice President of Product Development · *Dale LaFountain* Vice President of Information Technology · *Darlene Vogel* Senior Director of Print, Design, and Production · *Ken Lizzi* General Counsel · *Davey Estrada* Editorial Director · *Chris Warner* Senior Books Editor · *Diana Schutz* Executive Editor · *Cary Grazzini* Director of Print and Development · *Lia Ribacchi* Art Director · *Cara Niece* Director of Scheduling · *Tim Wiesch* Director of International Licensing · *Mark Bernardi* Director of Digital Publishing

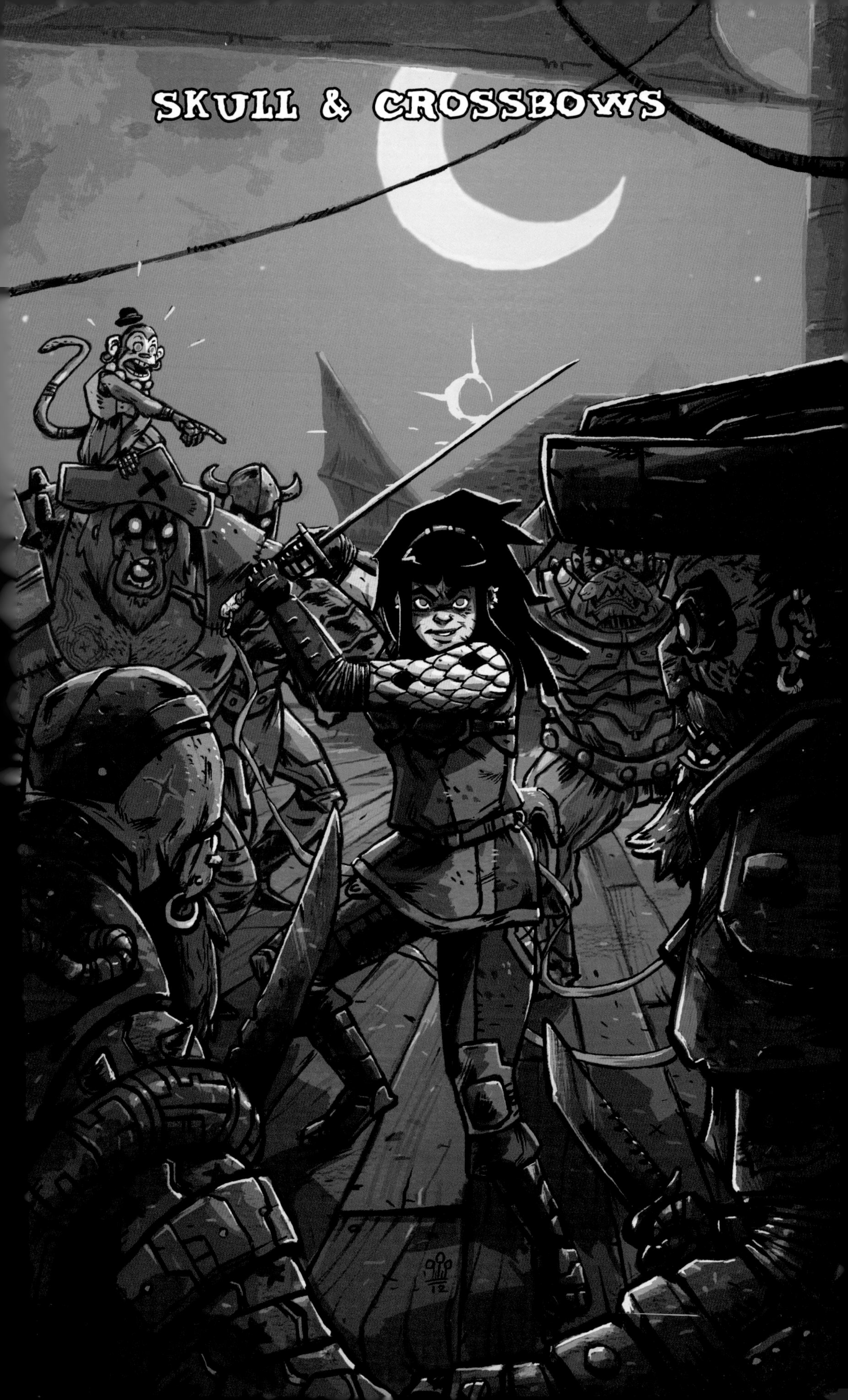
SKULL & CROSSBOWS

"GONNA HAVE TO GET A NEW *MONKEY*..."

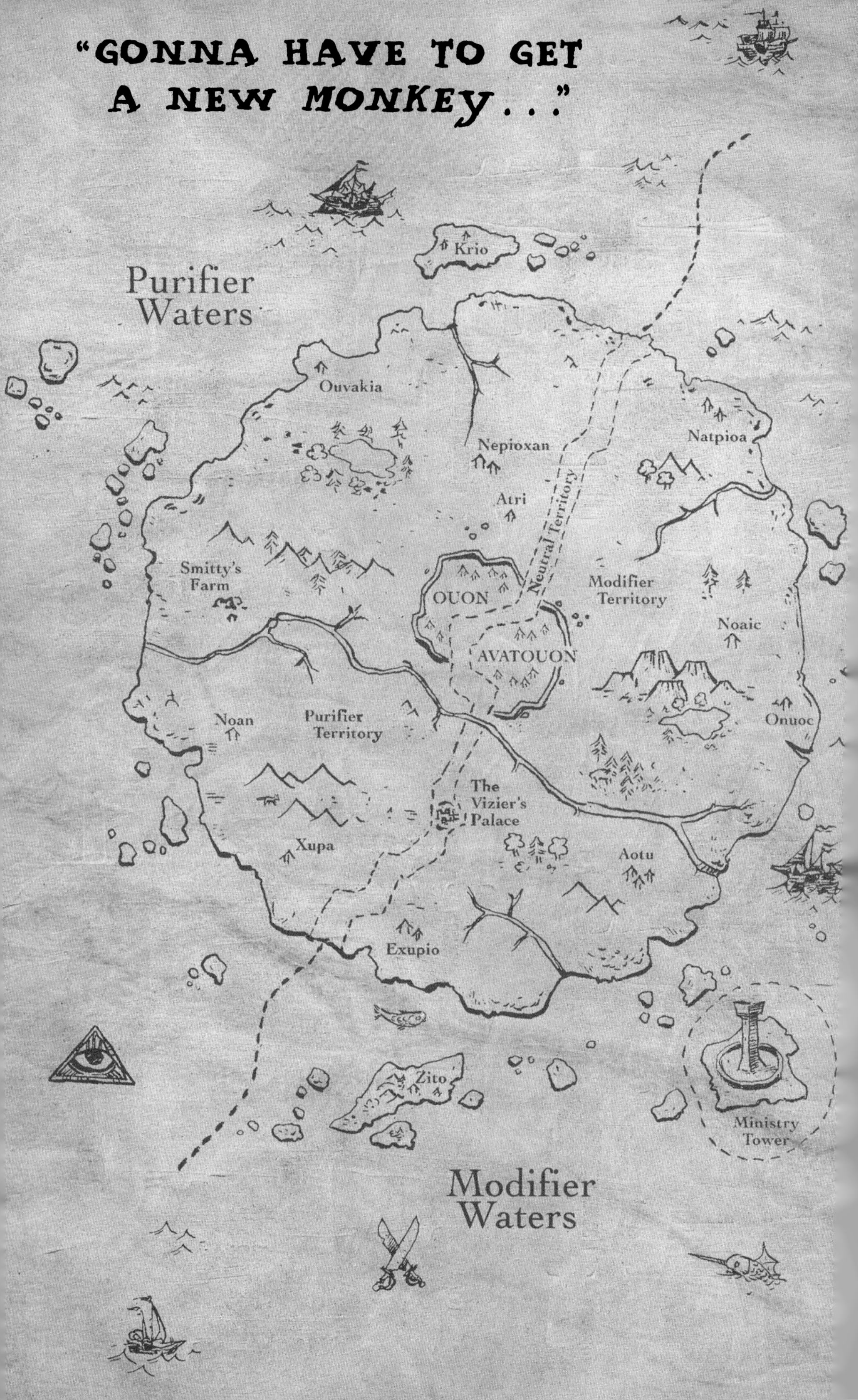

Krio
Purifier Waters
Ouvakia
Nepioxan
Natpioa
Atri
Neutral Territory
Smitty's Farm
OUON
Modifier Territory
Noaic
AVATOUON
Noan
Purifier Territory
Onuoc
The Vizier's Palace
Xupa
Aotu
Exupio
Zito
Ministry Tower
Modifier Waters

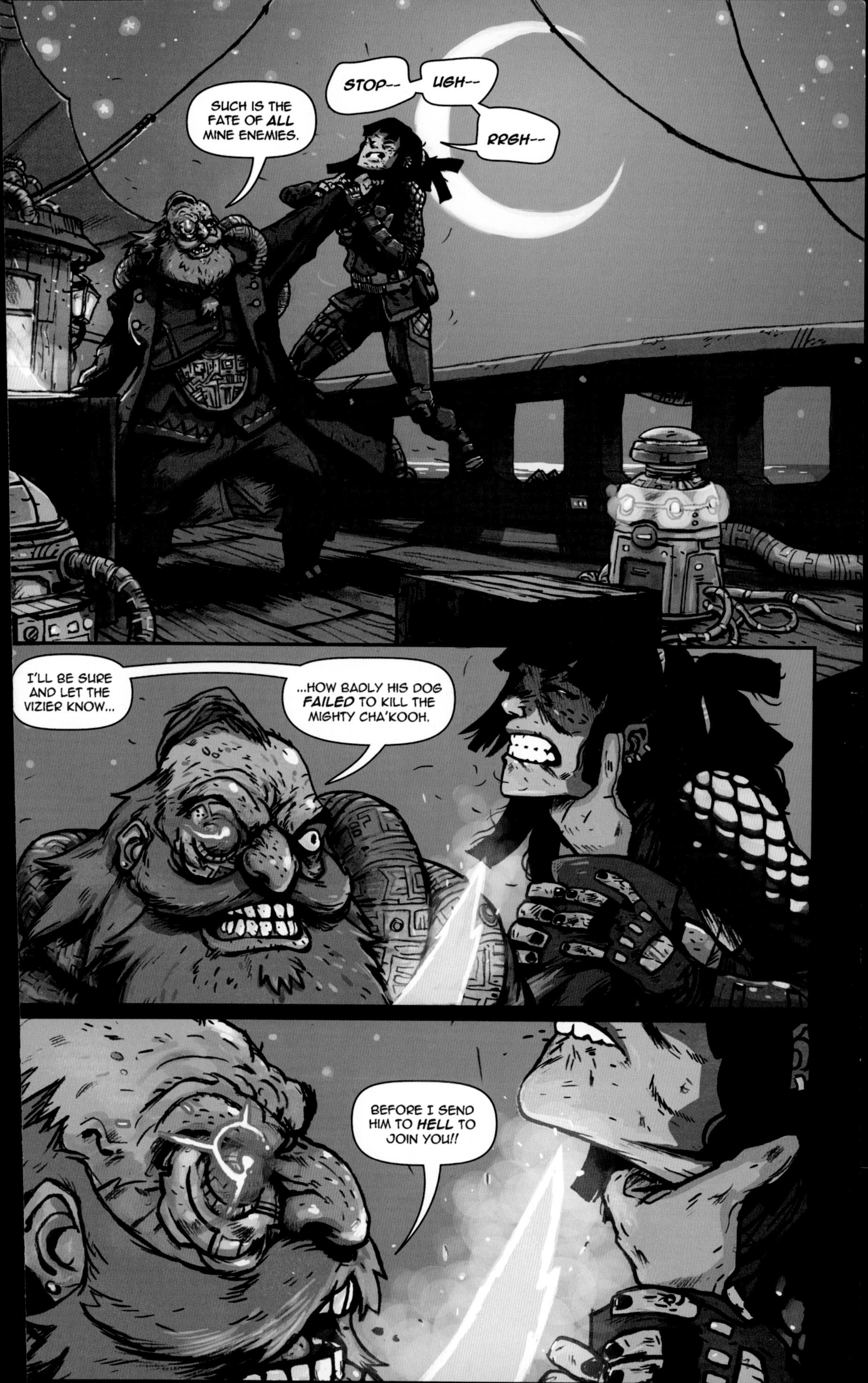
SUCH IS THE FATE OF ALL MINE ENEMIES.
STOP--
UGH--
RRGH--
I'LL BE SURE AND LET THE VIZIER KNOW...
...HOW BADLY HIS DOG FAILED TO KILL THE MIGHTY CHA'KOOH.
BEFORE I SEND HIM TO HELL TO JOIN YOU!!

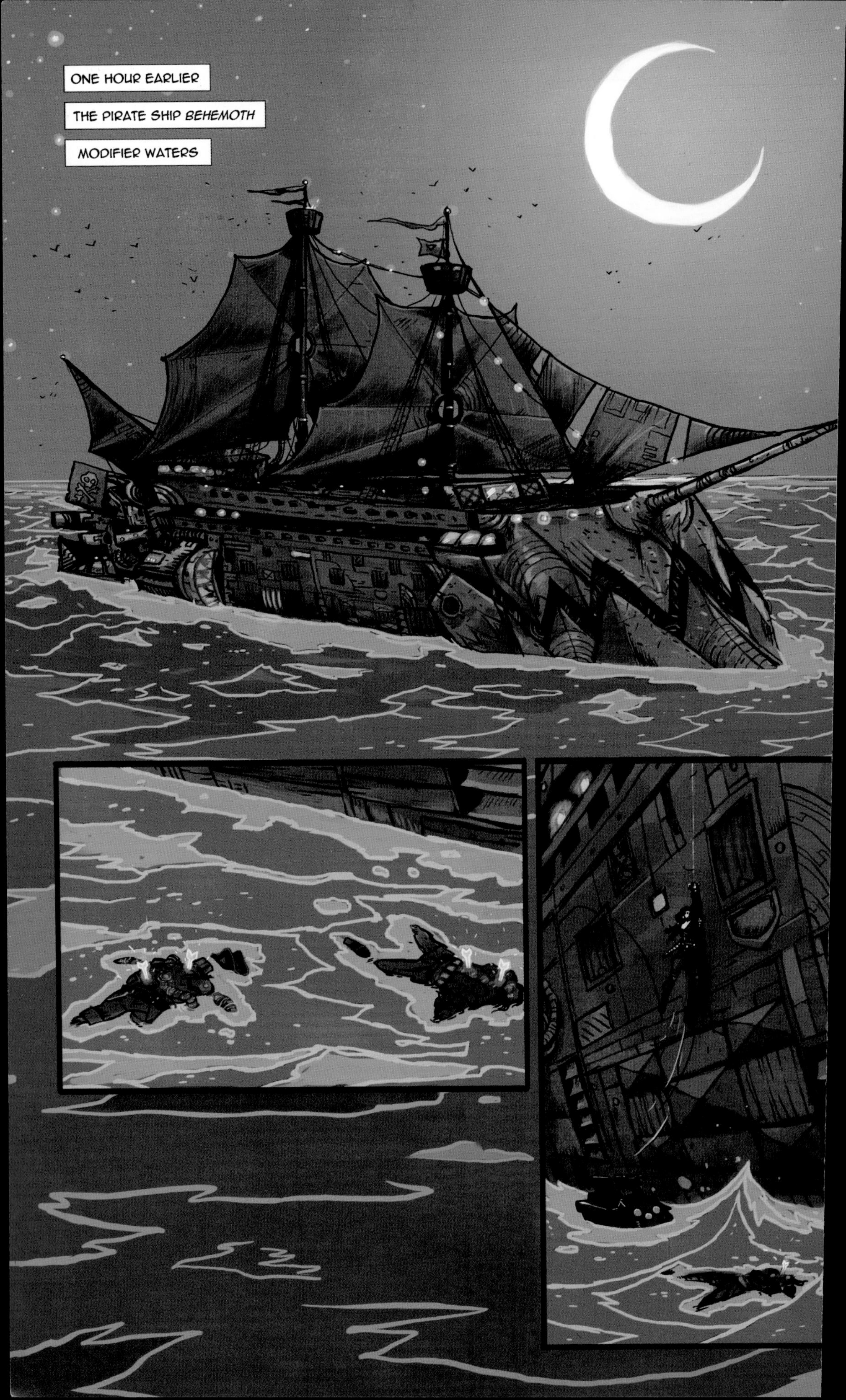
ONE HOUR EARLIER
THE PIRATE SHIP BEHEMOTH
MODIFIER WATERS

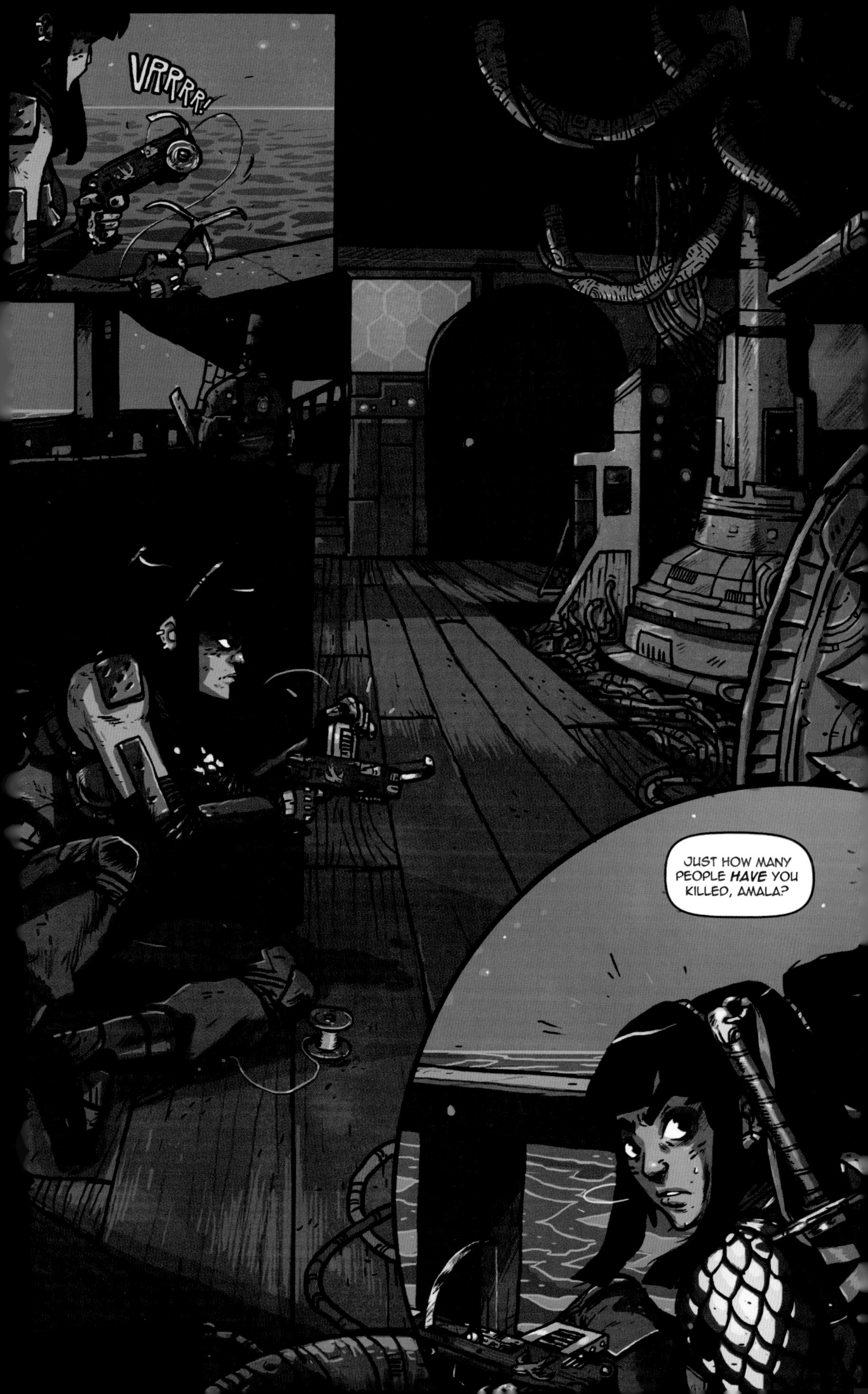
VRRRR!
JUST HOW MANY PEOPLE **HAVE** YOU KILLED, AMALA?

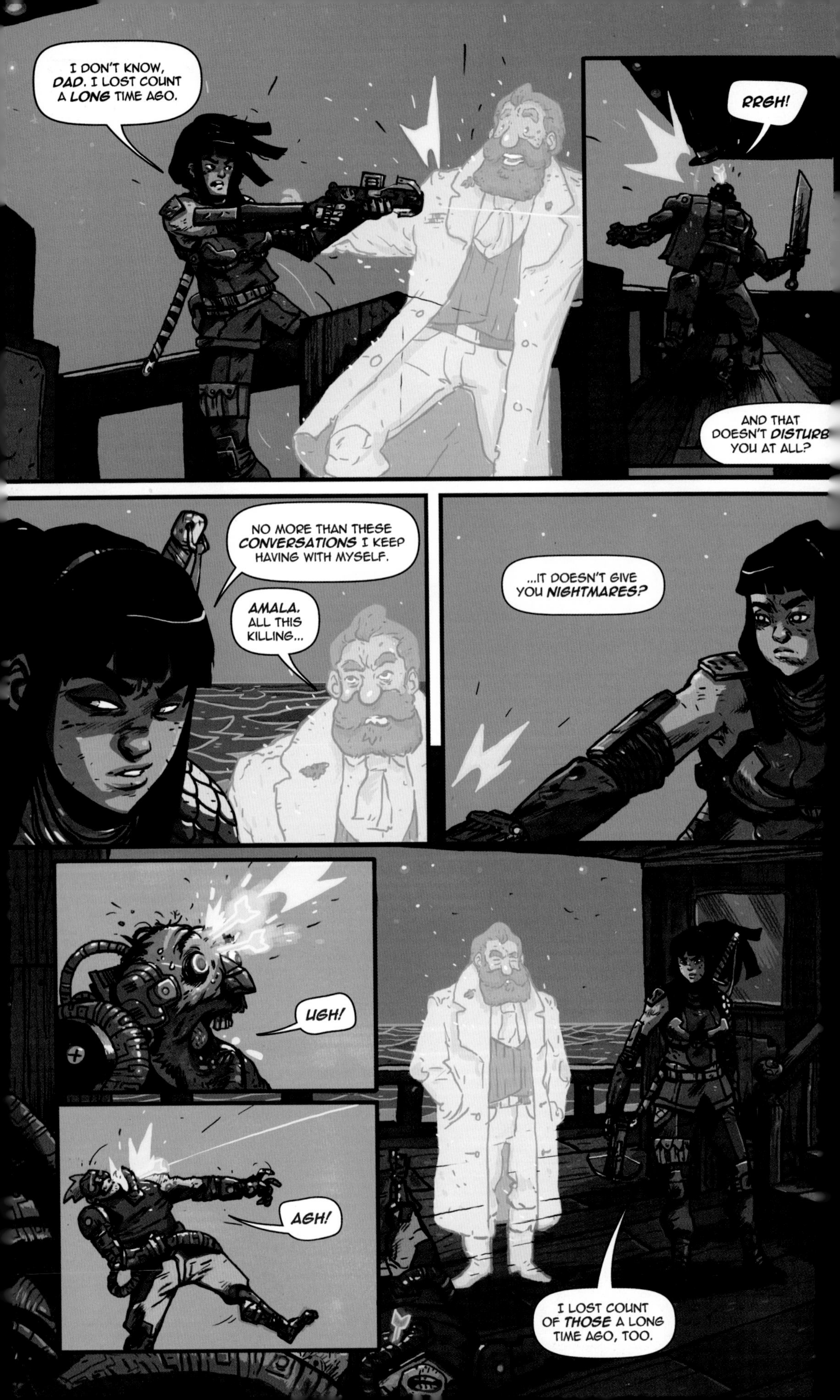
I DON'T KNOW, DAD. I LOST COUNT A LONG TIME AGO.
RRGH!
AND THAT DOESN'T DISTURB YOU AT ALL?
NO MORE THAN THESE CONVERSATIONS I KEEP HAVING WITH MYSELF.
AMALA. ALL THIS KILLING...
...IT DOESN'T GIVE YOU NIGHTMARES?
UGH!
AGH!
I LOST COUNT OF THOSE A LONG TIME AGO, TOO.

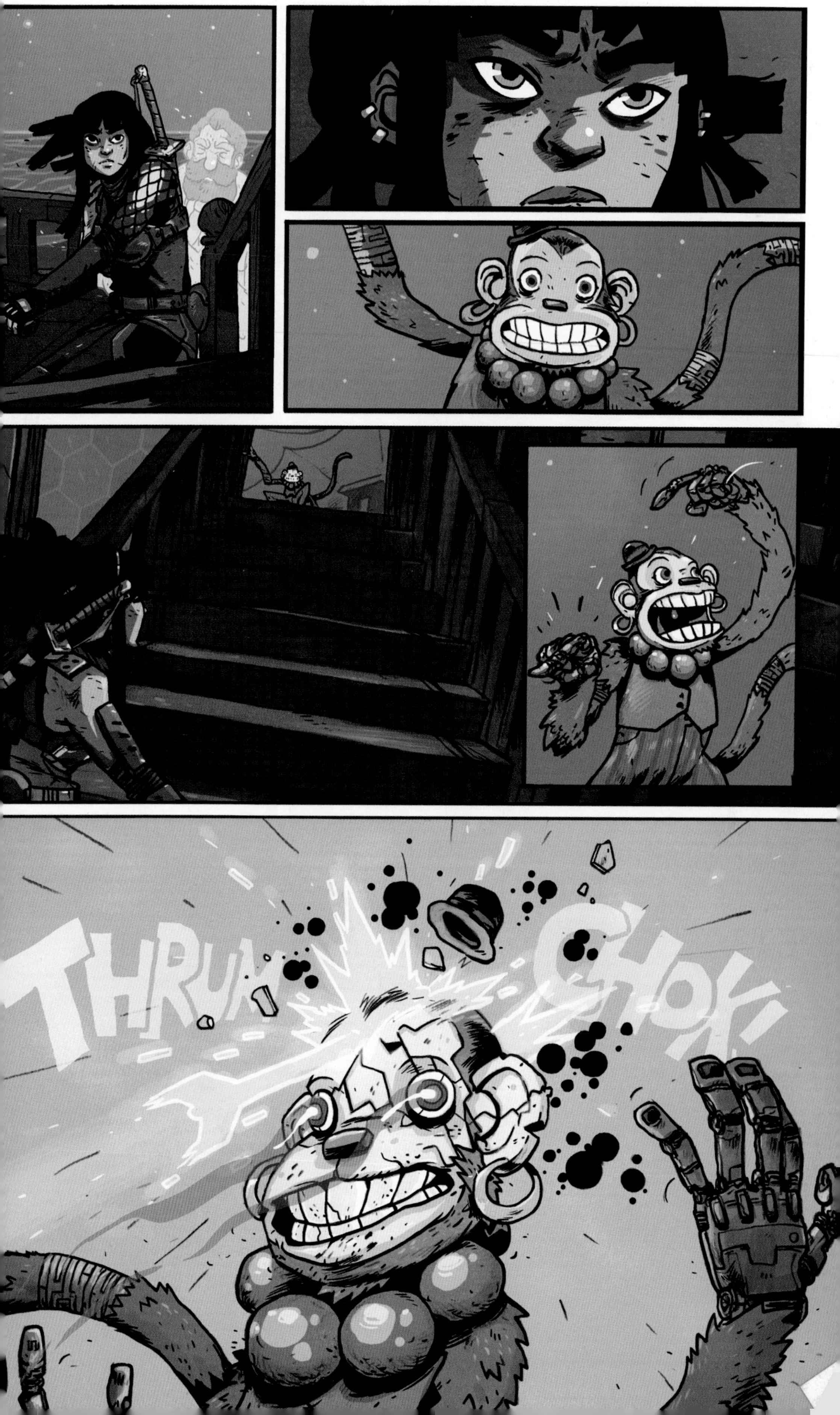
THRUM
CHOK!

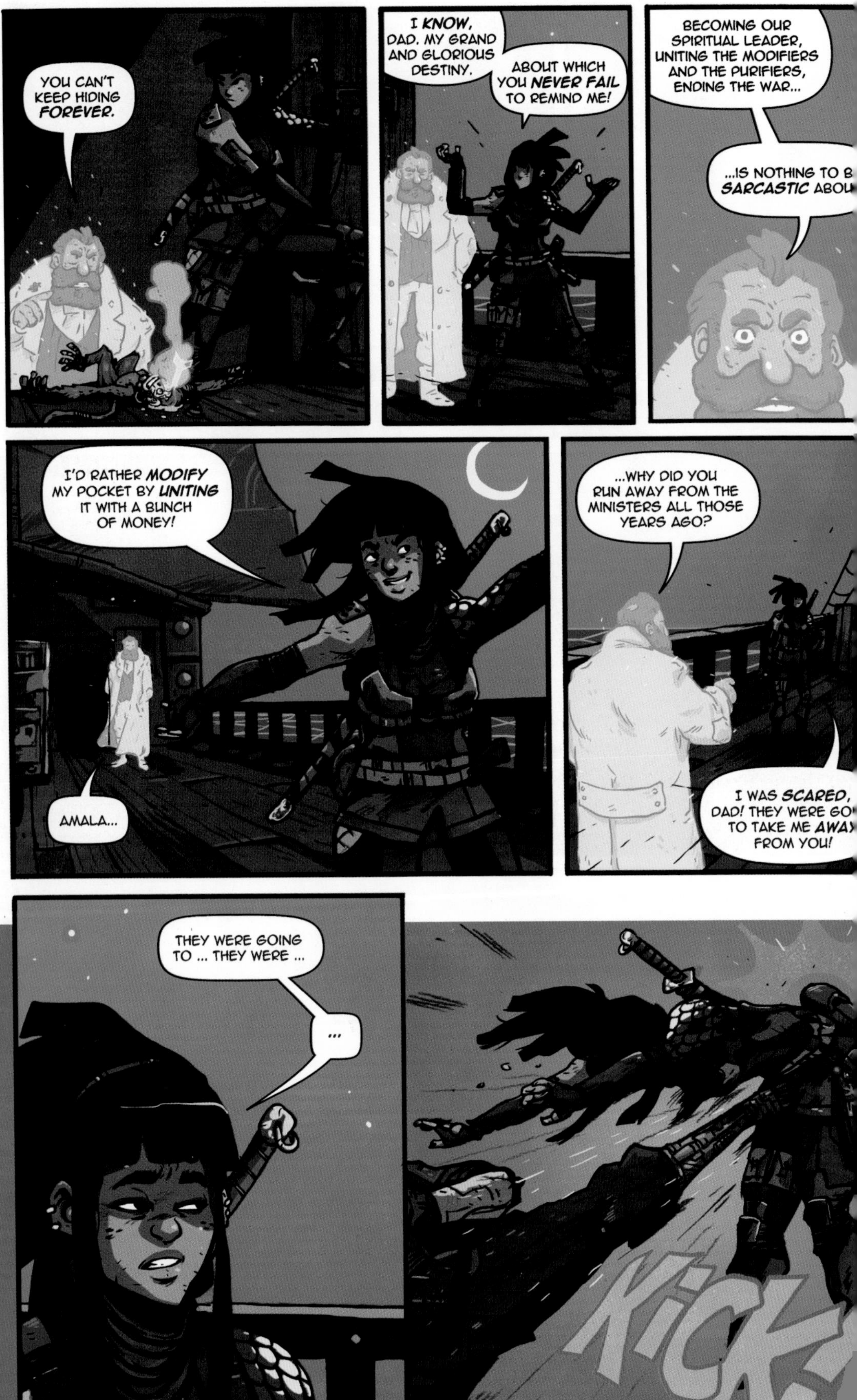

YOU CAN'T KEEP HIDING FOREVER.
I KNOW, DAD. MY GRAND AND GLORIOUS DESTINY.
ABOUT WHICH YOU NEVER FAIL TO REMIND ME!
BECOMING OUR SPIRITUAL LEADER, UNITING THE MODIFIERS AND THE PURIFIERS, ENDING THE WAR...
...IS NOTHING TO B
SARCASTIC ABOU
I'D RATHER MODIFY MY POCKET BY UNITING IT WITH A BUNCH OF MONEY!
AMALA...
...WHY DID YOU RUN AWAY FROM THE MINISTERS ALL THOSE YEARS AGO?
I WAS SCARED, DAD! THEY WERE GO
TO TAKE ME AWA
FROM YOU!
THEY WERE GOING TO ... THEY WERE ...
...
KICK

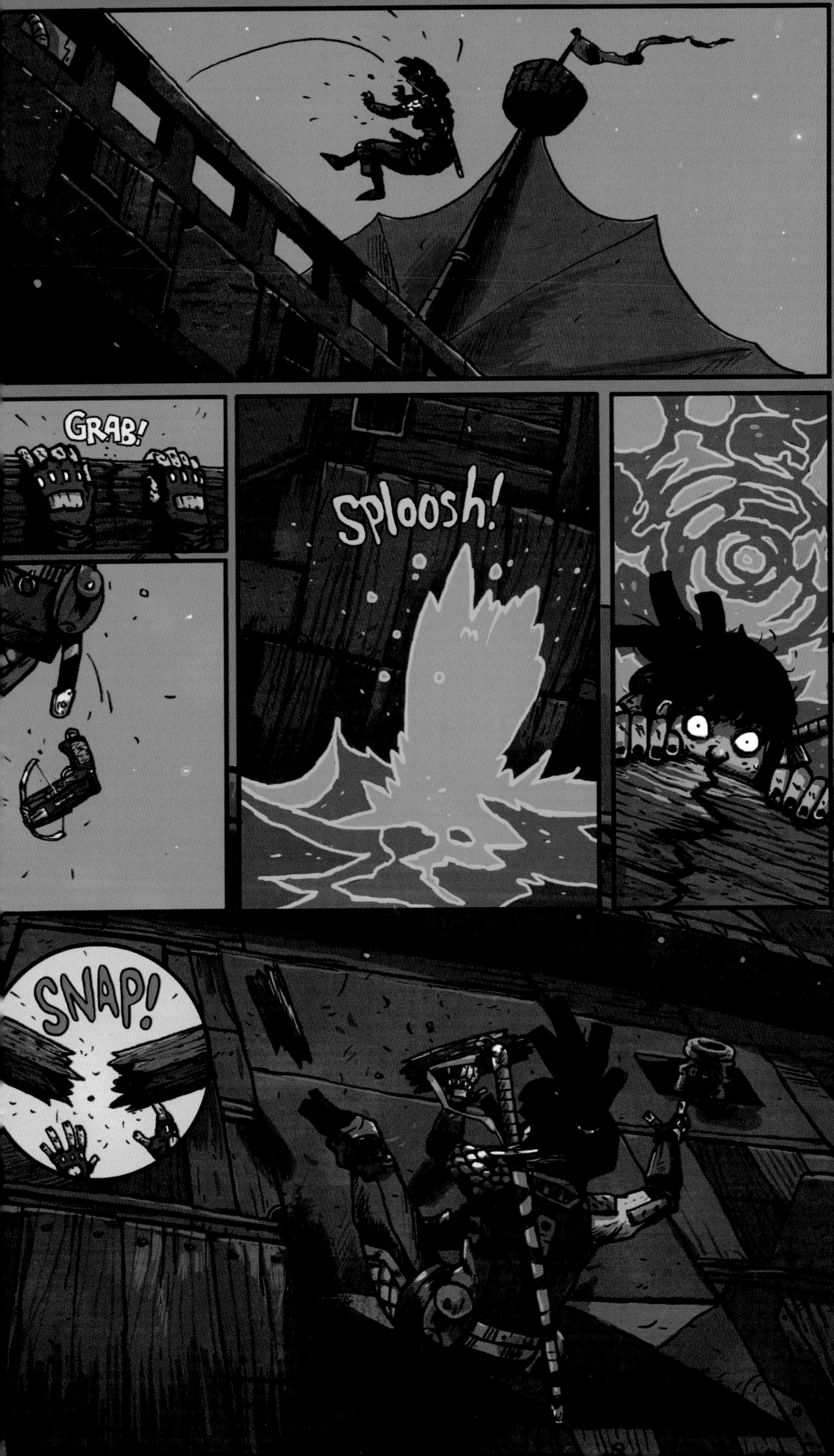
GRAB!
SPLOOSH!
SNAP!

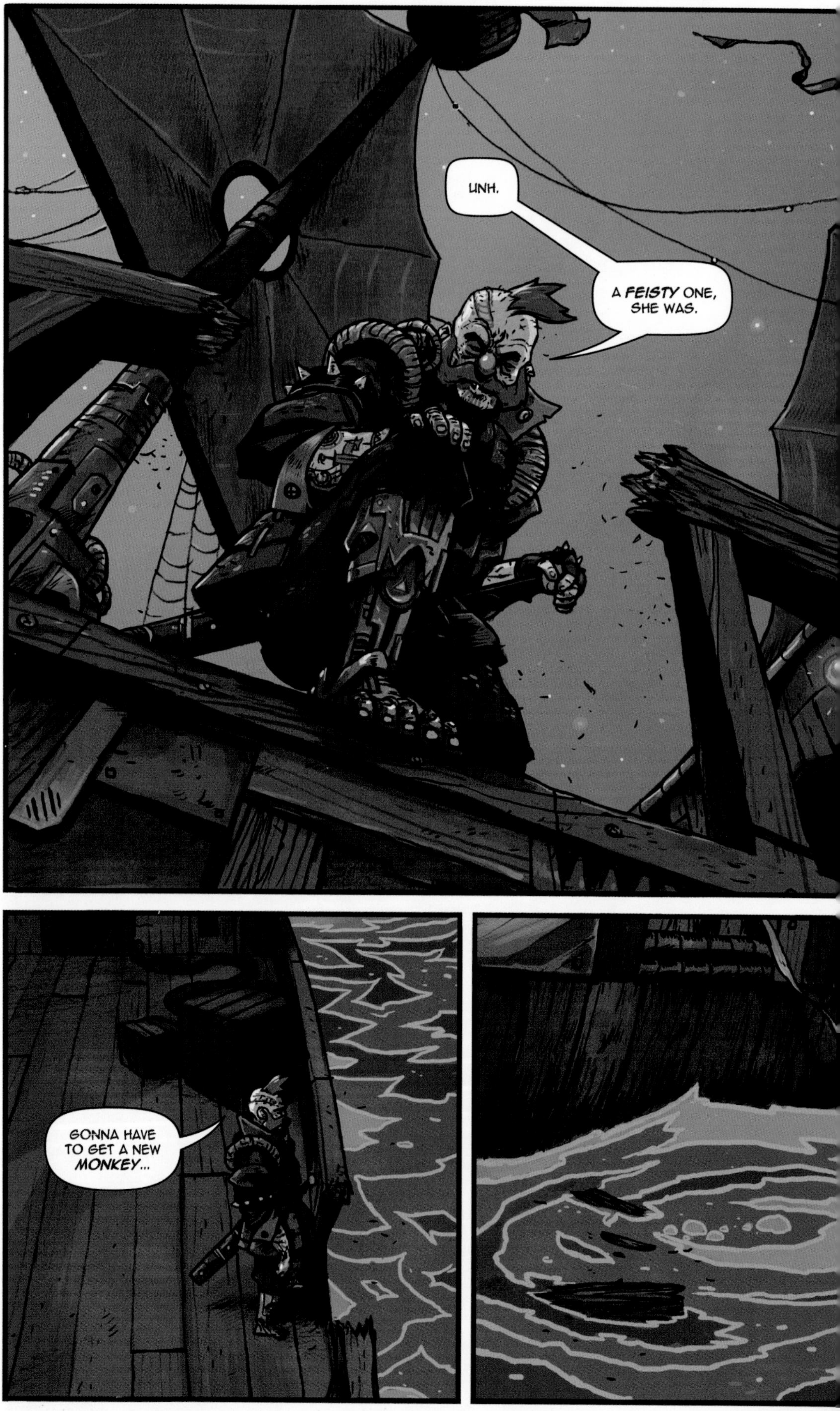
UNH.
A FEISTY ONE, SHE WAS.
GONNA HAVE TO GET A NEW MONKEY...

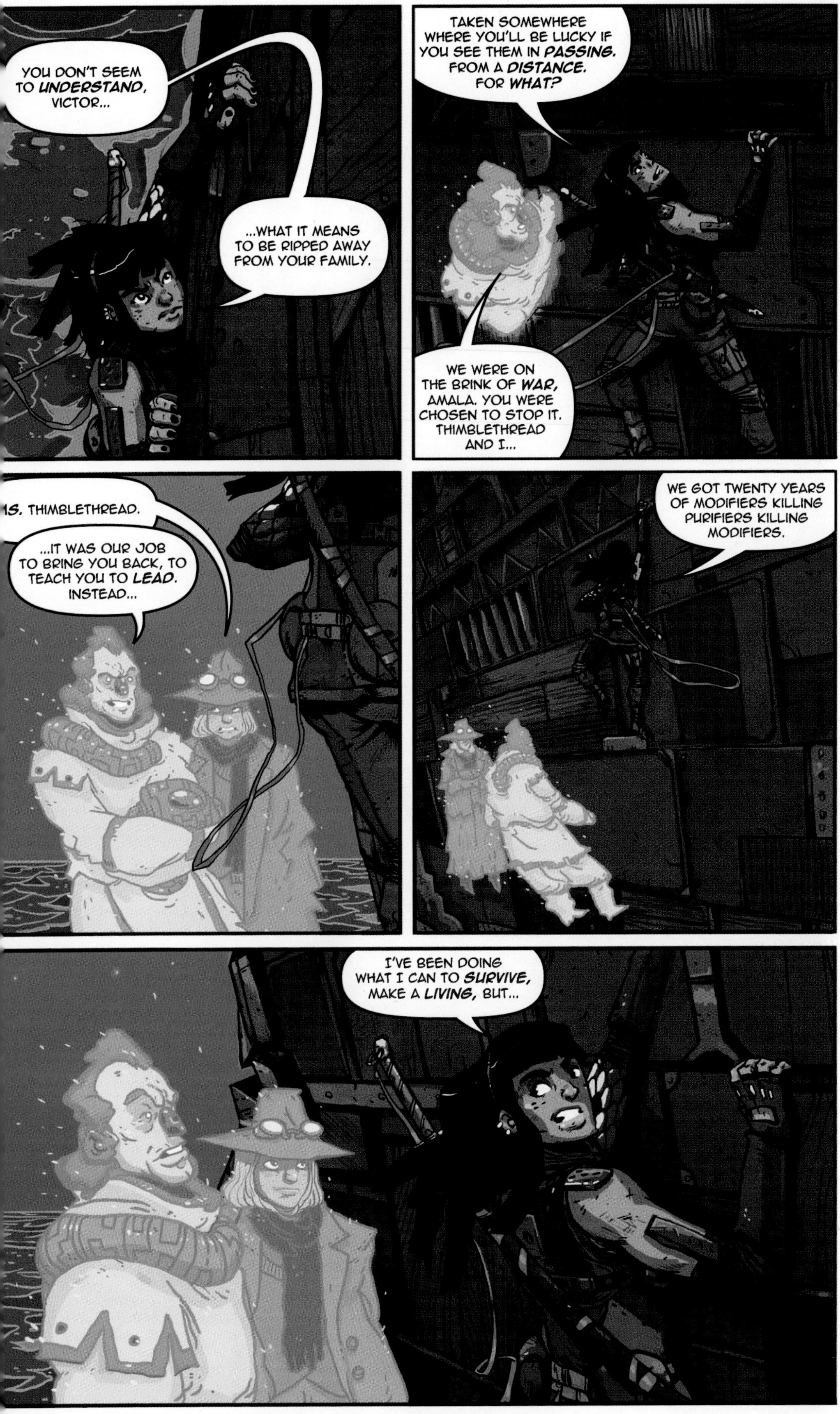
YOU DON'T SEEM TO UNDERSTAND, VICTOR...
...WHAT IT MEANS TO BE RIPPED AWAY FROM YOUR FAMILY.
TAKEN SOMEWHERE WHERE YOU'LL BE LUCKY IF YOU SEE THEM IN PASSING. FROM A DISTANCE. FOR WHAT?
WE WERE ON THE BRINK OF WAR, AMALA. YOU WERE CHOSEN TO STOP IT. THIMBLETHREAD AND I...
IS. THIMBLETHREAD.
...IT WAS OUR JOB TO BRING YOU BACK, TO TEACH YOU TO LEAD. INSTEAD...
WE GOT TWENTY YEARS OF MODIFIERS KILLING PURIFIERS KILLING MODIFIERS.
I'VE BEEN DOING WHAT I CAN TO SURVIVE, MAKE A LIVING, BUT...

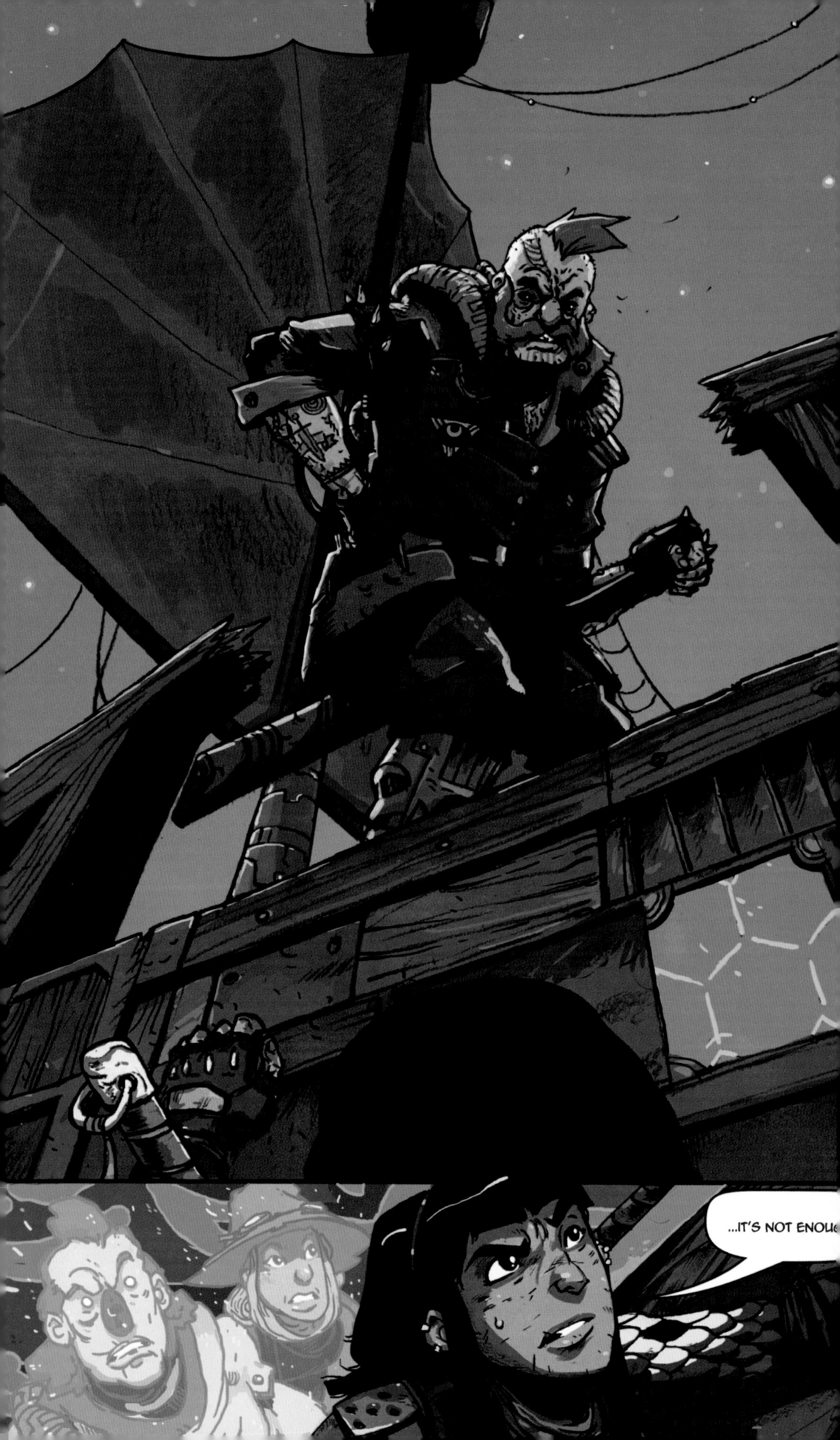
...IT'S NOT ENOU

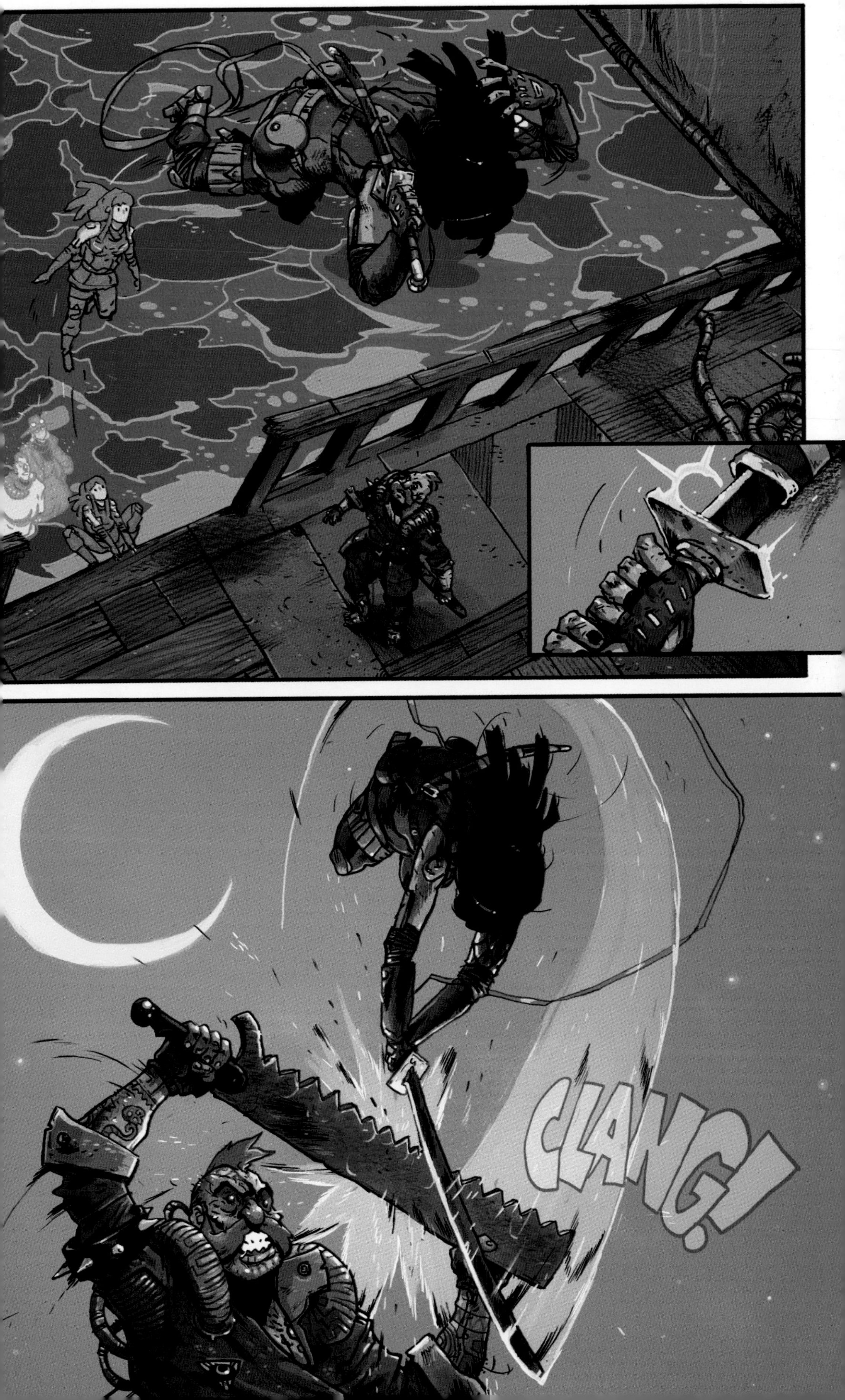
CLANG!

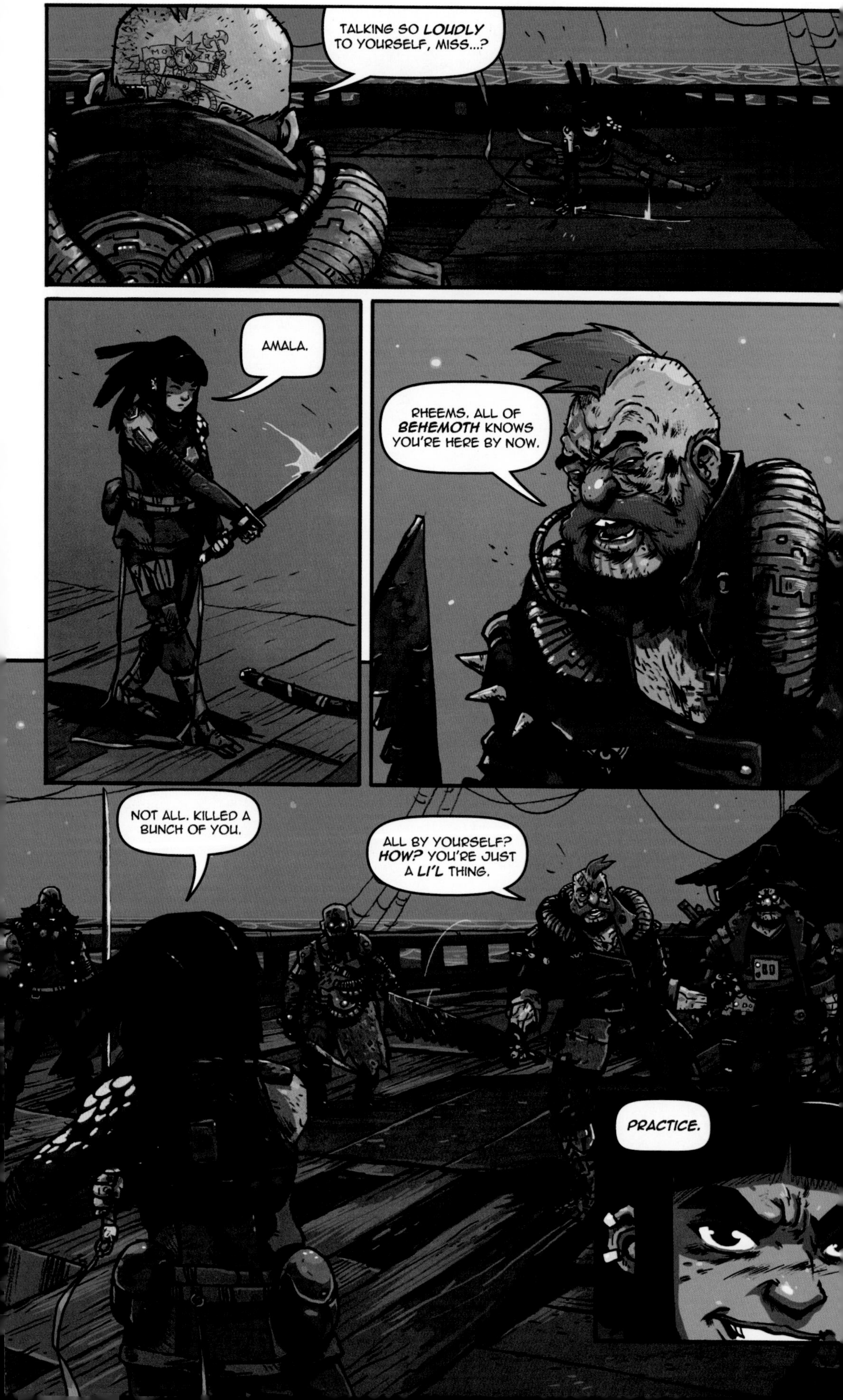
TALKING SO LOUDLY TO YOURSELF, MISS...?
AMALA.
RHEEMS. ALL OF BEHEMOTH KNOWS YOU'RE HERE BY NOW.
NOT ALL. KILLED A BUNCH OF YOU.
ALL BY YOURSELF? HOW? YOU'RE JUST A LI'L THING.
PRACTICE.

KICK!

THE *VIZIER* HIRED YOU, EH?

OOF!

I'VE HEARD TALES OF A NEW ASSASSIN. SOMEONE *DIFFERENT!*

I'M NOT EXACTLY NEW. HE'S LETTING WORD GET OUT.

AAAAHH!

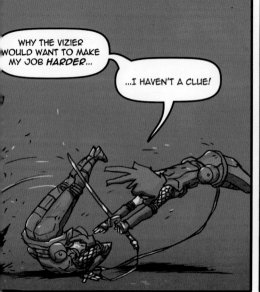

WHY THE VIZIER WOULD WANT TO MAKE MY JOB *HARDER*...

...I HAVEN'T A CLUE!

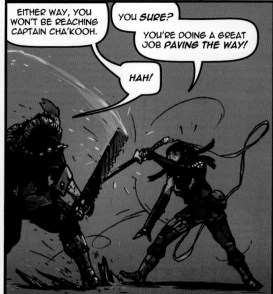

EITHER WAY, YOU WON'T BE REACHING CAPTAIN CHA'KOOH.

YOU *SURE?*

YOU'RE DOING A GREAT JOB *PAVING THE WAY!*

HAH!

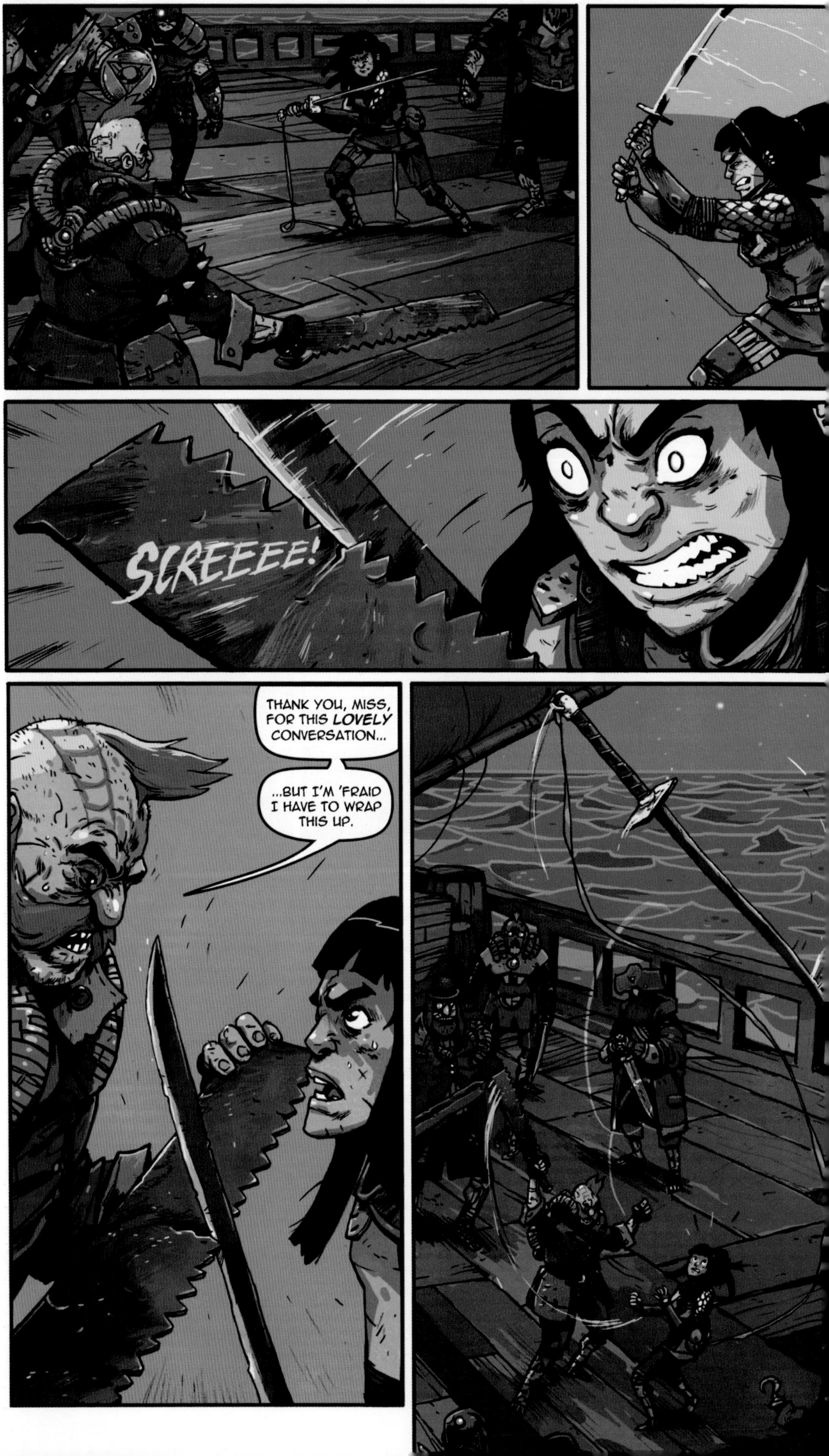
SCREEEE!
THANK YOU, MISS, FOR THIS LOVELY CONVERSATION...
...BUT I'M 'FRAID I HAVE TO WRAP THIS UP.

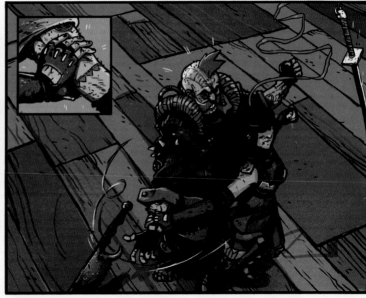

OW'S THAT FOR
RAPPING IT UP?

SHOULD I TIE
A BOW ON IT?

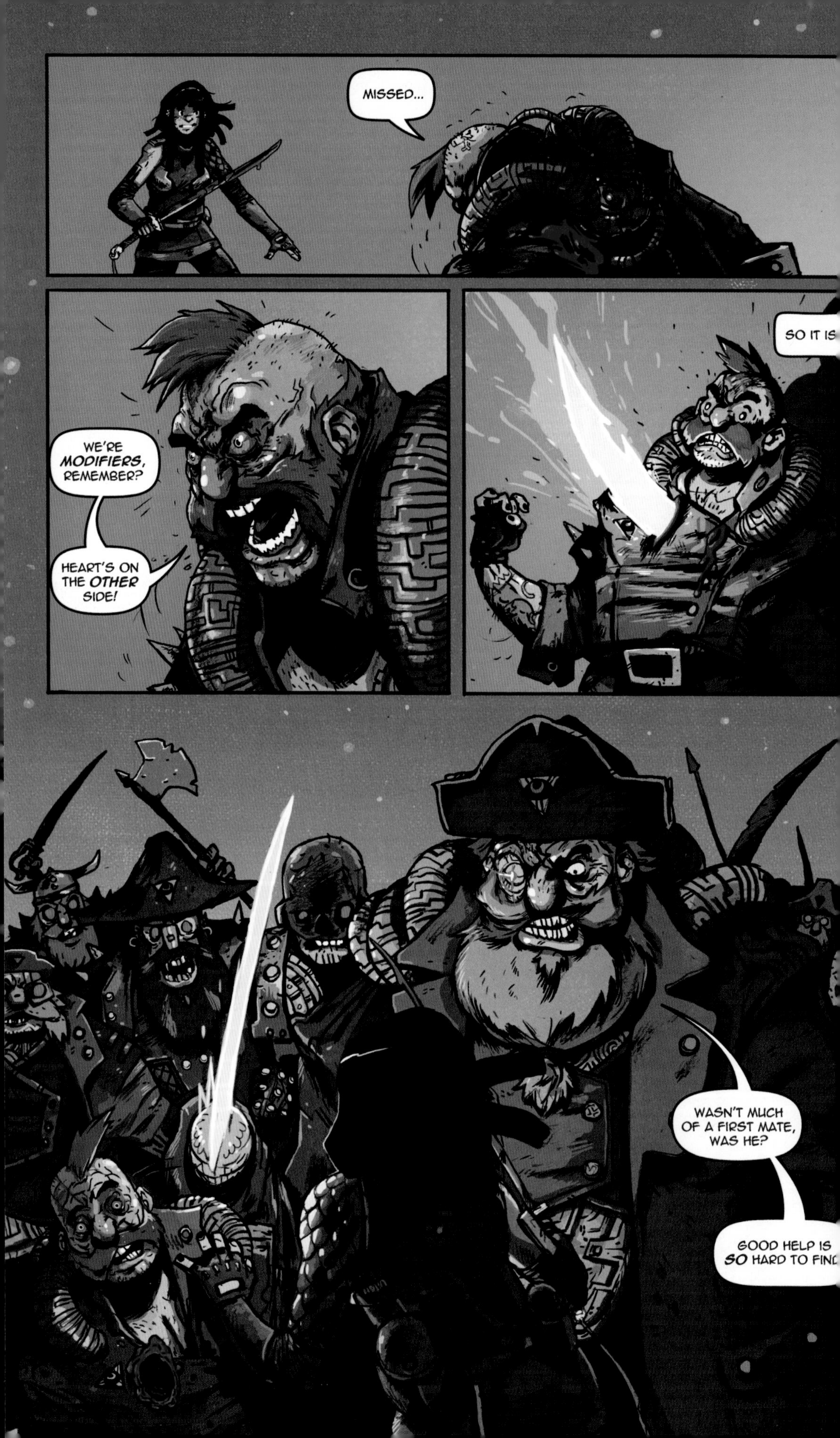
MISSED...
WE'RE *MODIFIERS*, REMEMBER?
HEART'S ON THE *OTHER* SIDE!
SO IT IS
WASN'T MUCH OF A FIRST MATE, WAS HE?
GOOD HELP IS *SO* HARD TO FIND

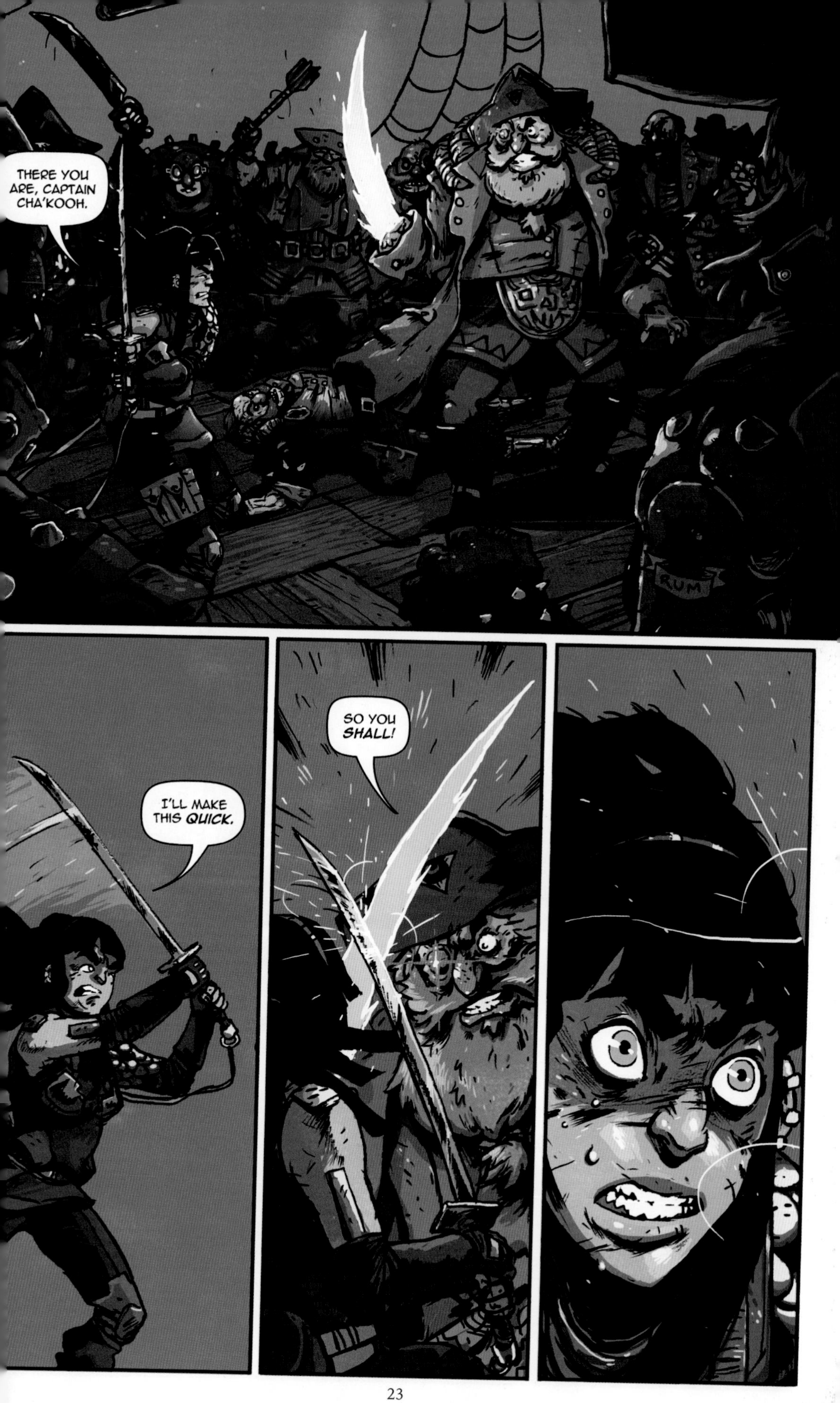
THERE YOU ARE, CAPTAIN CHA'KOOH.
RUM
I'LL MAKE THIS QUICK.
SO YOU SHALL!

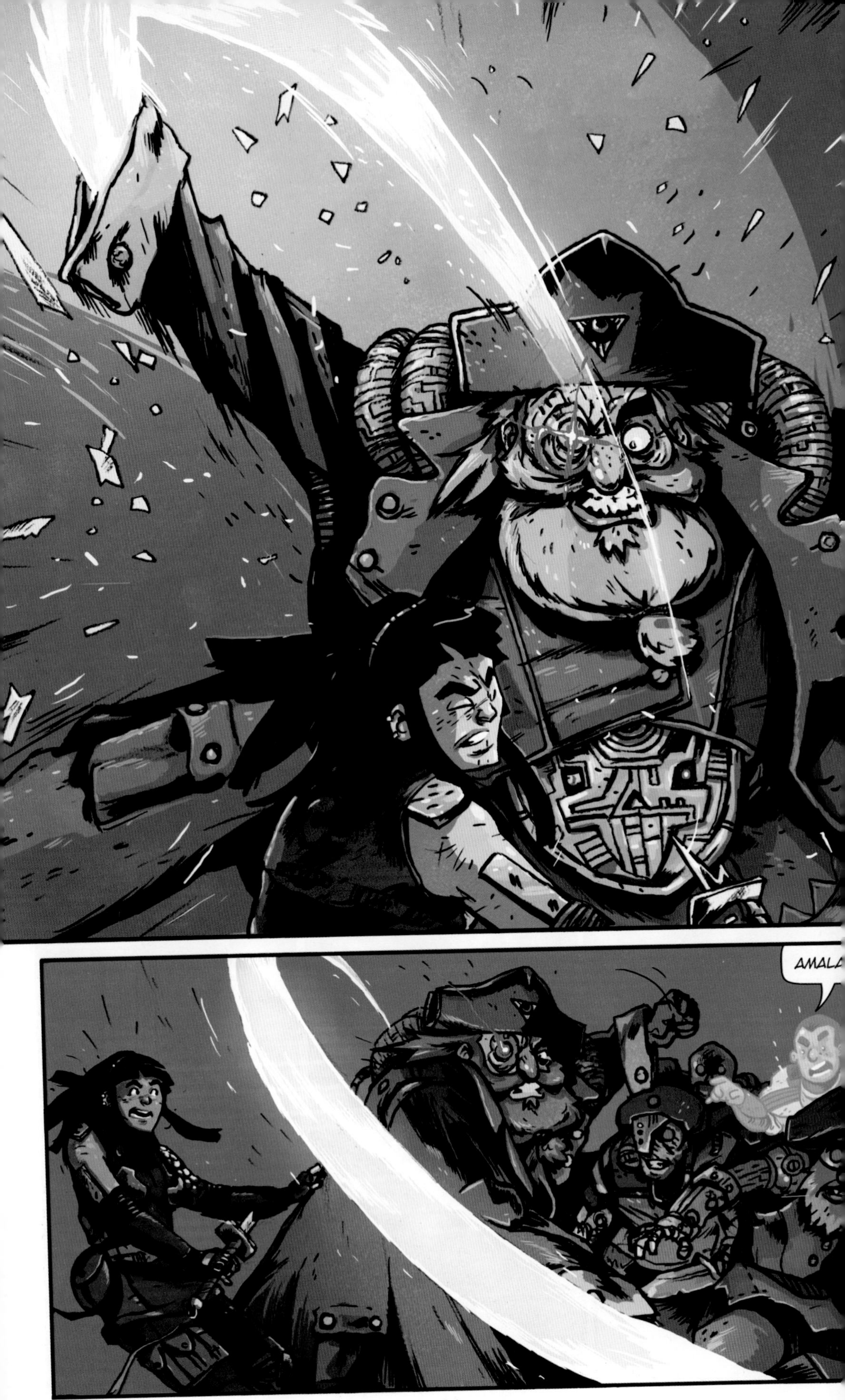
AMALA

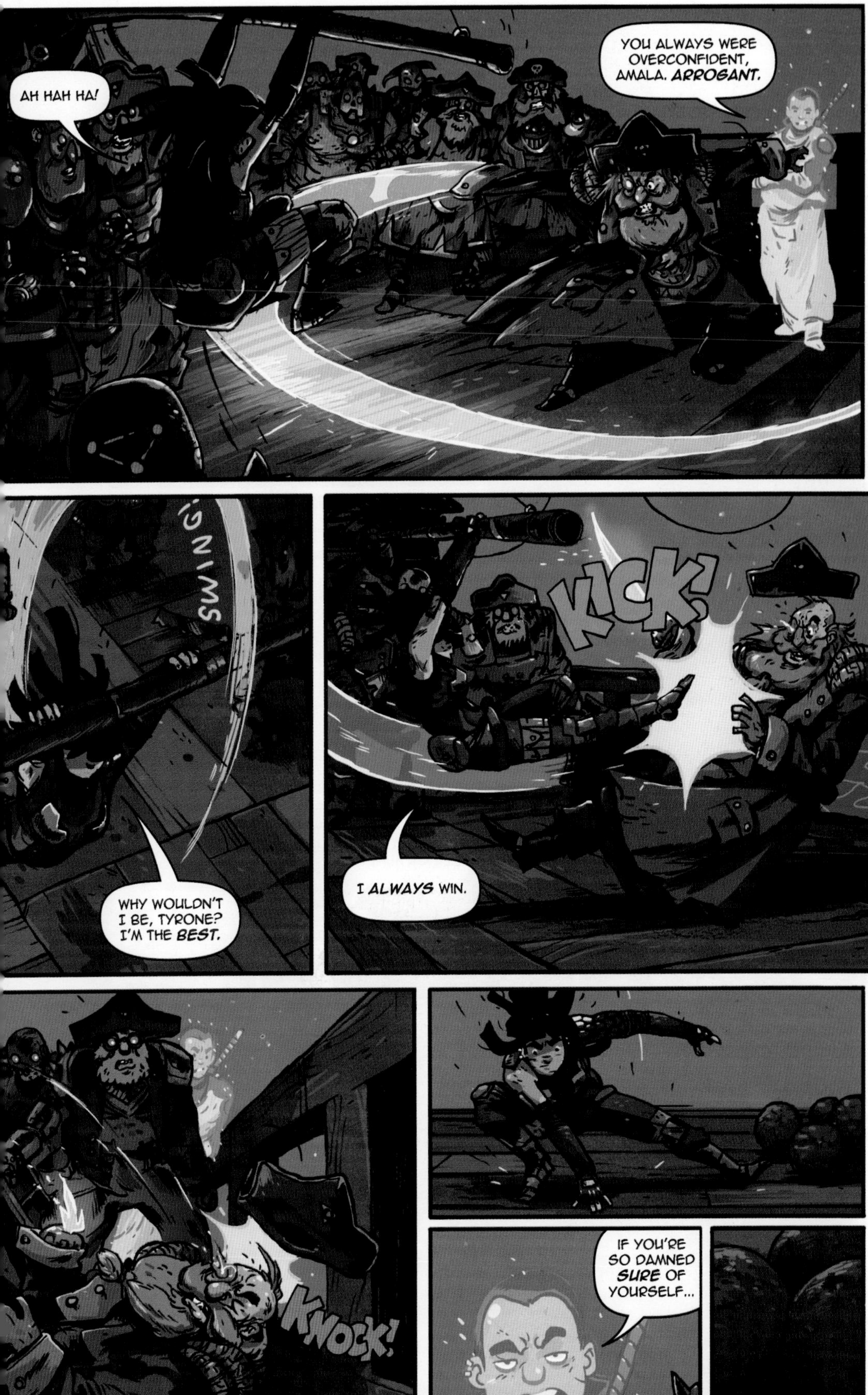
AH HAH HA!
YOU ALWAYS WERE OVERCONFIDENT, AMALA. ARROGANT.
SWING!
WHY WOULDN'T I BE, TYRONE? I'M THE BEST.
KICK!
I ALWAYS WIN.
KNOCK!
IF YOU'RE SO DAMNED SURE OF YOURSELF...

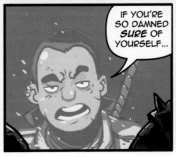

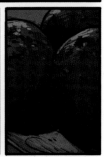

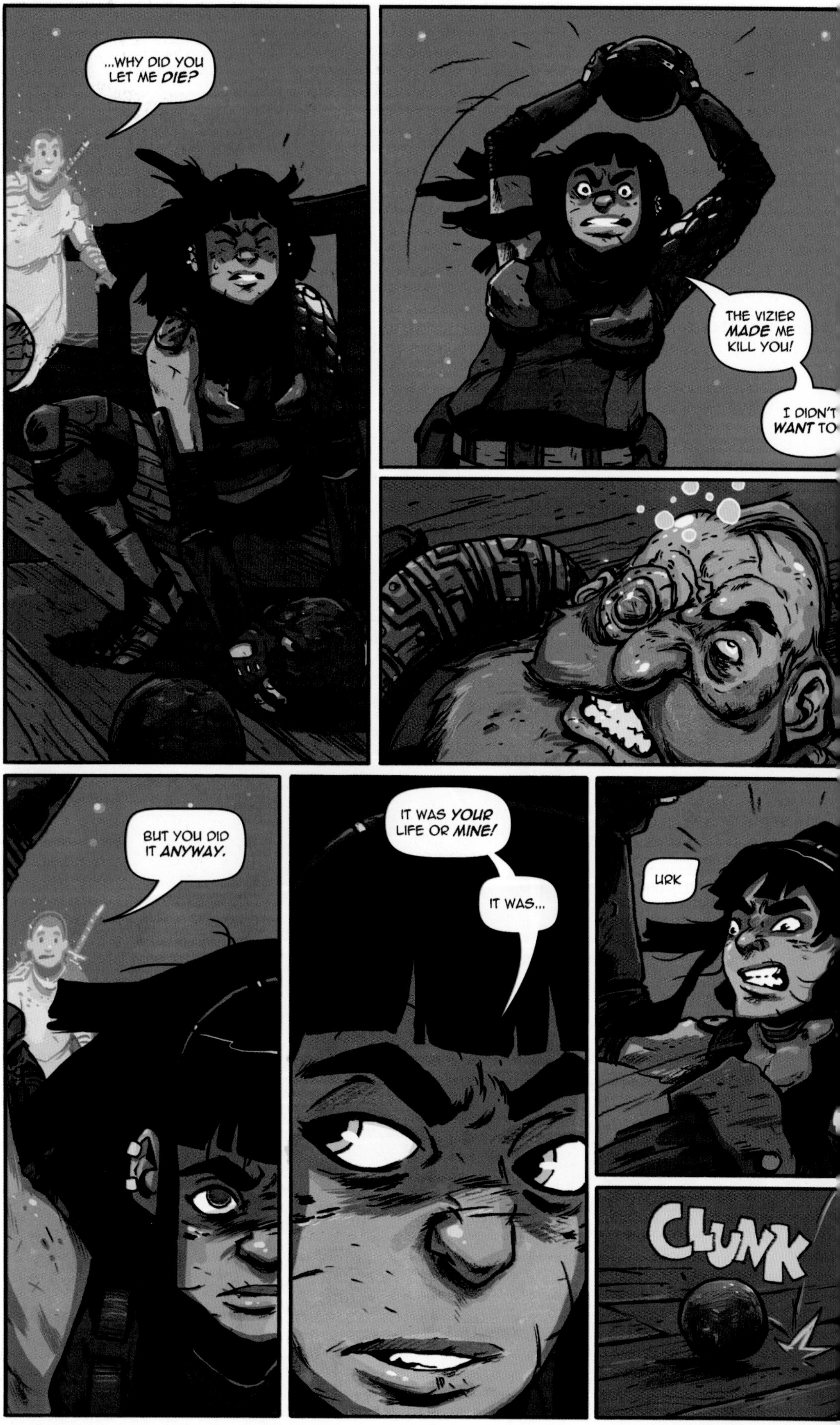
...WHY DID YOU LET ME DIE?
THE VIZIER MADE ME KILL YOU!
I DIDN'T WANT TO
BUT YOU DID IT ANYWAY.
IT WAS YOUR LIFE OR MINE!
IT WAS...
URK
CLUNK

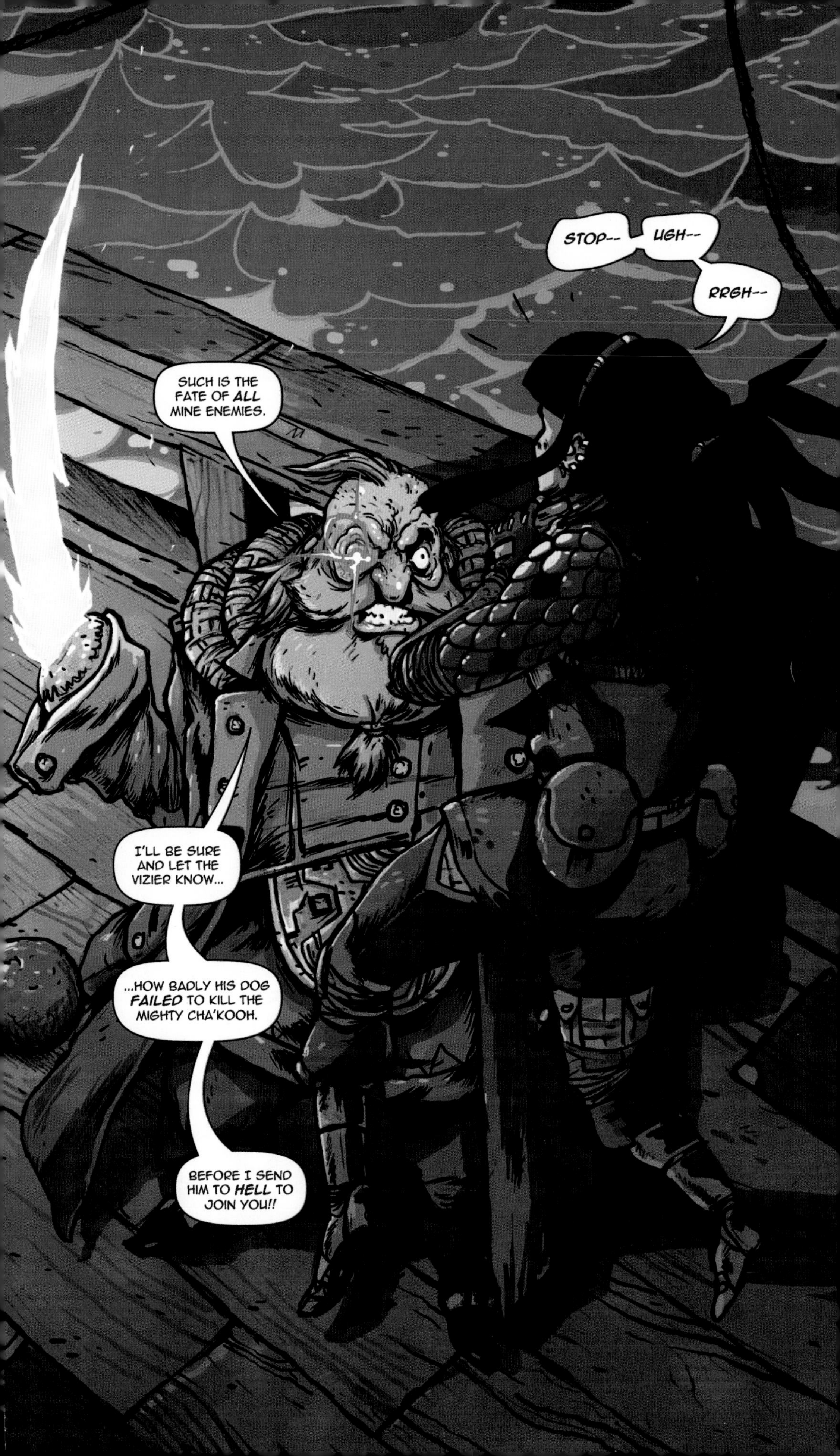
STOP-- UGH--
RRGH--
SUCH IS THE FATE OF ALL MINE ENEMIES.
I'LL BE SURE AND LET THE VIZIER KNOW...
...HOW BADLY HIS DOG FAILED TO KILL THE MIGHTY CHA'KOOH.
BEFORE I SEND HIM TO HELL TO JOIN YOU!!

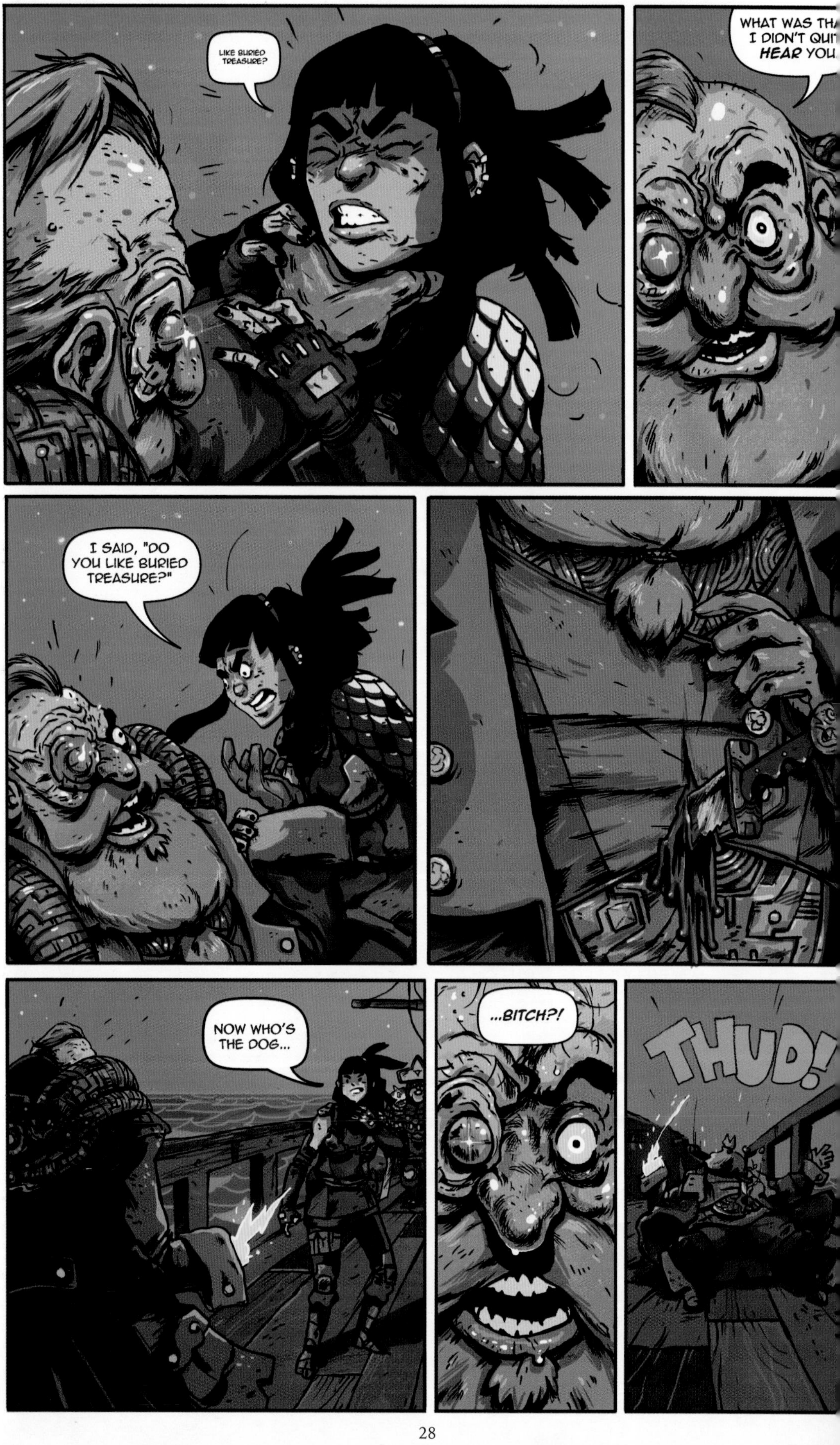
LIKE BURIED TREASURE?
WHAT WAS THA I DIDN'T QUIT HEAR YOU
I SAID, "DO YOU LIKE BURIED TREASURE?"
NOW WHO'S THE DOG...
...BITCH?!
THUD!

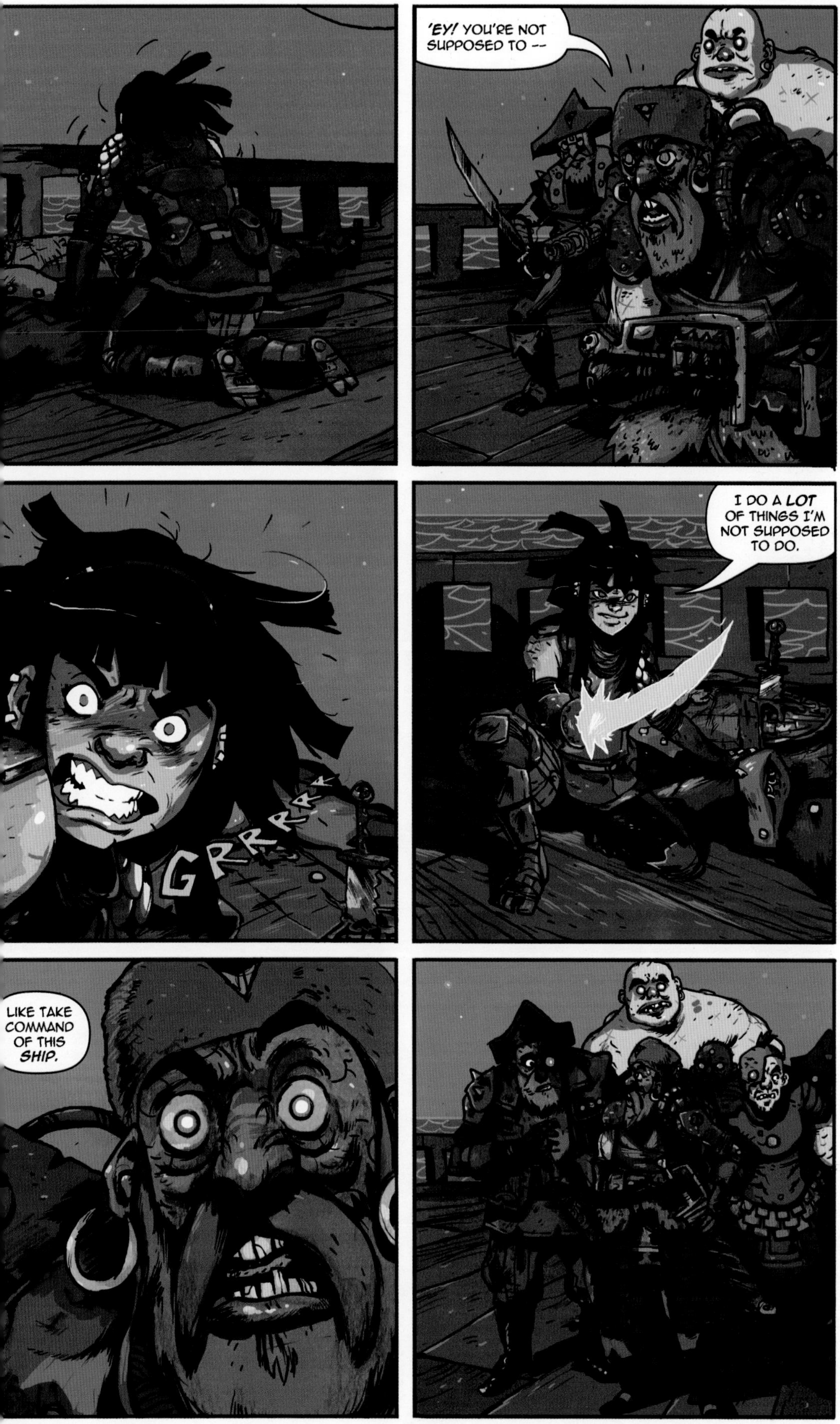
'EY! YOU'RE NOT SUPPOSED TO --
GRRRAAK
I DO A LOT OF THINGS I'M NOT SUPPOSED TO DO.
LIKE TAKE COMMAND OF THIS SHIP.

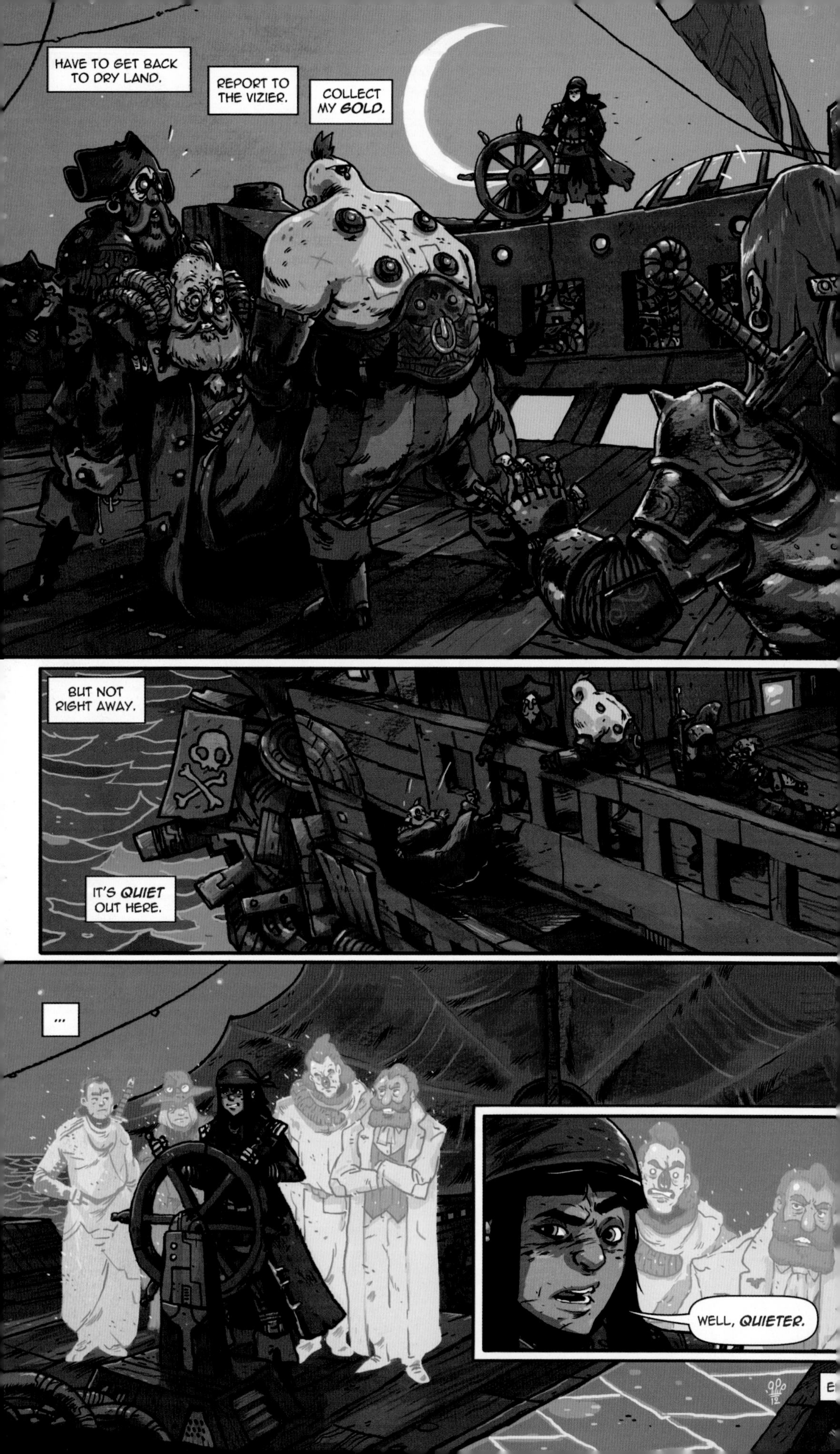
HAVE TO GET BACK TO DRY LAND.
REPORT TO THE VIZIER.
COLLECT MY GOLD.
BUT NOT RIGHT AWAY.
IT'S QUIET OUT HERE.
...
WELL, QUIETER.

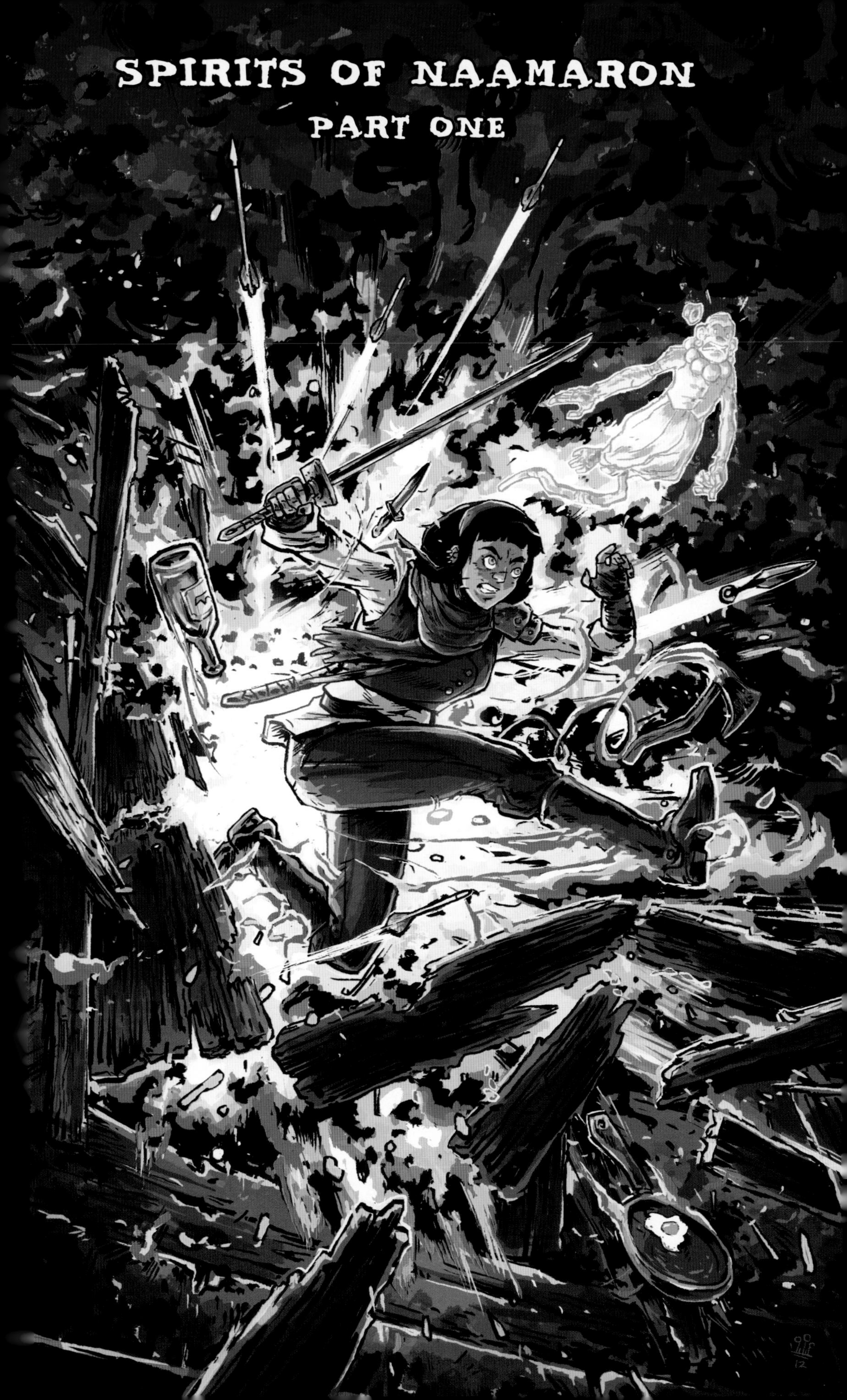
SPIRITS OF NAAMARON
PART ONE

"DAMN, I KINDA *LIKED* THAT PLACE."

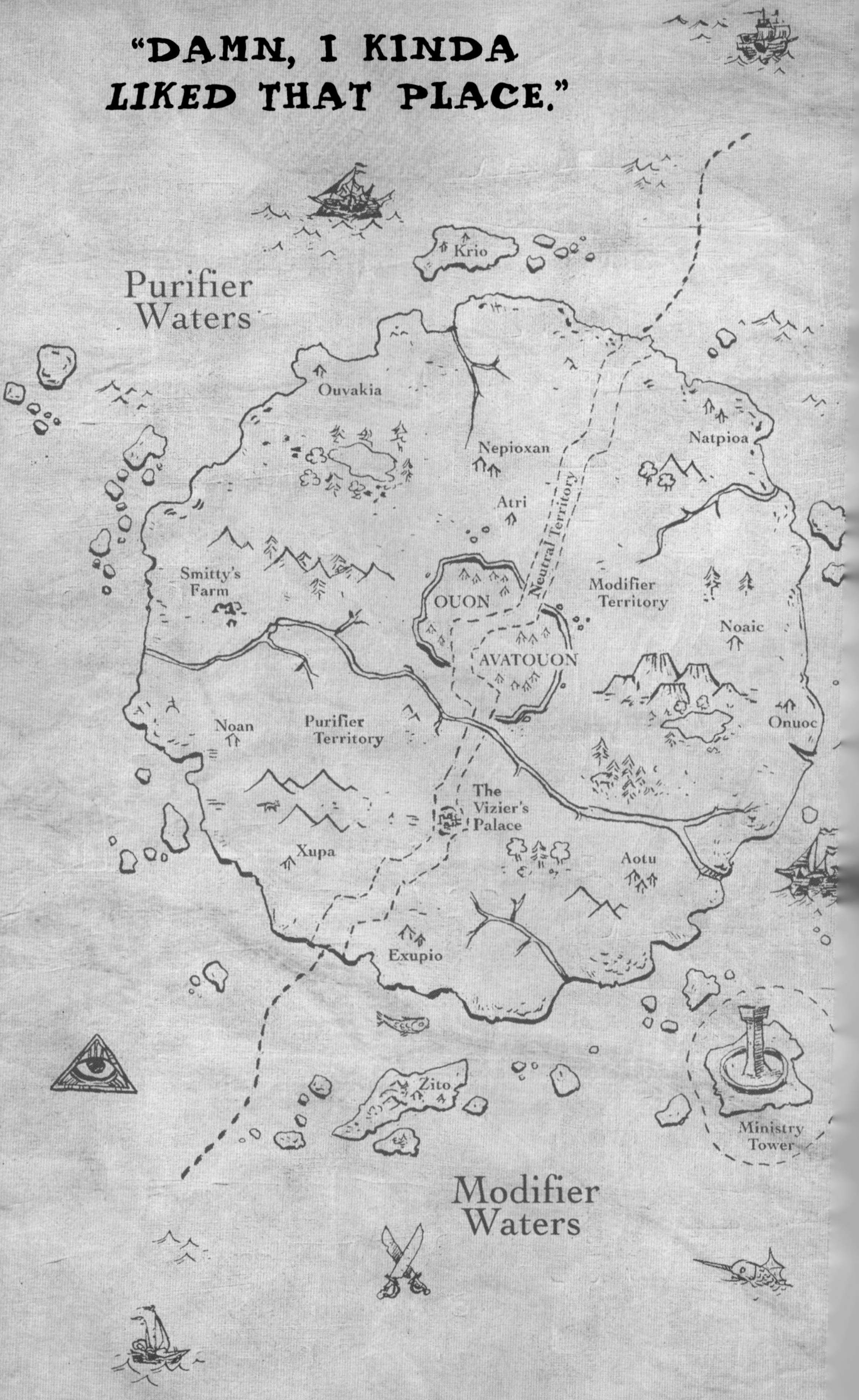
Purifier Waters
Krio
Ouvakia
Nepioxan
Natpioa
Atri
Neutral Territory
Smitty's Farm
OUON
Modifier Territory
Noaic
AVATOUON
Noan
Purifier Territory
Onuoc
The Vizier's Palace
Xupa
Aotu
Exupio
Zito
Ministry Tower
Modifier Waters

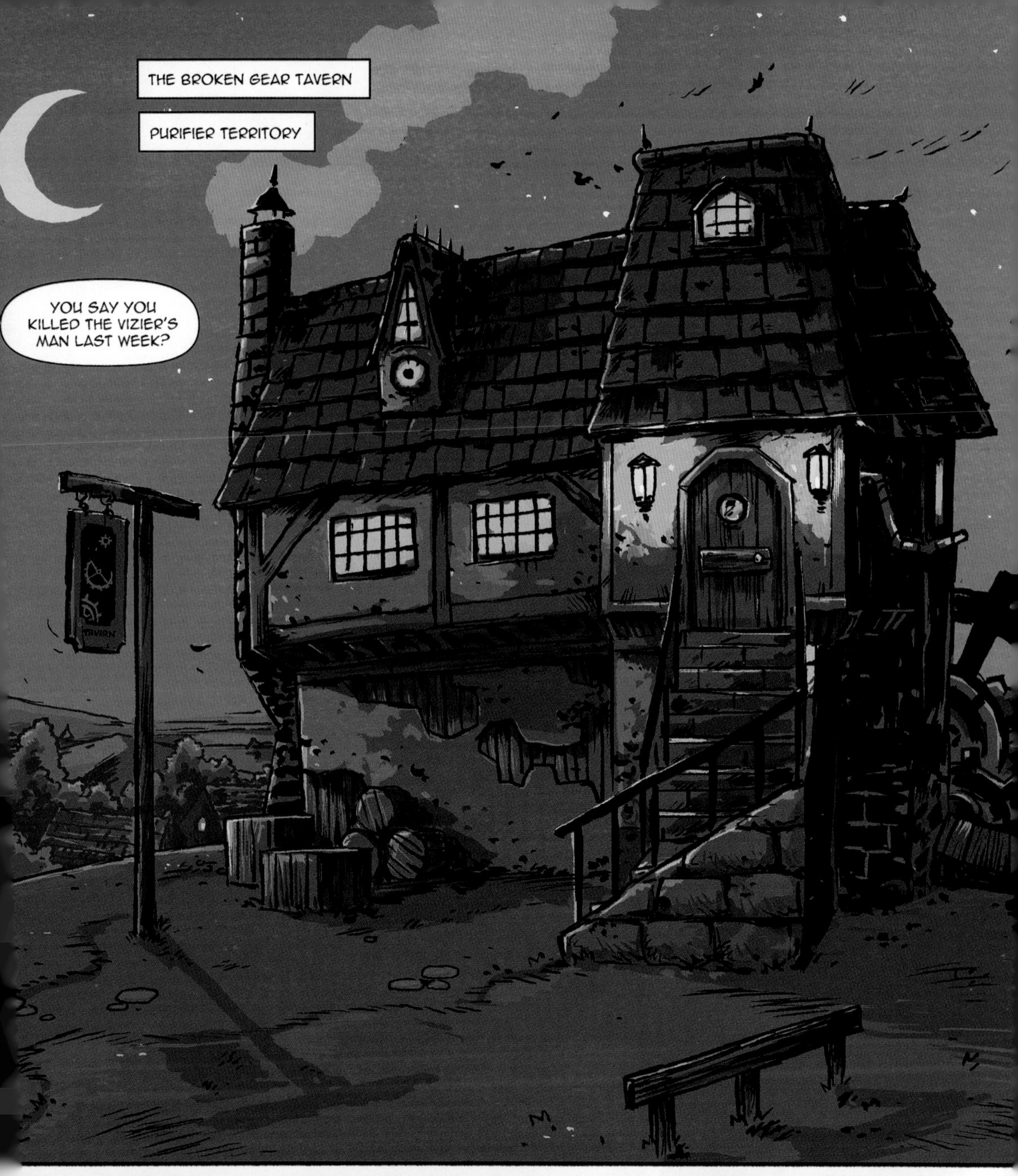
THE BROKEN GEAR TAVERN
PURIFIER TERRITORY
YOU SAY YOU KILLED THE VIZIER'S MAN LAST WEEK?
TAVERN

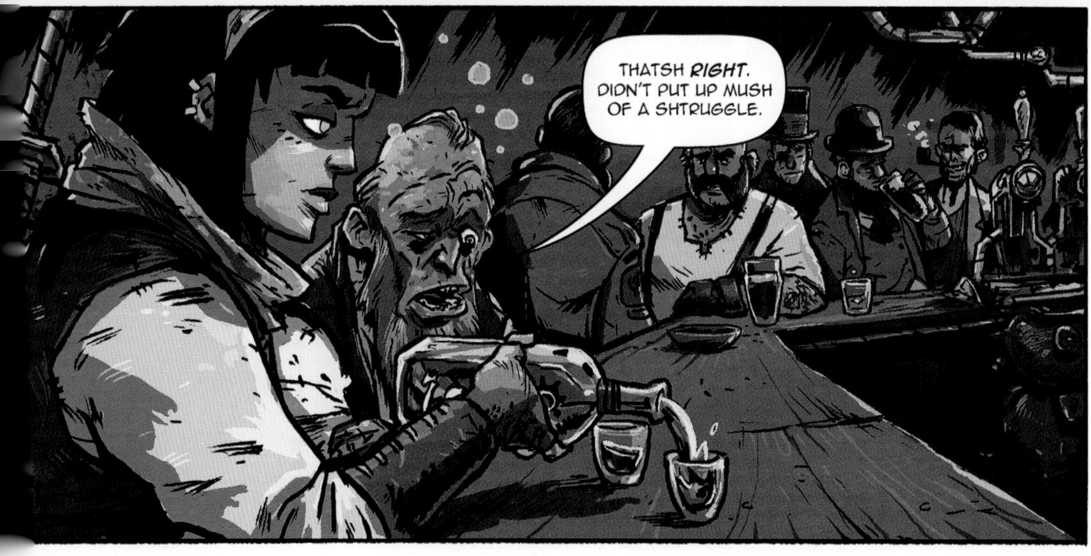
THATSH ***RIGHT***. DIDN'T PUT UP MUSH OF A SHTRUGGLE.

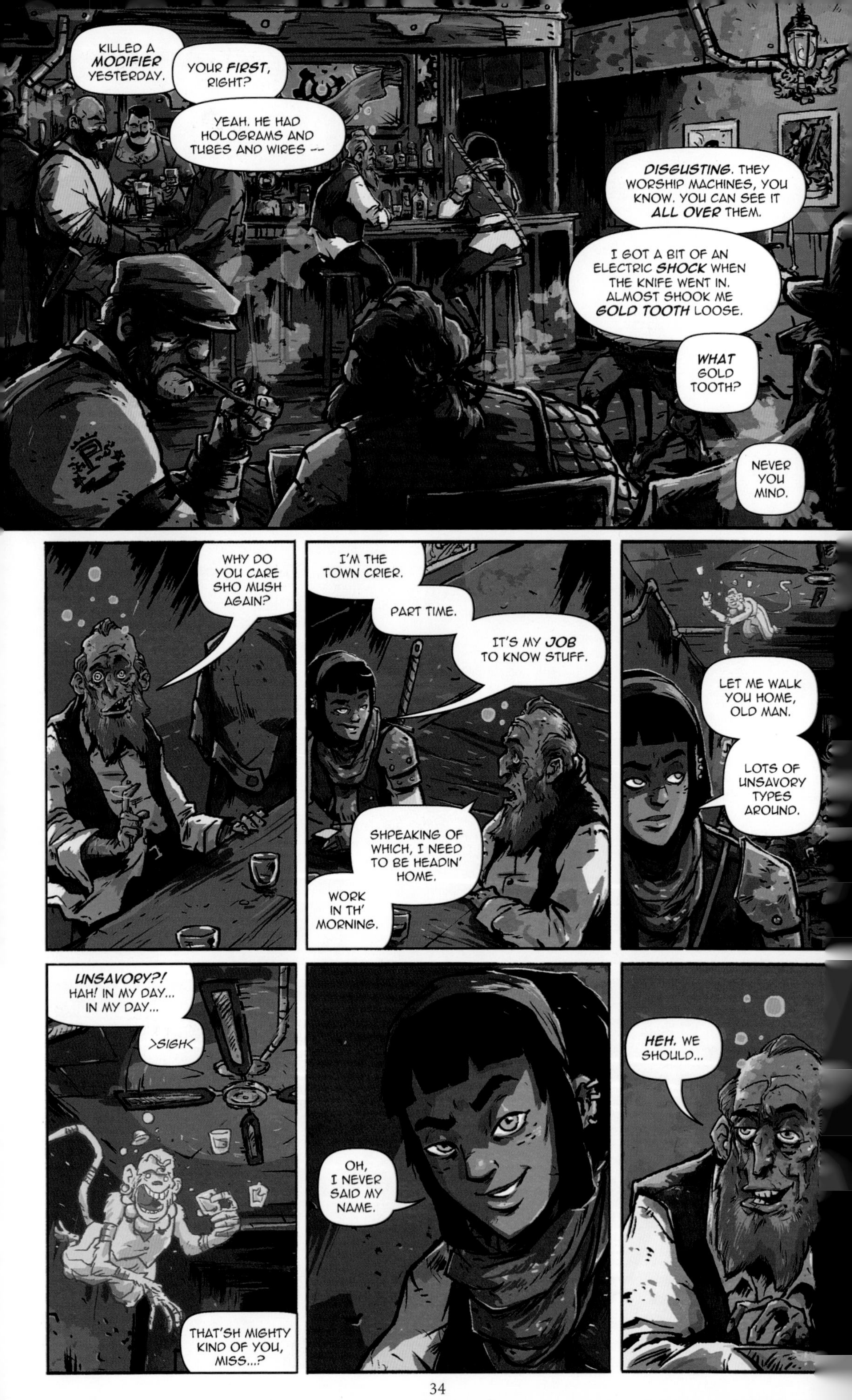
KILLED A MODIFIER YESTERDAY.
YOUR FIRST, RIGHT?
YEAH. HE HAD HOLOGRAMS AND TUBES AND WIRES --
DISGUSTING. THEY WORSHIP MACHINES, YOU KNOW. YOU CAN SEE IT ALL OVER THEM.
I GOT A BIT OF AN ELECTRIC SHOCK WHEN THE KNIFE WENT IN. ALMOST SHOOK ME GOLD TOOTH LOOSE.
WHAT GOLD TOOTH?
NEVER YOU MIND.
WHY DO YOU CARE SHO MUSH AGAIN?
I'M THE TOWN CRIER.
PART TIME.
IT'S MY JOB TO KNOW STUFF.
SHPEAKING OF WHICH, I NEED TO BE HEADIN' HOME.
WORK IN TH' MORNING.
LET ME WALK YOU HOME, OLD MAN.
LOTS OF UNSAVORY TYPES AROUND.
UNSAVORY?! HAH! IN MY DAY... IN MY DAY...
>SIGH<
THAT'SH MIGHTY KIND OF YOU, MISS...?
OH, I NEVER SAID MY NAME.
HEH. WE SHOULD...

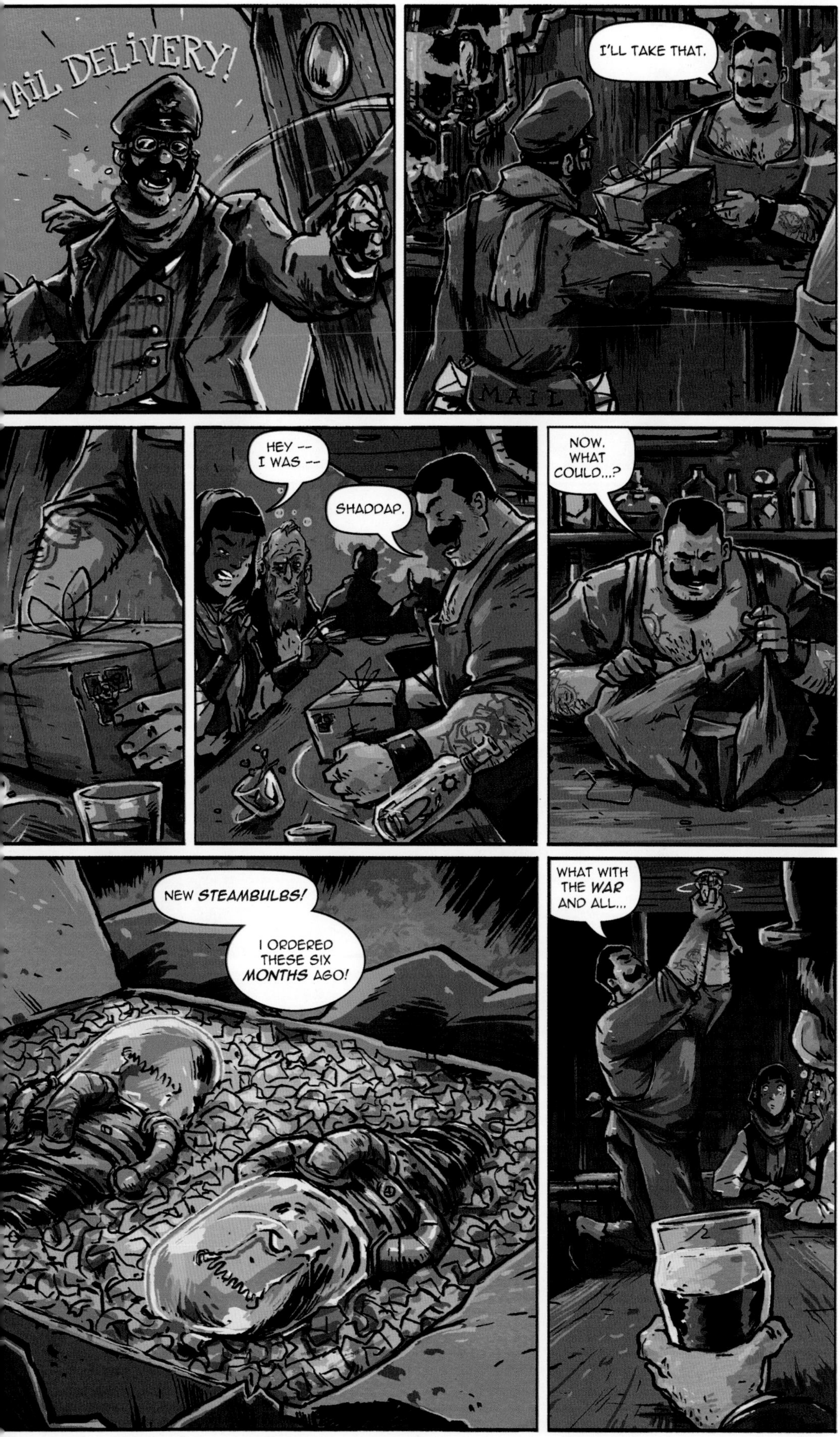
MAIL DELIVERY!
I'LL TAKE THAT.
MAIL
HEY -- I WAS --
SHADDAP.
NOW. WHAT COULD...?
NEW STEAMBULBS!
I ORDERED THESE SIX MONTHS AGO!
WHAT WITH THE WAR AND ALL...

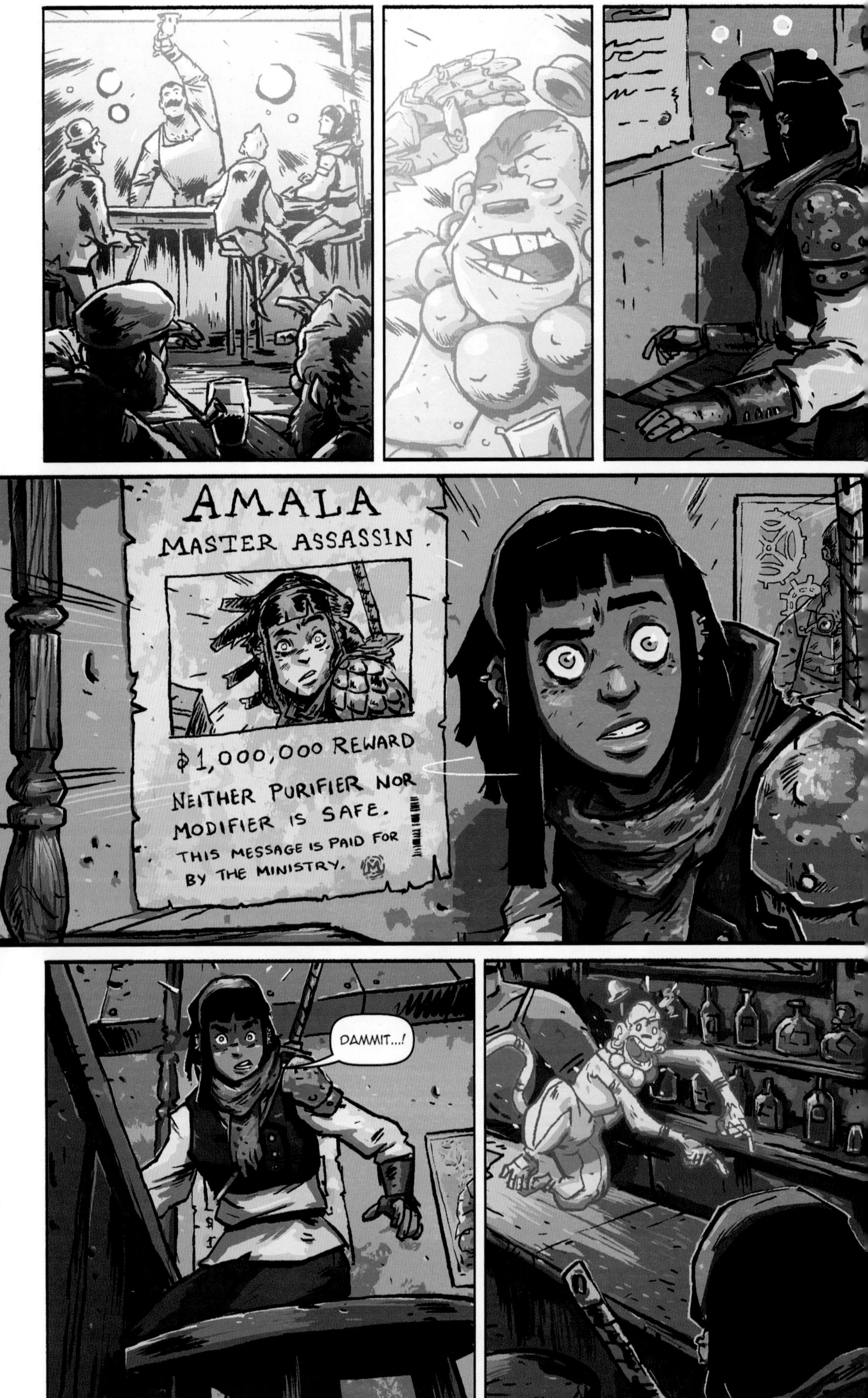
AMALA
MASTER ASSASSIN
$1,000,000 REWARD
NEITHER PURIFIER NOR MODIFIER IS SAFE.
THIS MESSAGE IS PAID FOR BY THE MINISTRY.
DAMMIT...!

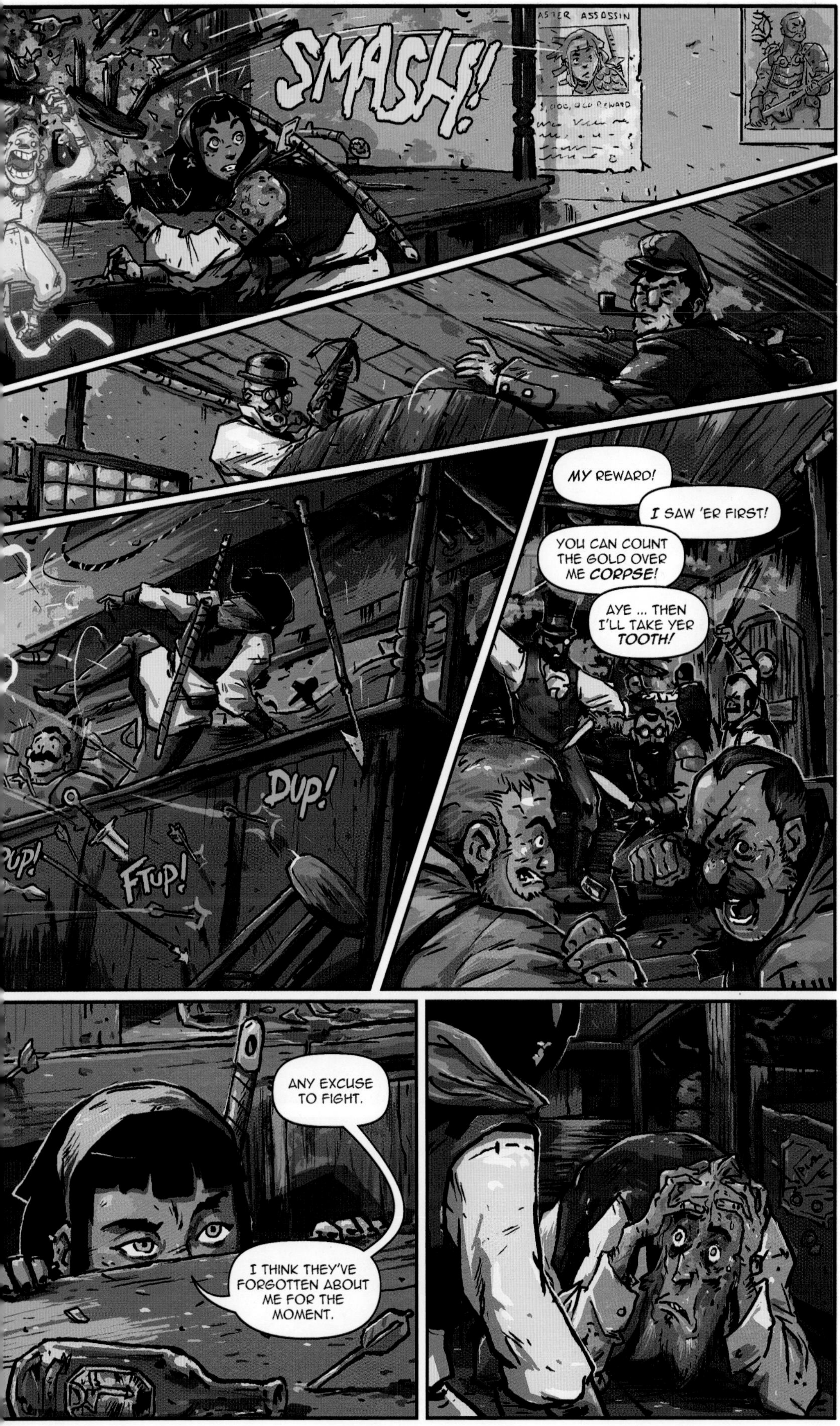
SMASH!
ASTER ASSASSIN
MY REWARD!
I SAW 'ER FIRST!
YOU CAN COUNT THE GOLD OVER ME CORPSE!
AYE ... THEN I'LL TAKE YER TOOTH!
DUP!
FTUP!
ANY EXCUSE TO FIGHT.
I THINK THEY'VE FORGOTTEN ABOUT ME FOR THE MOMENT.

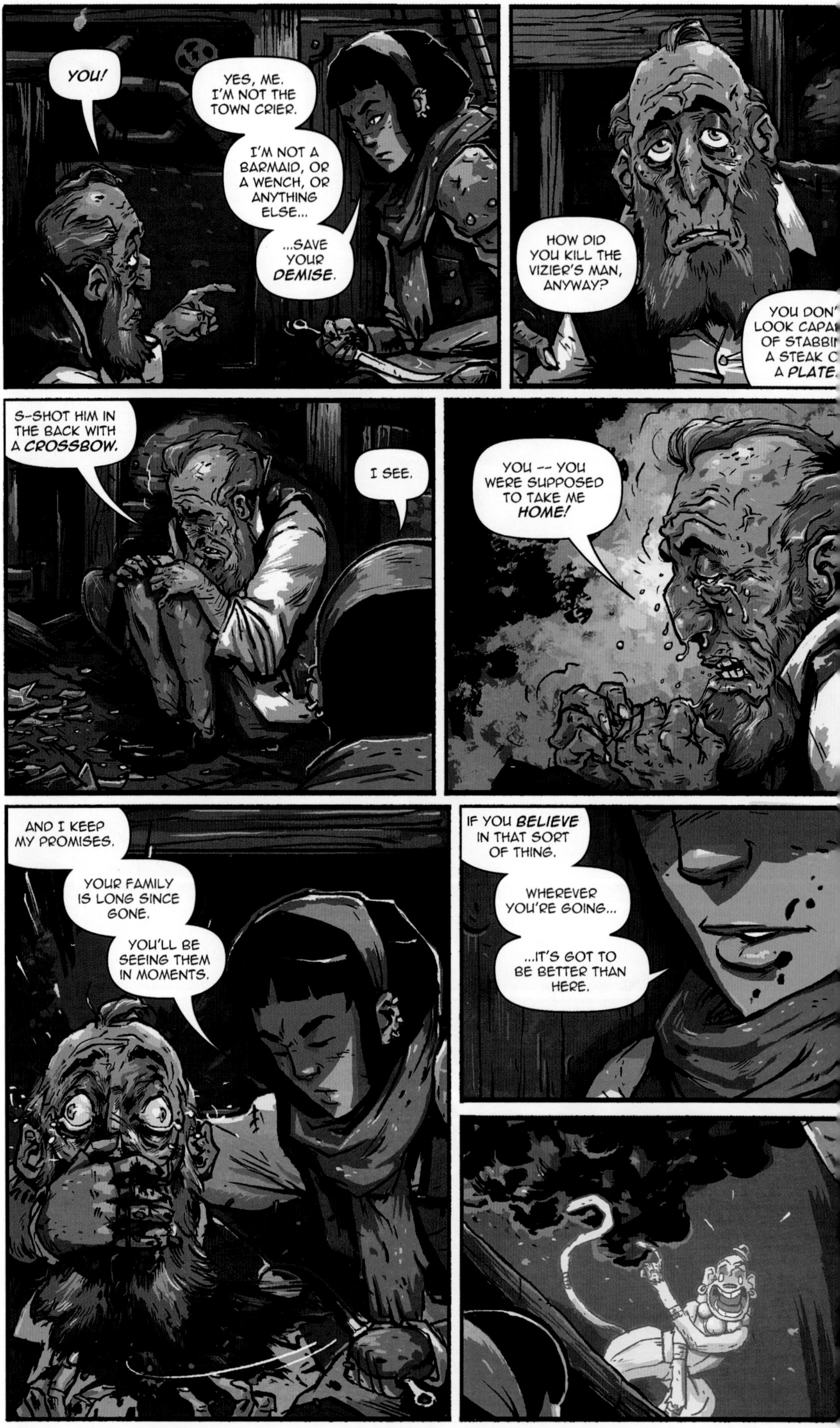
YOU!
YES, ME. I'M NOT THE TOWN CRIER.
I'M NOT A BARMAID, OR A WENCH, OR ANYTHING ELSE...
...SAVE YOUR DEMISE.
HOW DID YOU KILL THE VIZIER'S MAN, ANYWAY?
YOU DON' LOOK CAPA OF STABBI A STEAK C A PLATE.
S-SHOT HIM IN THE BACK WITH A CROSSBOW.
I SEE.
YOU -- YOU WERE SUPPOSED TO TAKE ME HOME!
AND I KEEP MY PROMISES.
YOUR FAMILY IS LONG SINCE GONE.
YOU'LL BE SEEING THEM IN MOMENTS.
IF YOU BELIEVE IN THAT SORT OF THING.
WHEREVER YOU'RE GOING...
...IT'S GOT TO BE BETTER THAN HERE.

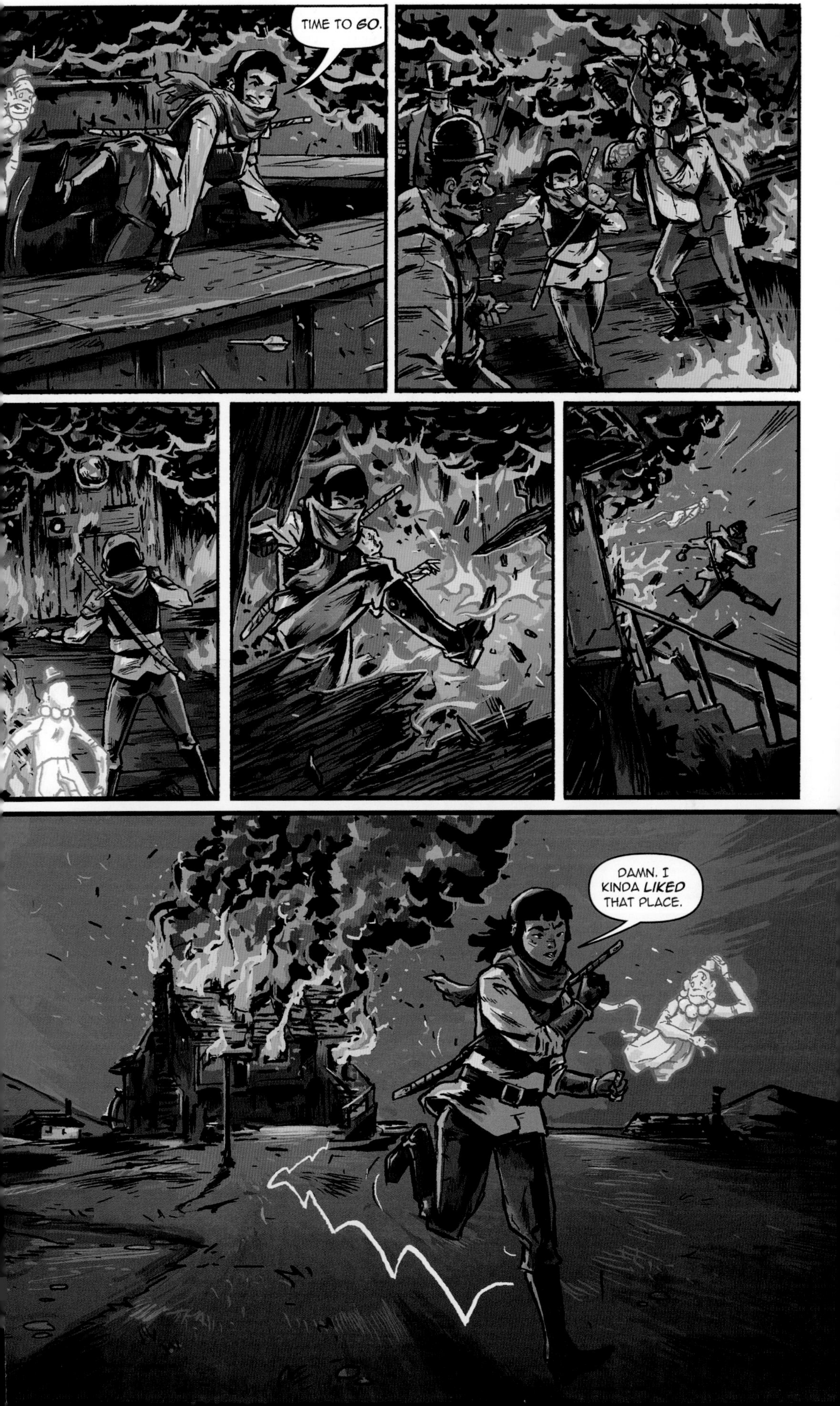
TIME TO GO.
DAMN. I KINDA LIKED THAT PLACE.

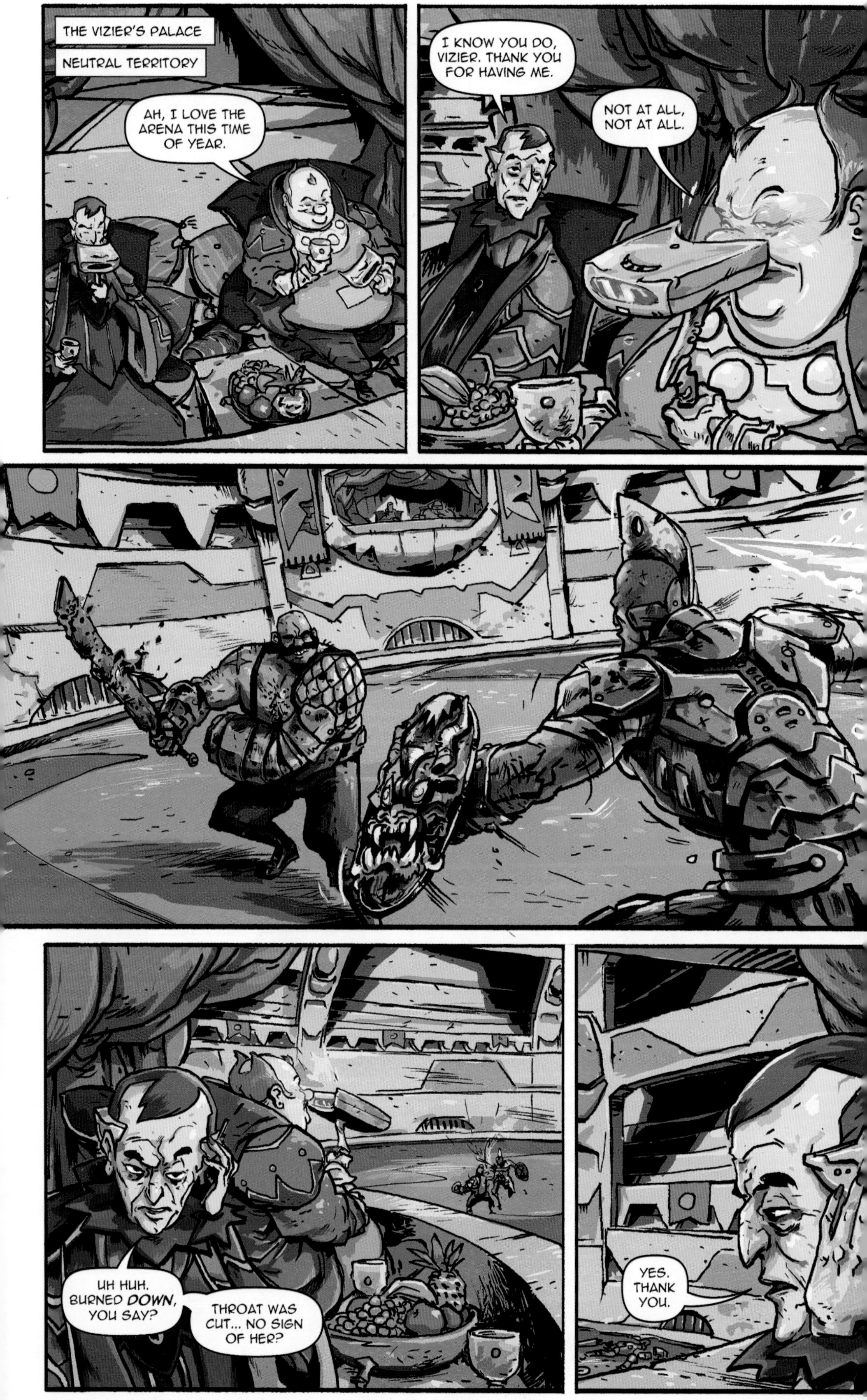
THE VIZIER'S PALACE
NEUTRAL TERRITORY
AH, I LOVE THE ARENA THIS TIME OF YEAR.
I KNOW YOU DO, VIZIER. THANK YOU FOR HAVING ME.
NOT AT ALL, NOT AT ALL.
UH HUH. BURNED *DOWN*, YOU SAY?
THROAT WAS CUT... NO SIGN OF HER?
YES. THANK YOU.

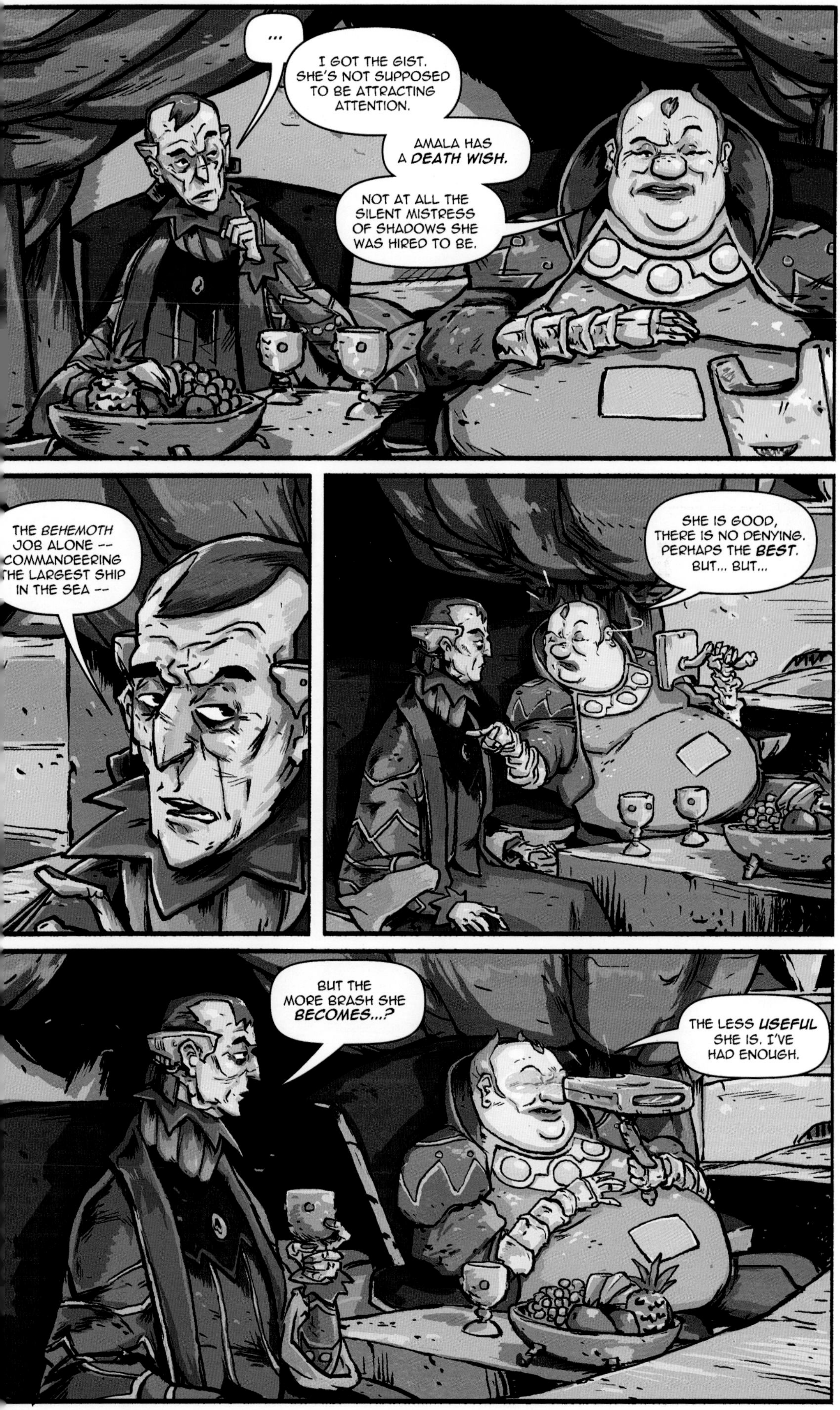
...
I GOT THE GIST. SHE'S NOT SUPPOSED TO BE ATTRACTING ATTENTION.
AMALA HAS A *DEATH WISH.*
NOT AT ALL THE SILENT MISTRESS OF SHADOWS SHE WAS HIRED TO BE.
THE *BEHEMOTH* JOB ALONE -- COMMANDEERING THE LARGEST SHIP IN THE SEA --
SHE IS GOOD, THERE IS NO DENYING. PERHAPS THE *BEST.* BUT... BUT...
BUT THE MORE BRASH SHE *BECOMES...?*
THE LESS *USEFUL* SHE IS. I'VE HAD ENOUGH.

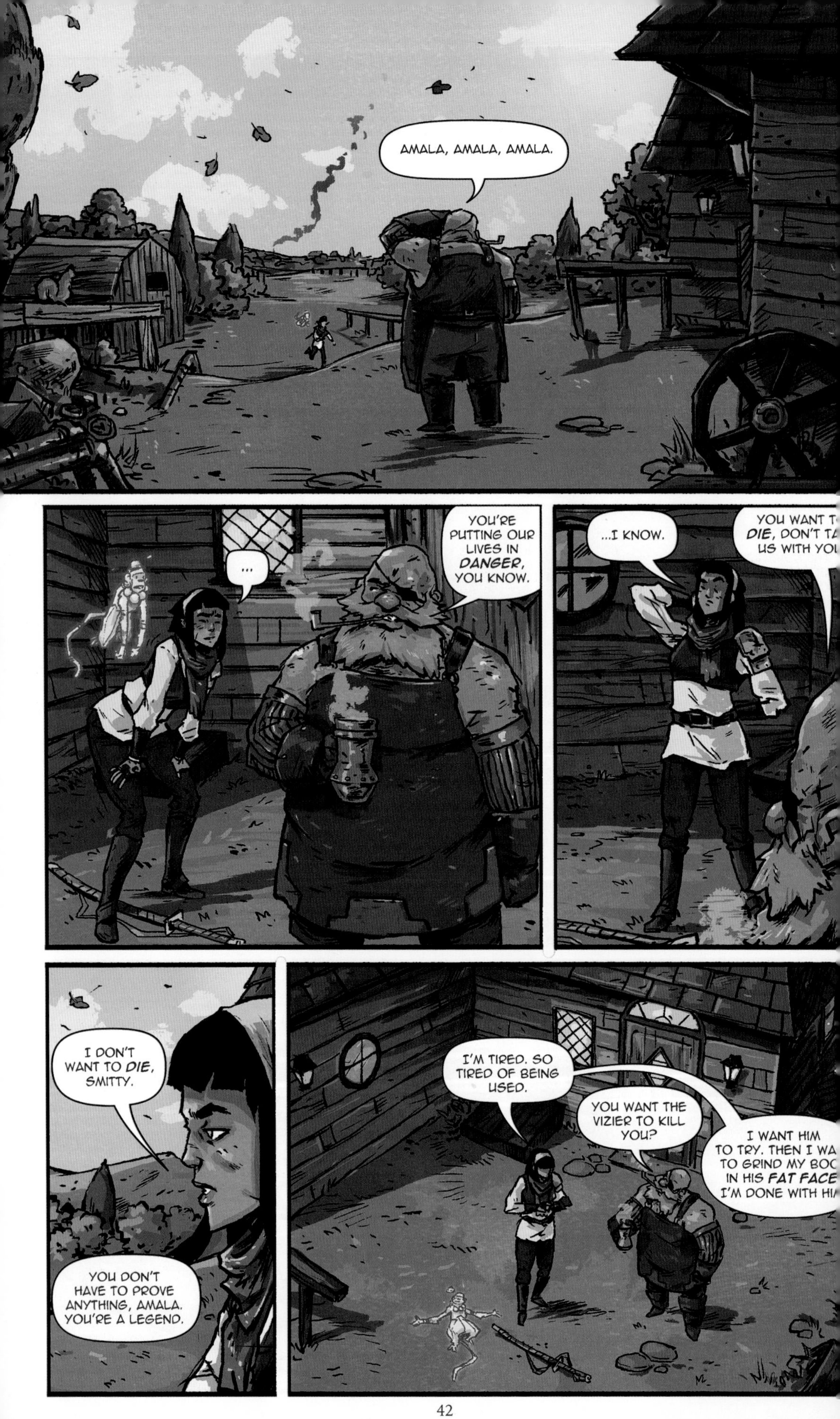
AMALA, AMALA, AMALA.
...
YOU'RE PUTTING OUR LIVES IN *DANGER*, YOU KNOW.
...I KNOW.
YOU WANT T *DIE*, DON'T TA US WITH YOU
I DON'T WANT TO *DIE*, SMITTY.
YOU DON'T HAVE TO PROVE ANYTHING, AMALA. YOU'RE A LEGEND.
I'M TIRED. SO TIRED OF BEING USED.
YOU WANT THE VIZIER TO KILL YOU?
I WANT HIM TO TRY. THEN I WA TO GRIND MY BOO IN HIS *FAT FACE* I'M DONE WITH HI

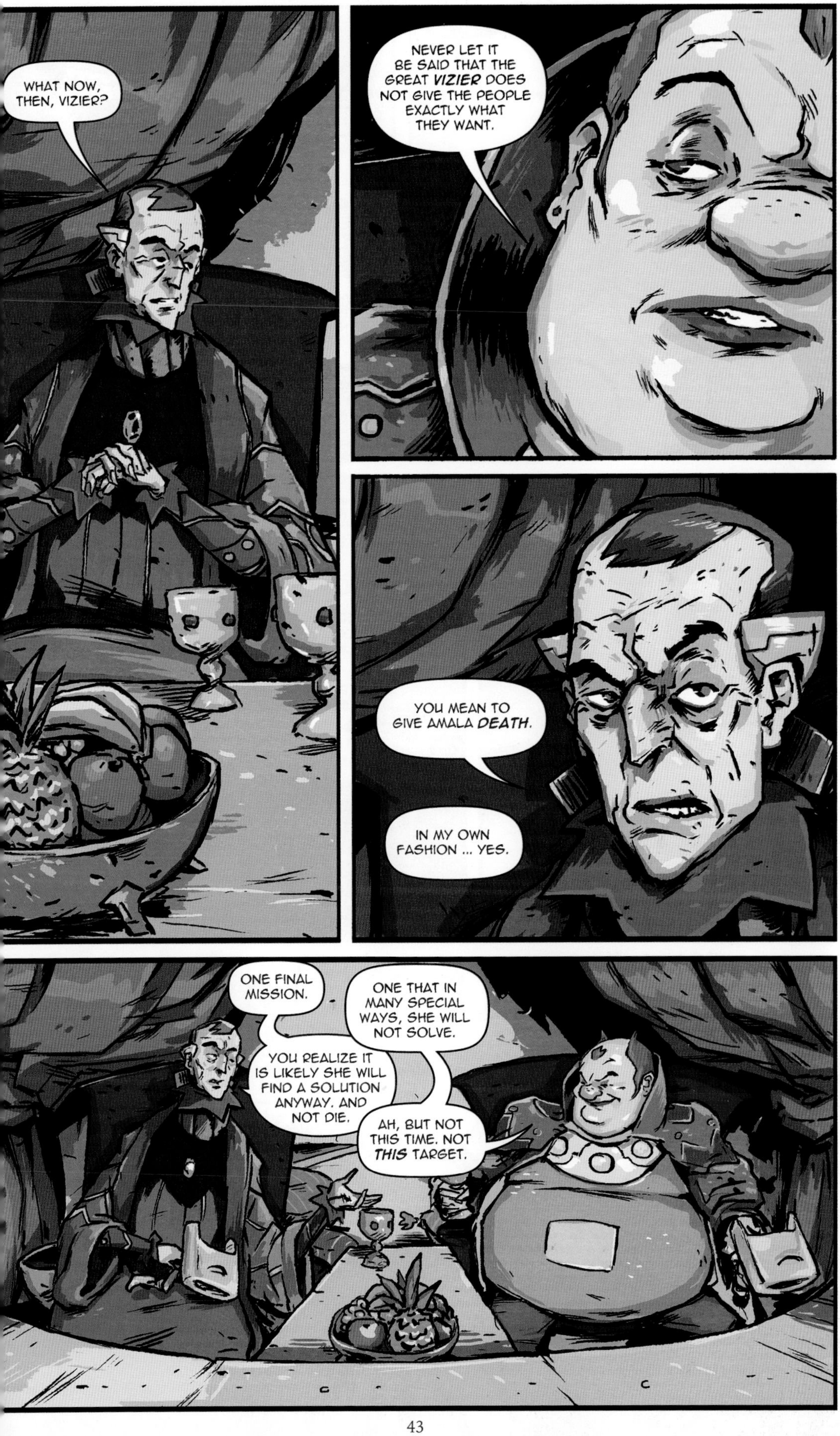
WHAT NOW, THEN, VIZIER?
NEVER LET IT BE SAID THAT THE GREAT VIZIER DOES NOT GIVE THE PEOPLE EXACTLY WHAT THEY WANT.
YOU MEAN TO GIVE AMALA DEATH.
IN MY OWN FASHION ... YES.
ONE FINAL MISSION.
ONE THAT IN MANY SPECIAL WAYS, SHE WILL NOT SOLVE.
YOU REALIZE IT IS LIKELY SHE WILL FIND A SOLUTION ANYWAY. AND NOT DIE.
AH, BUT NOT THIS TIME. NOT THIS TARGET.

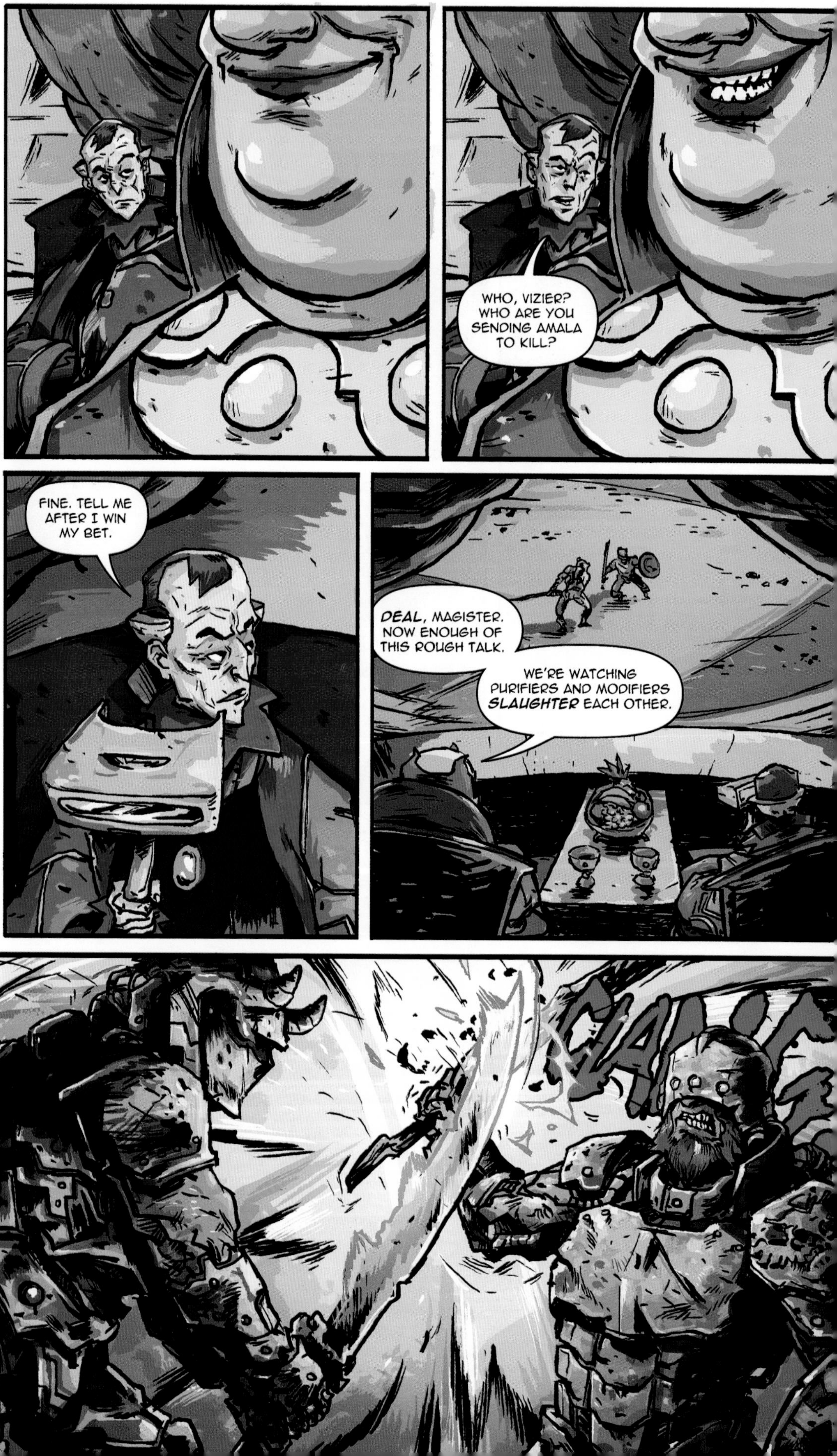
WHO, VIZIER? WHO ARE YOU SENDING AMALA TO KILL?
FINE. TELL ME AFTER I WIN MY BET.
DEAL, MAGISTER. NOW ENOUGH OF THIS ROUGH TALK.
WE'RE WATCHING PURIFIERS AND MODIFIERS SLAUGHTER EACH OTHER.

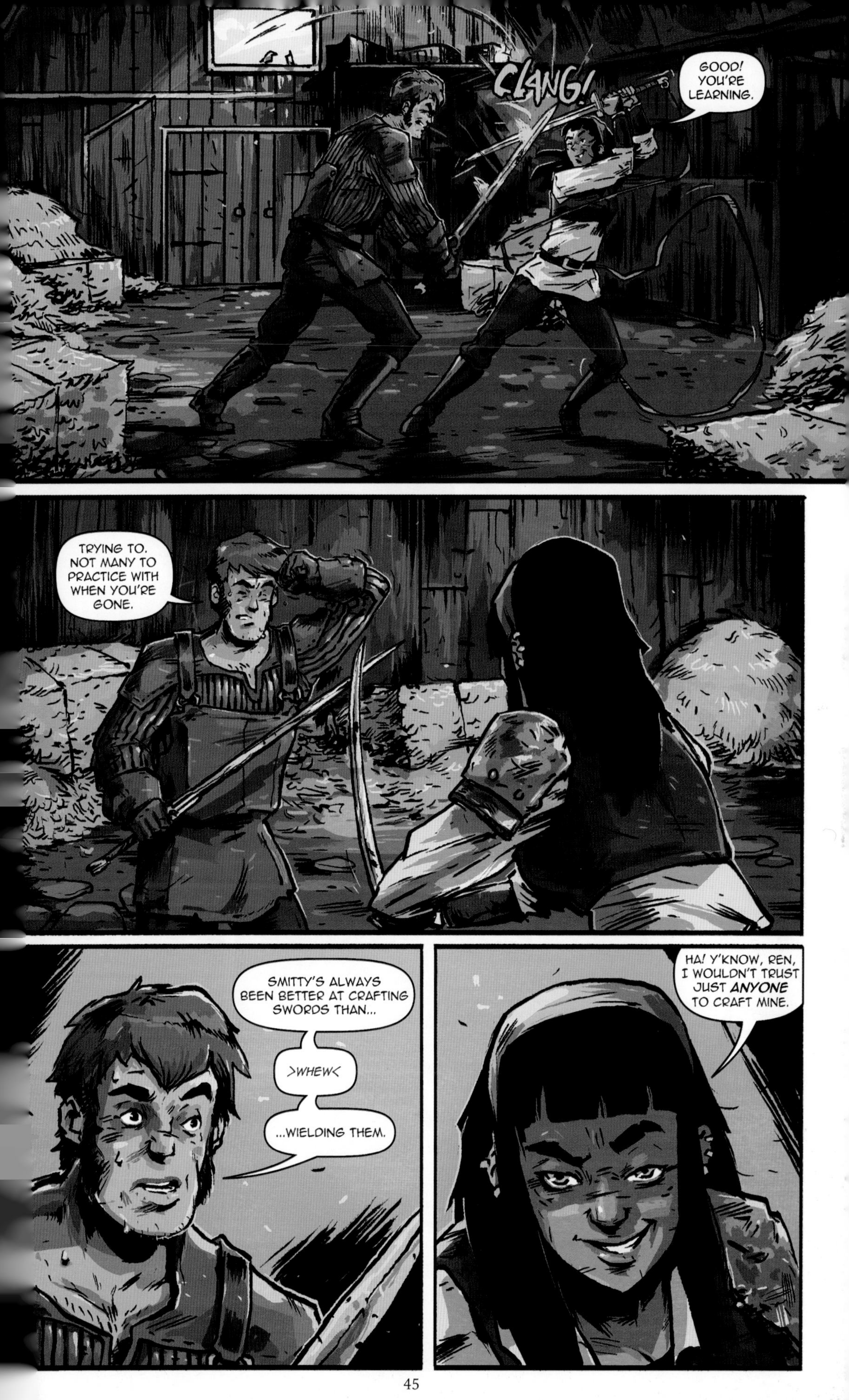
CLANG!
GOOD! YOU'RE LEARNING.
TRYING TO. NOT MANY TO PRACTICE WITH WHEN YOU'RE GONE.
SMITTY'S ALWAYS BEEN BETTER AT CRAFTING SWORDS THAN...
>WHEW<
...WIELDING THEM.
HA! Y'KNOW, REN, I WOULDN'T TRUST JUST ANYONE TO CRAFT MINE.

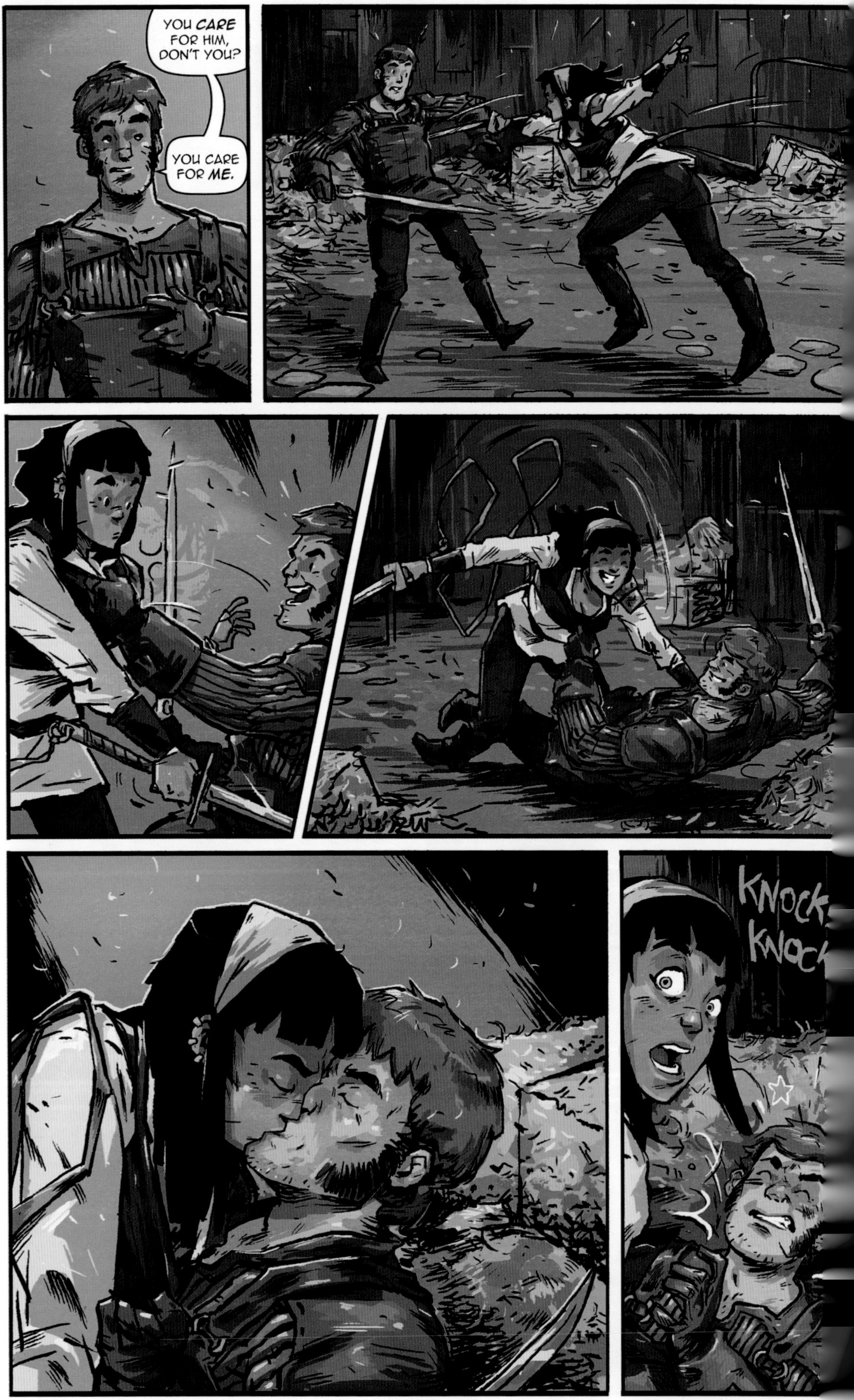
YOU CARE FOR HIM, DON'T YOU?
YOU CARE FOR ME.
KNOCK
KNOCK

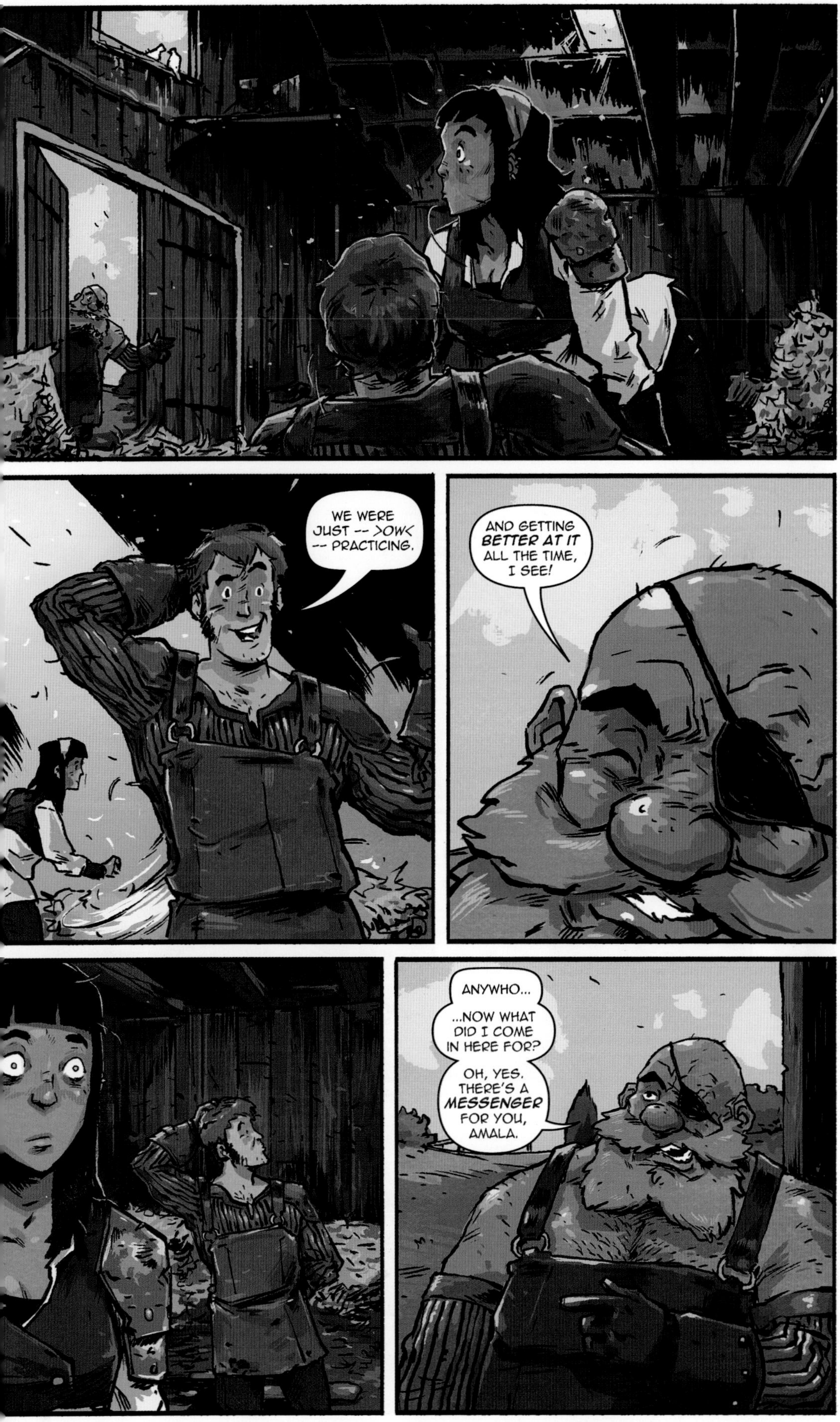
WE WERE JUST -- >OW< -- PRACTICING.
AND GETTING BETTER AT IT ALL THE TIME, I SEE!
ANYWHO...
...NOW WHAT DID I COME IN HERE FOR?
OH, YES. THERE'S A MESSENGER FOR YOU, AMALA.

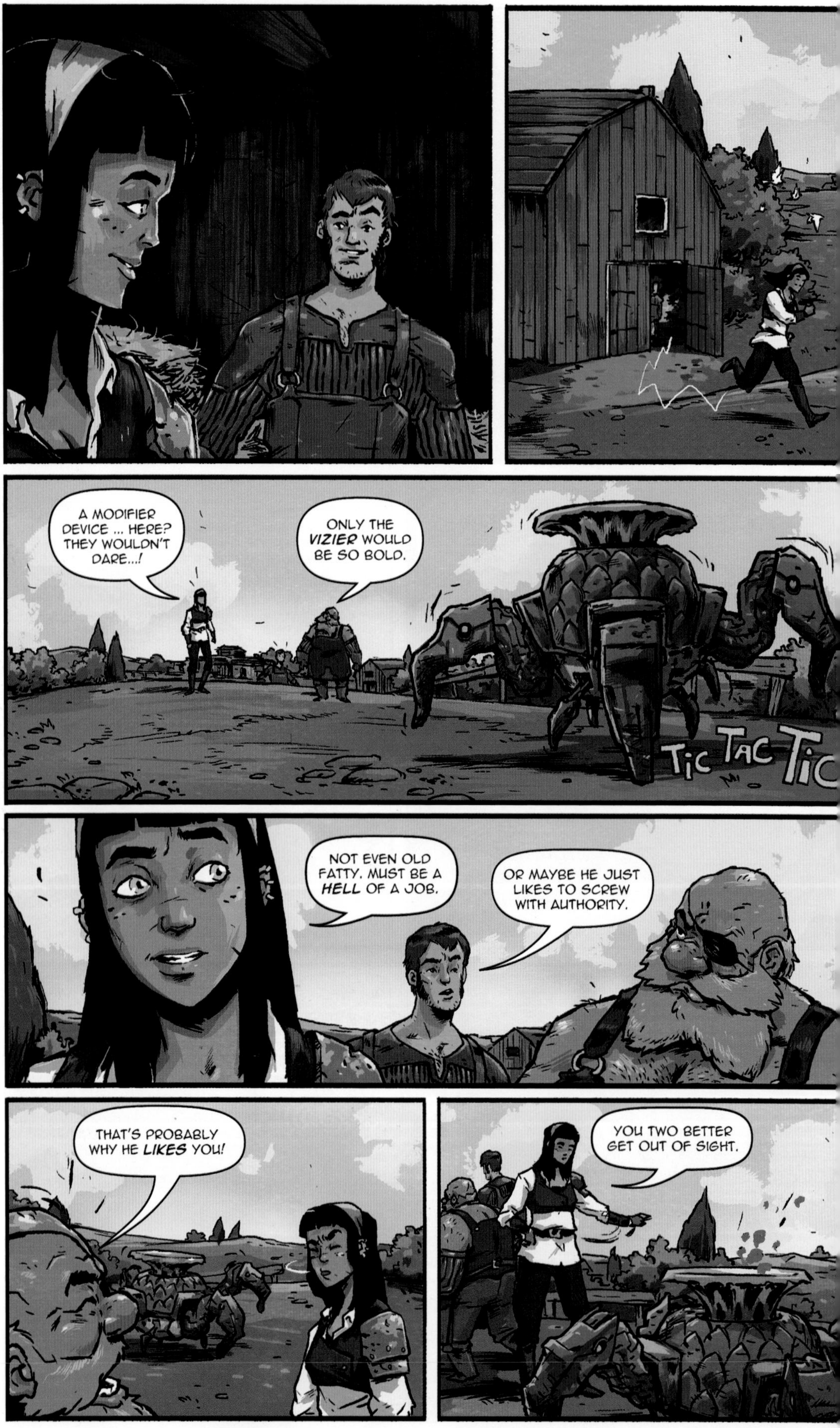
A MODIFIER DEVICE ... HERE? THEY WOULDN'T DARE...!
ONLY THE VIZIER WOULD BE SO BOLD.
TIC TAC TIC
NOT EVEN OLD FATTY. MUST BE A HELL OF A JOB.
OR MAYBE HE JUST LIKES TO SCREW WITH AUTHORITY.
THAT'S PROBABLY WHY HE LIKES YOU!
YOU TWO BETTER GET OUT OF SIGHT.

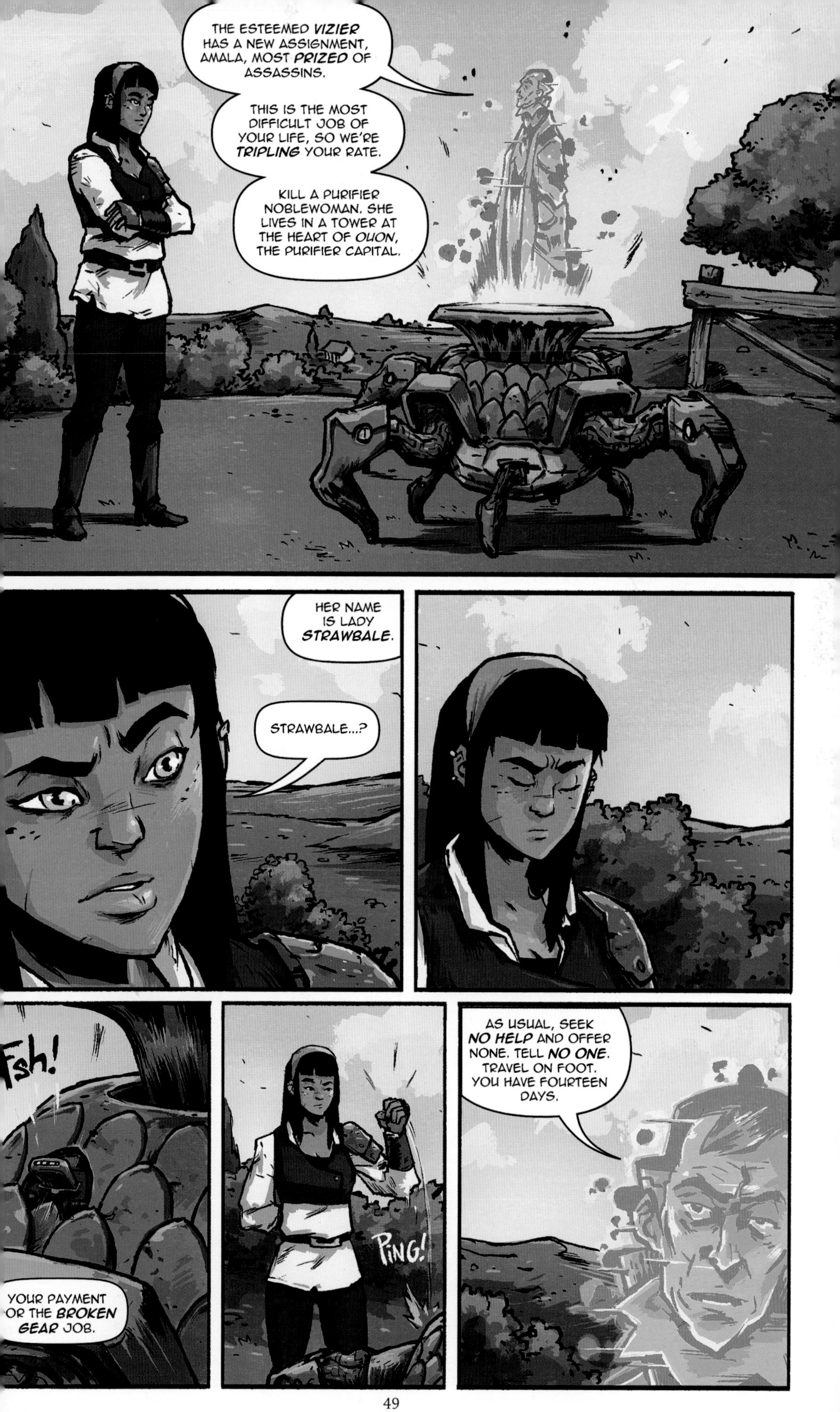
THE ESTEEMED VIZIER HAS A NEW ASSIGNMENT, AMALA, MOST PRIZED OF ASSASSINS.
THIS IS THE MOST DIFFICULT JOB OF YOUR LIFE, SO WE'RE TRIPLING YOUR RATE.
KILL A PURIFIER NOBLEWOMAN. SHE LIVES IN A TOWER AT THE HEART OF OUON, THE PURIFIER CAPITAL.
HER NAME IS LADY STRAWBALE.
STRAWBALE...?
Fsh!
YOUR PAYMENT FOR THE BROKEN GEAR JOB.
PING!
AS USUAL, SEEK NO HELP AND OFFER NONE. TELL NO ONE. TRAVEL ON FOOT. YOU HAVE FOURTEEN DAYS.

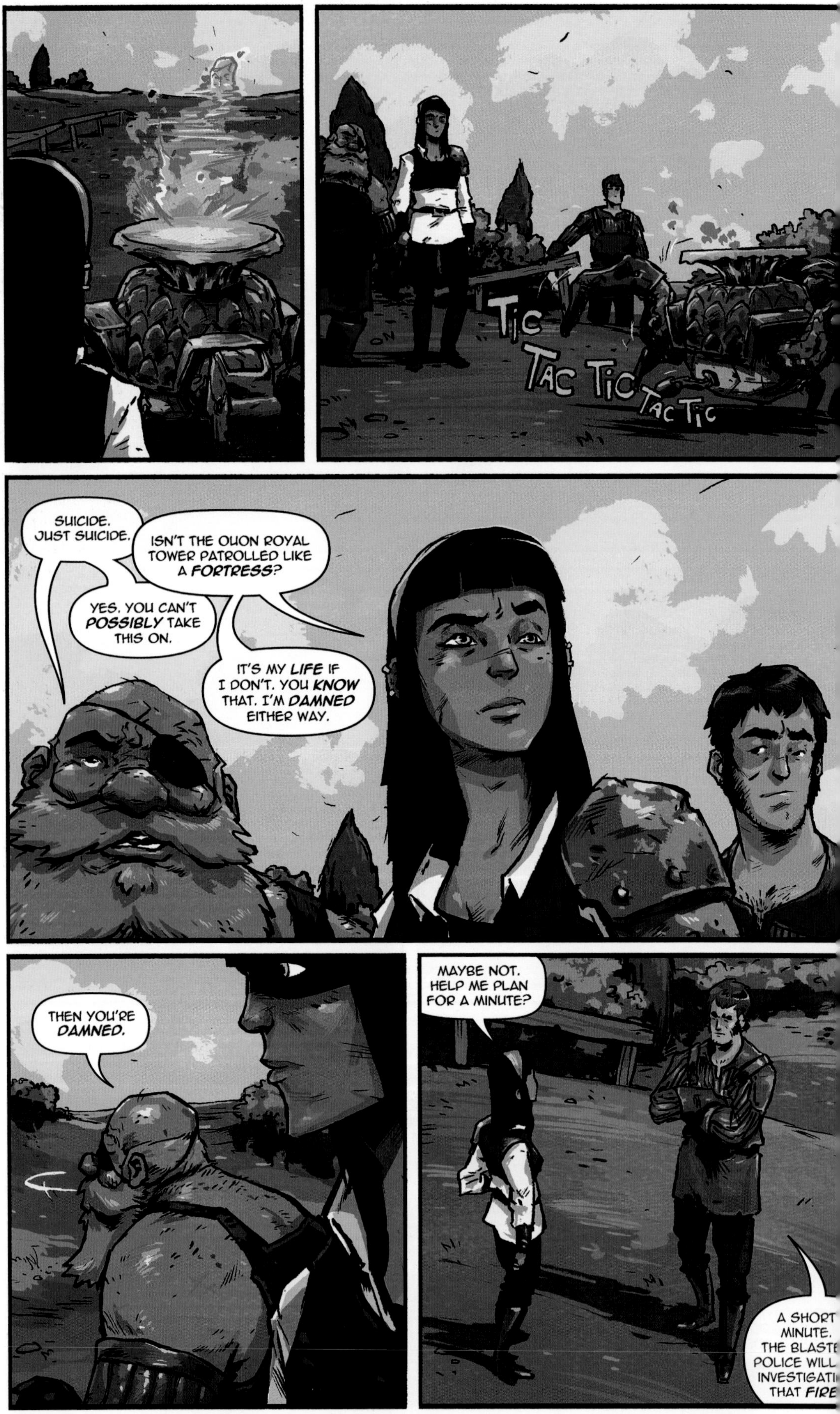
TIC
TAC TIC TAC TIC
SUICIDE. JUST SUICIDE.
ISN'T THE OUON ROYAL TOWER PATROLLED LIKE A FORTRESS?
YES. YOU CAN'T POSSIBLY TAKE THIS ON.
IT'S MY LIFE IF I DON'T. YOU KNOW THAT. I'M DAMNED EITHER WAY.
THEN YOU'RE DAMNED.
MAYBE NOT. HELP ME PLAN FOR A MINUTE?
A SHORT MINUTE. THE BLASTE POLICE WILL INVESTIGAT THAT FIRE

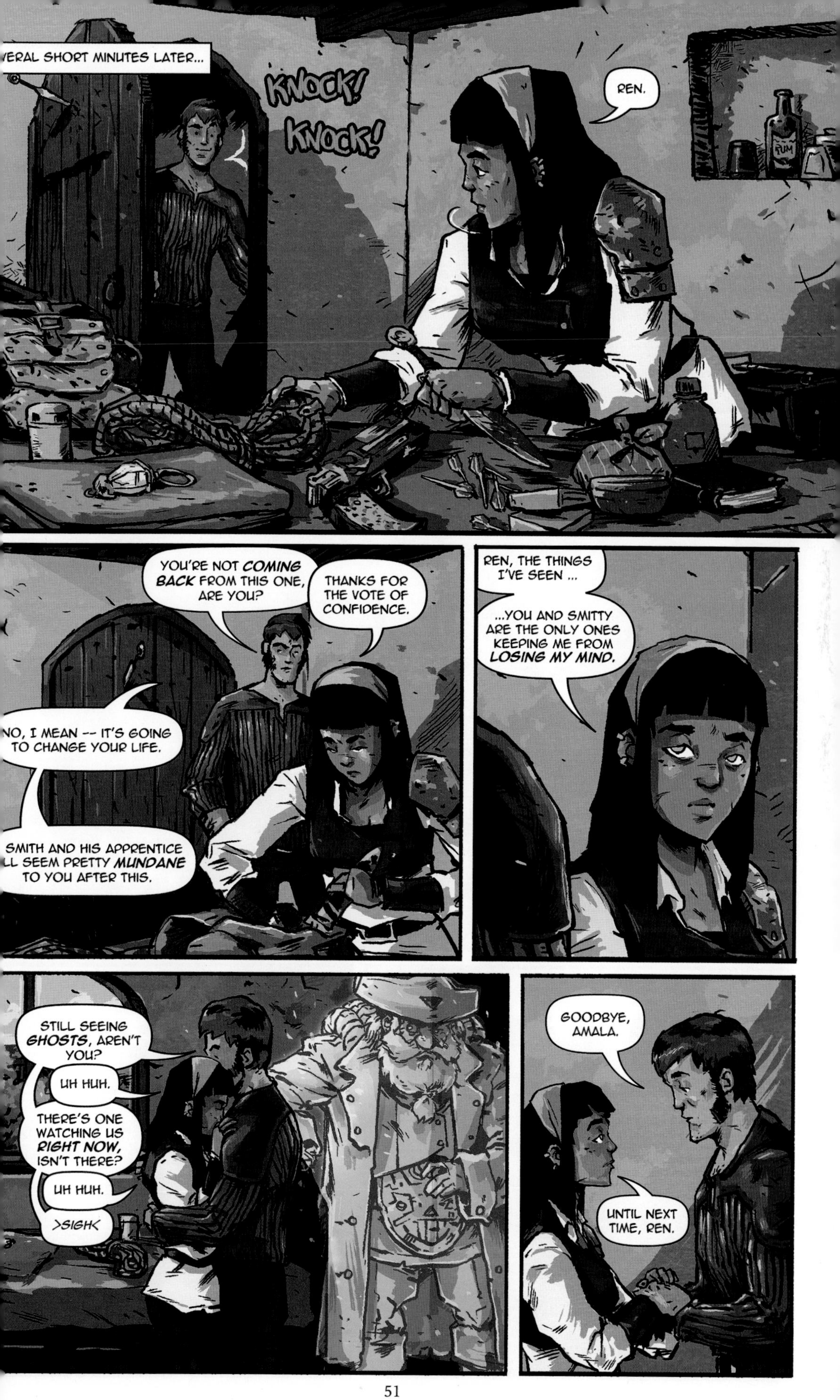
VERAL SHORT MINUTES LATER...
KNOCK!
KNOCK!
REN.
RUM
YOU'RE NOT COMING BACK FROM THIS ONE, ARE YOU?
THANKS FOR THE VOTE OF CONFIDENCE.
NO, I MEAN -- IT'S GOING TO CHANGE YOUR LIFE.
SMITH AND HIS APPRENTICE LL SEEM PRETTY MUNDANE TO YOU AFTER THIS.
REN, THE THINGS I'VE SEEN ...
...YOU AND SMITTY ARE THE ONLY ONES KEEPING ME FROM LOSING MY MIND.
STILL SEEING GHOSTS, AREN'T YOU?
UH HUH.
THERE'S ONE WATCHING US RIGHT NOW, ISN'T THERE?
UH HUH.
>SIGH<
GOODBYE, AMALA.
UNTIL NEXT TIME, REN.

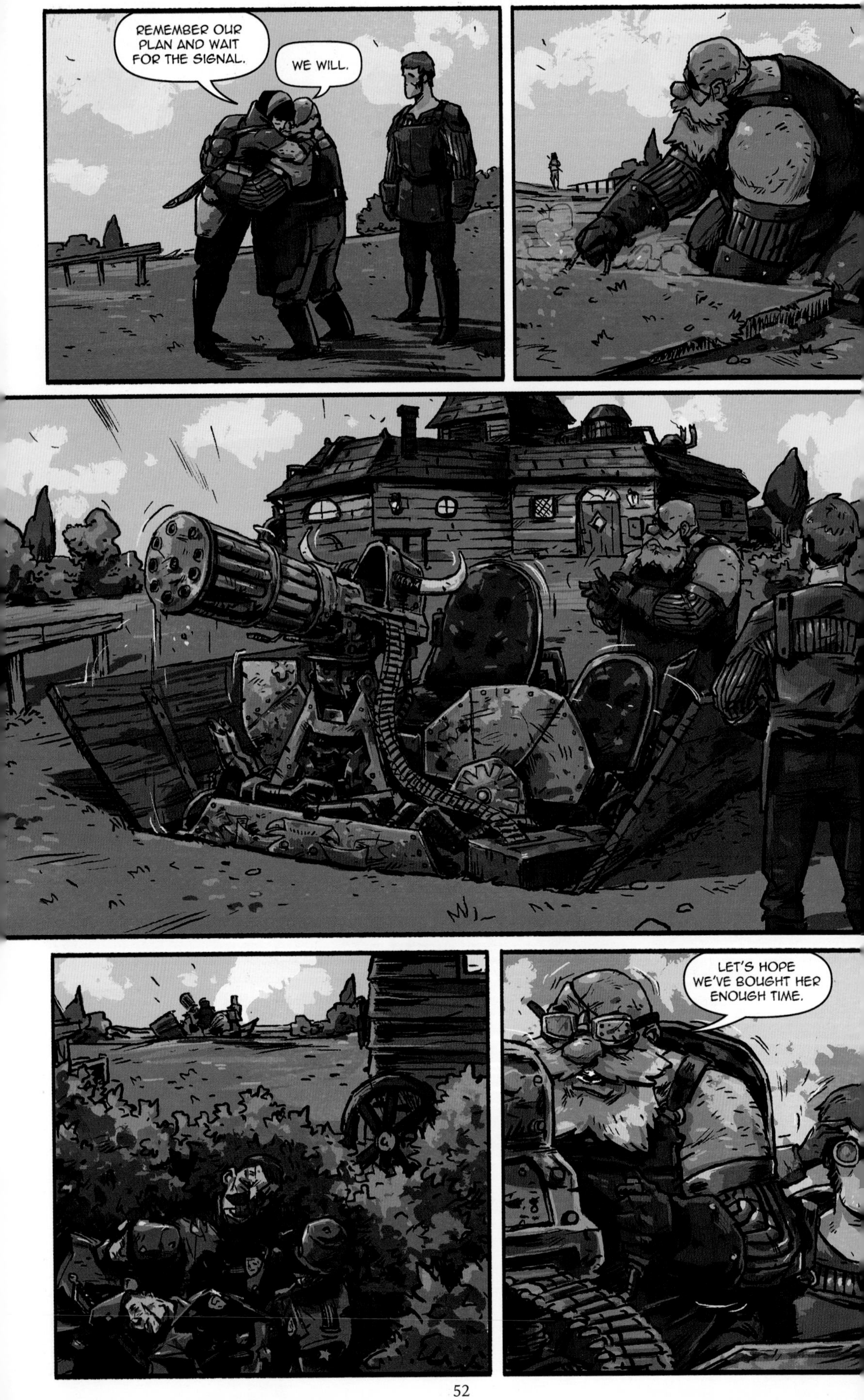
REMEMBER OUR PLAN AND WAIT FOR THE SIGNAL.
WE WILL.
LET'S HOPE WE'VE BOUGHT HER ENOUGH TIME.

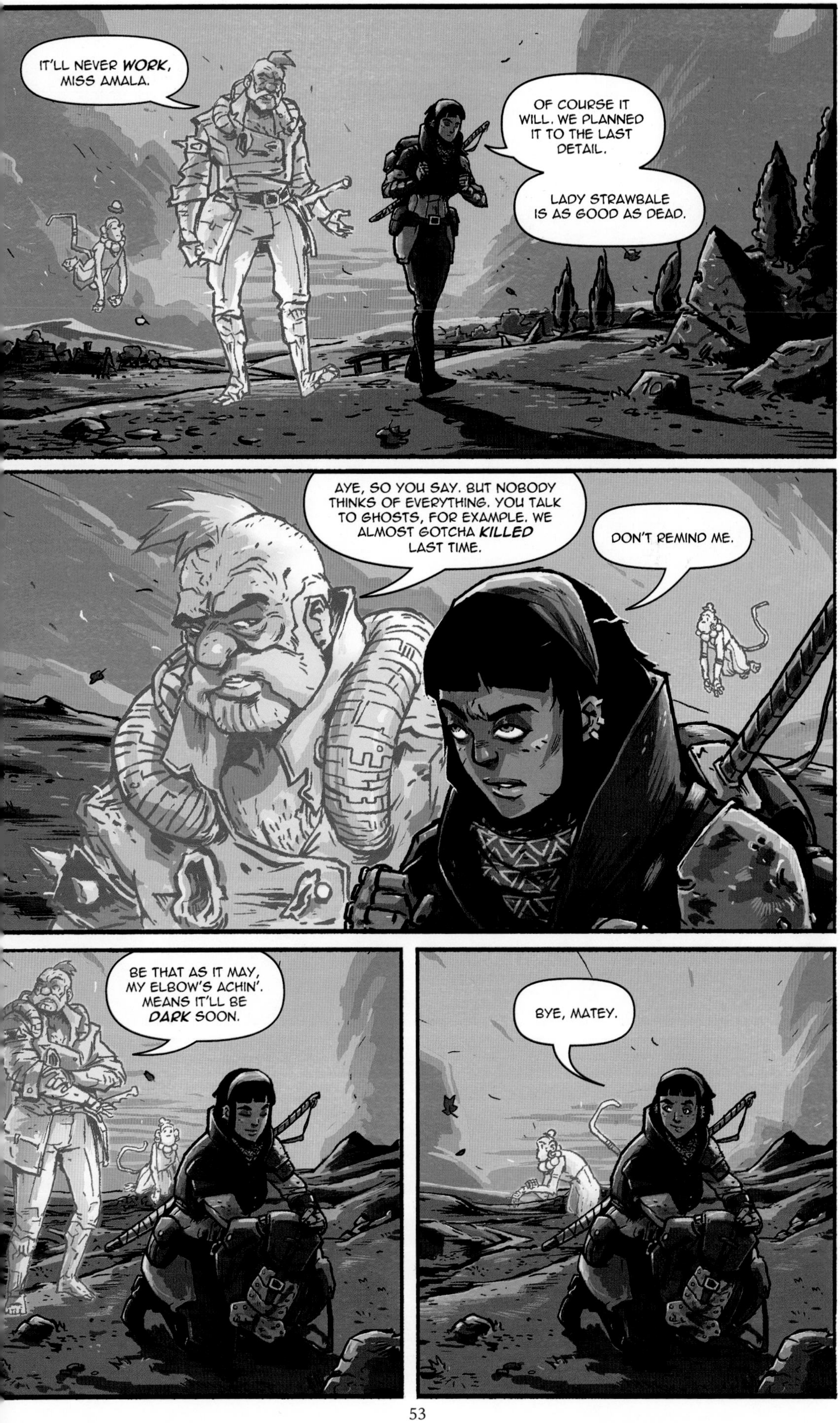
IT'LL NEVER *WORK*, MISS AMALA.
OF COURSE IT WILL. WE PLANNED IT TO THE LAST DETAIL.
LADY STRAWBALE IS AS GOOD AS DEAD.
AYE, SO YOU SAY. BUT NOBODY THINKS OF EVERYTHING. YOU TALK TO GHOSTS, FOR EXAMPLE. WE ALMOST GOTCHA *KILLED* LAST TIME.
DON'T REMIND ME.
BE THAT AS IT MAY, MY ELBOW'S ACHIN'. MEANS IT'LL BE *DARK* SOON.
BYE, MATEY.

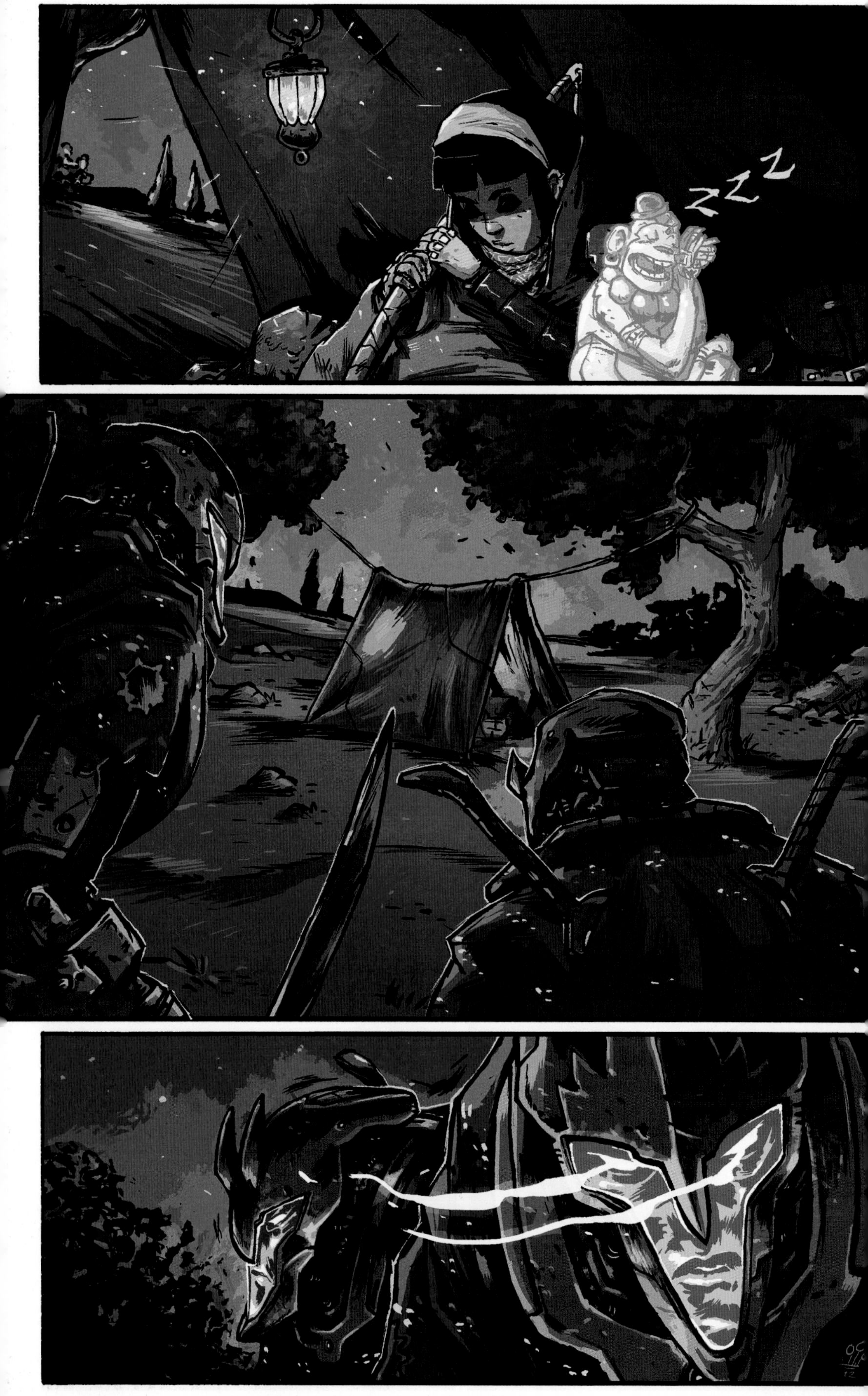
ZZZ

SPIRITS OF NAAMARON

PART TWO

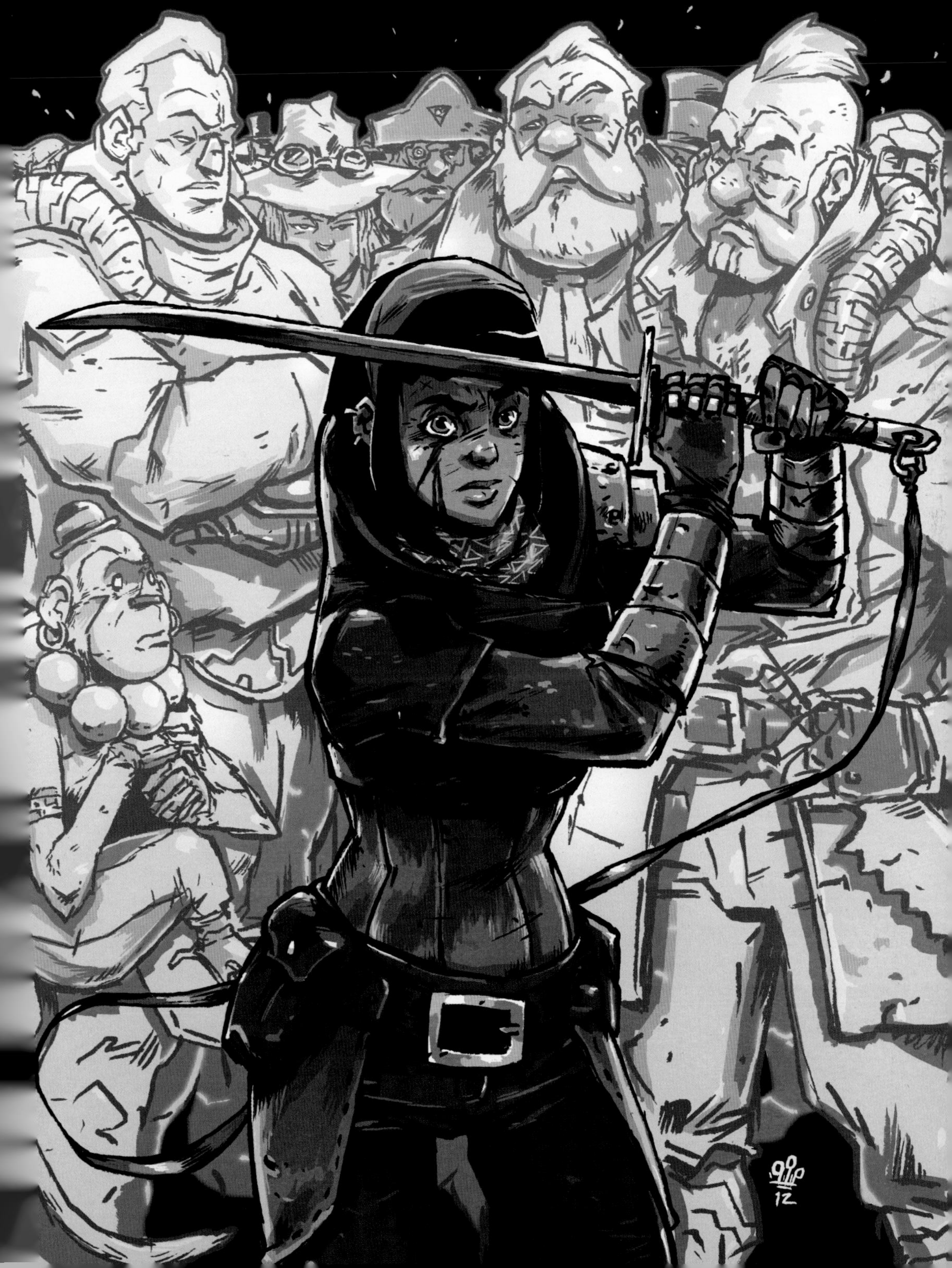

"LET ME INTRODUCE YOU TO SOME FRIENDS OF MINE."

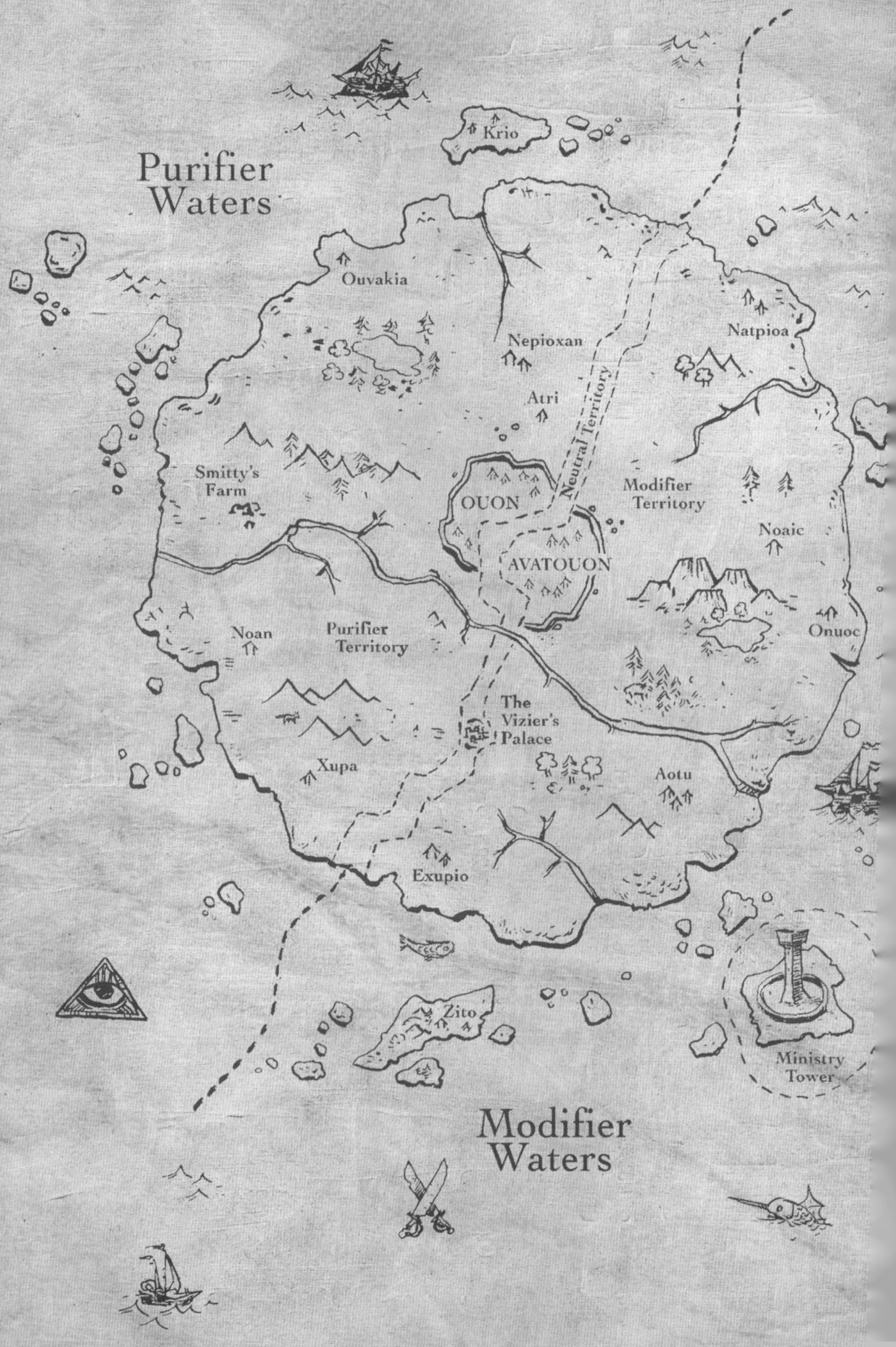

Purifier Waters
Krio
Ouvakia
Nepioxan
Natpioa
Atri
Neutral Territory
Smitty's Farm
OUON
Modifier Territory
Noaic
AVATOUON
Noan
Purifier Territory
Onuoc
The Vizier's Palace
Xupa
Aotu
Exupio
Zito
Ministry Tower
Modifier Waters

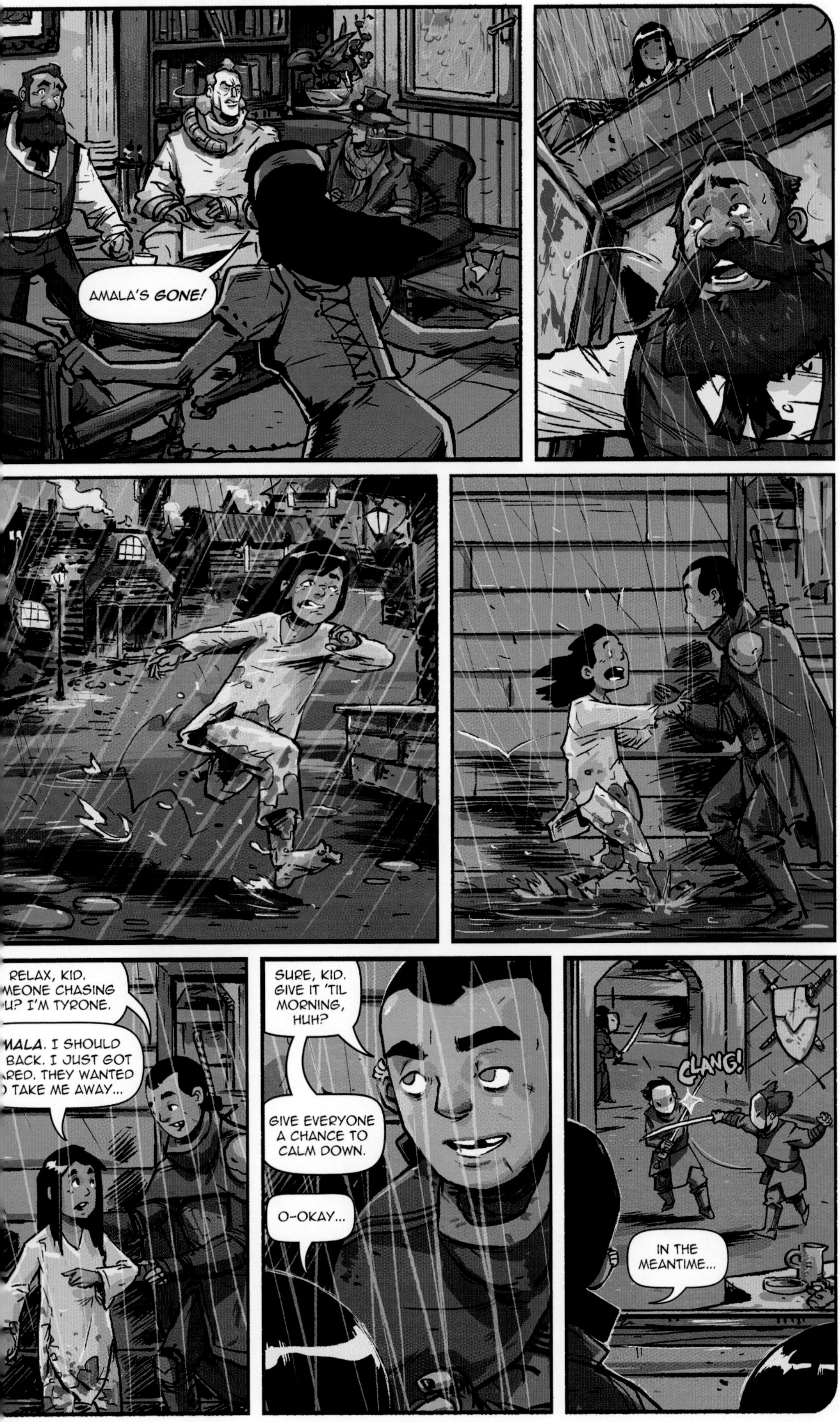
AMALA'S GONE!
RELAX, KID. MEONE CHASING U? I'M TYRONE.
MALA. I SHOULD BACK. I JUST GOT RED. THEY WANTED TAKE ME AWAY...
SURE, KID. GIVE IT 'TIL MORNING, HUH?
GIVE EVERYONE A CHANCE TO CALM DOWN.
O-OKAY...
CLANG!
IN THE MEANTIME...

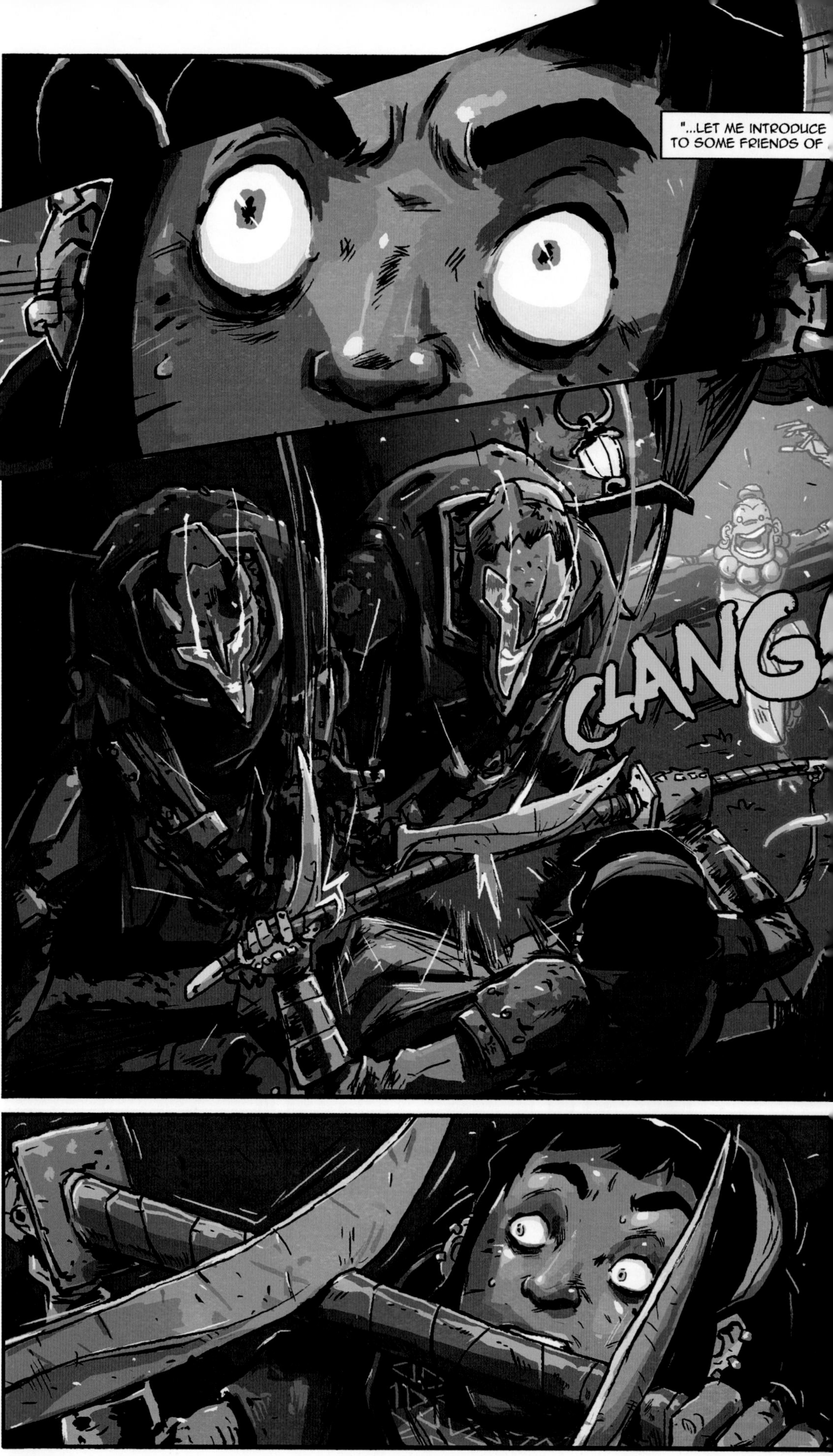
"...LET ME INTRODUCE
TO SOME FRIENDS OF
CLANG

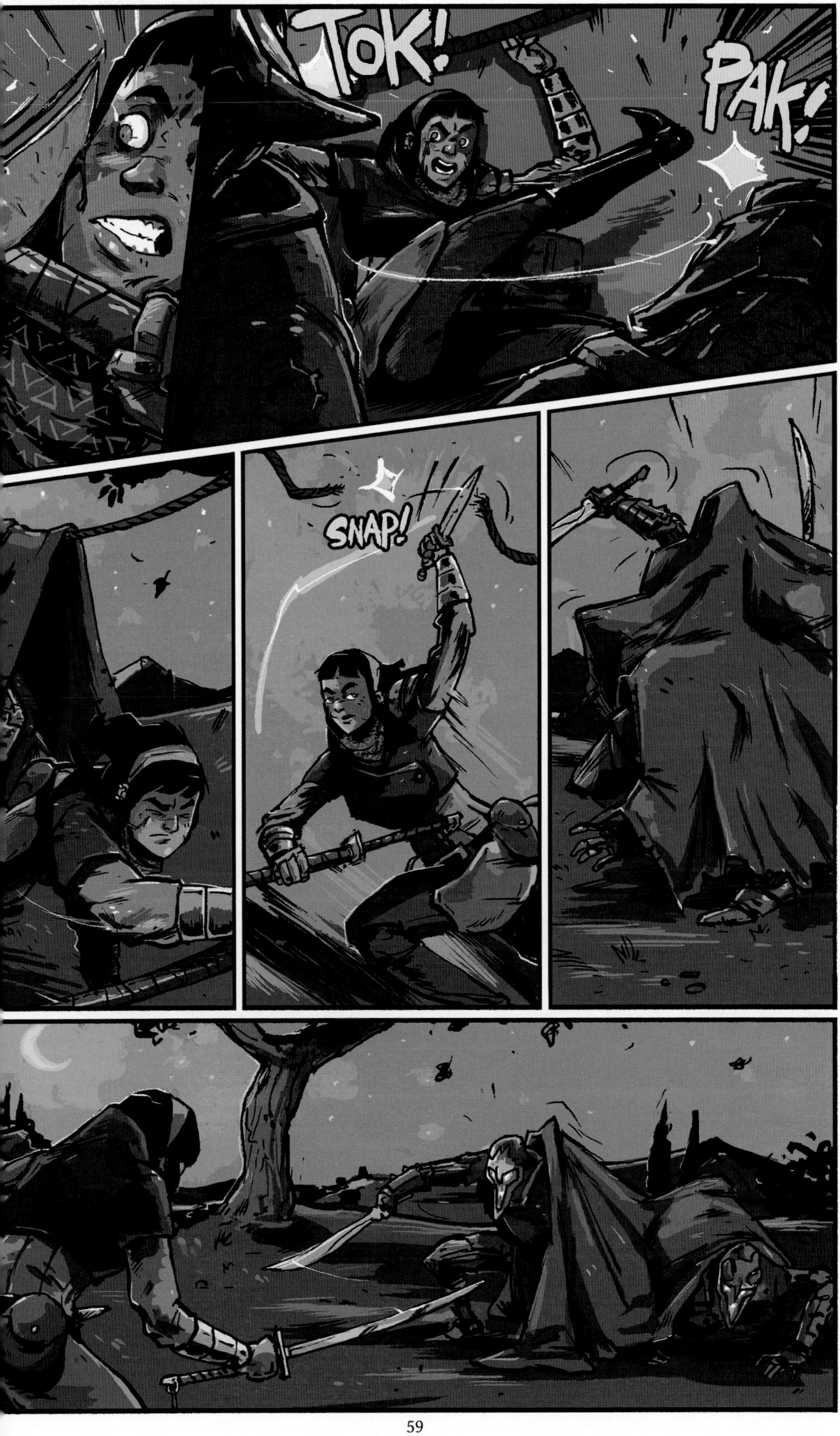
TOK!
PAK!
SNAP!

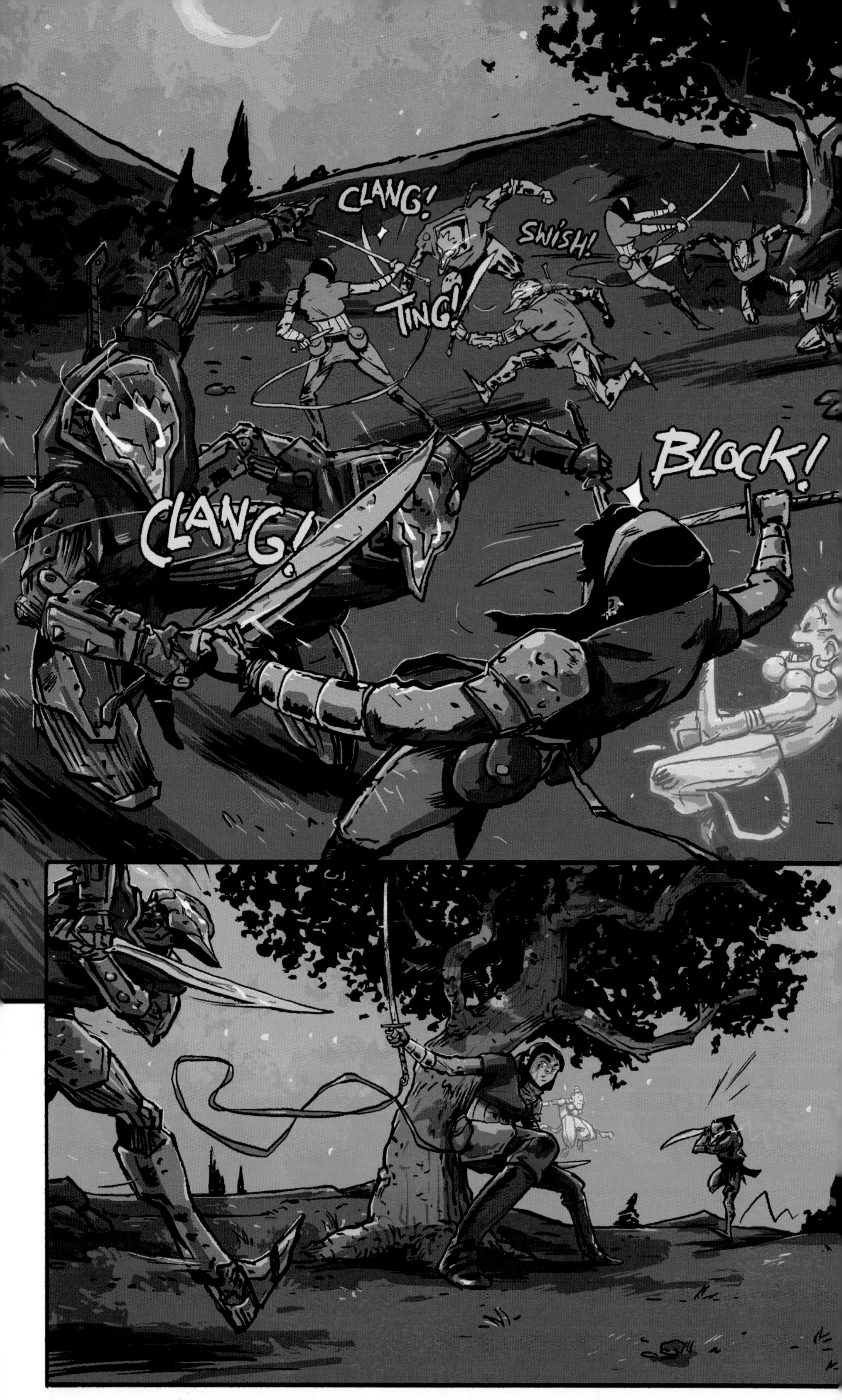
CLANG!
SWISH!
TING!
BLOCK!
CLANG!

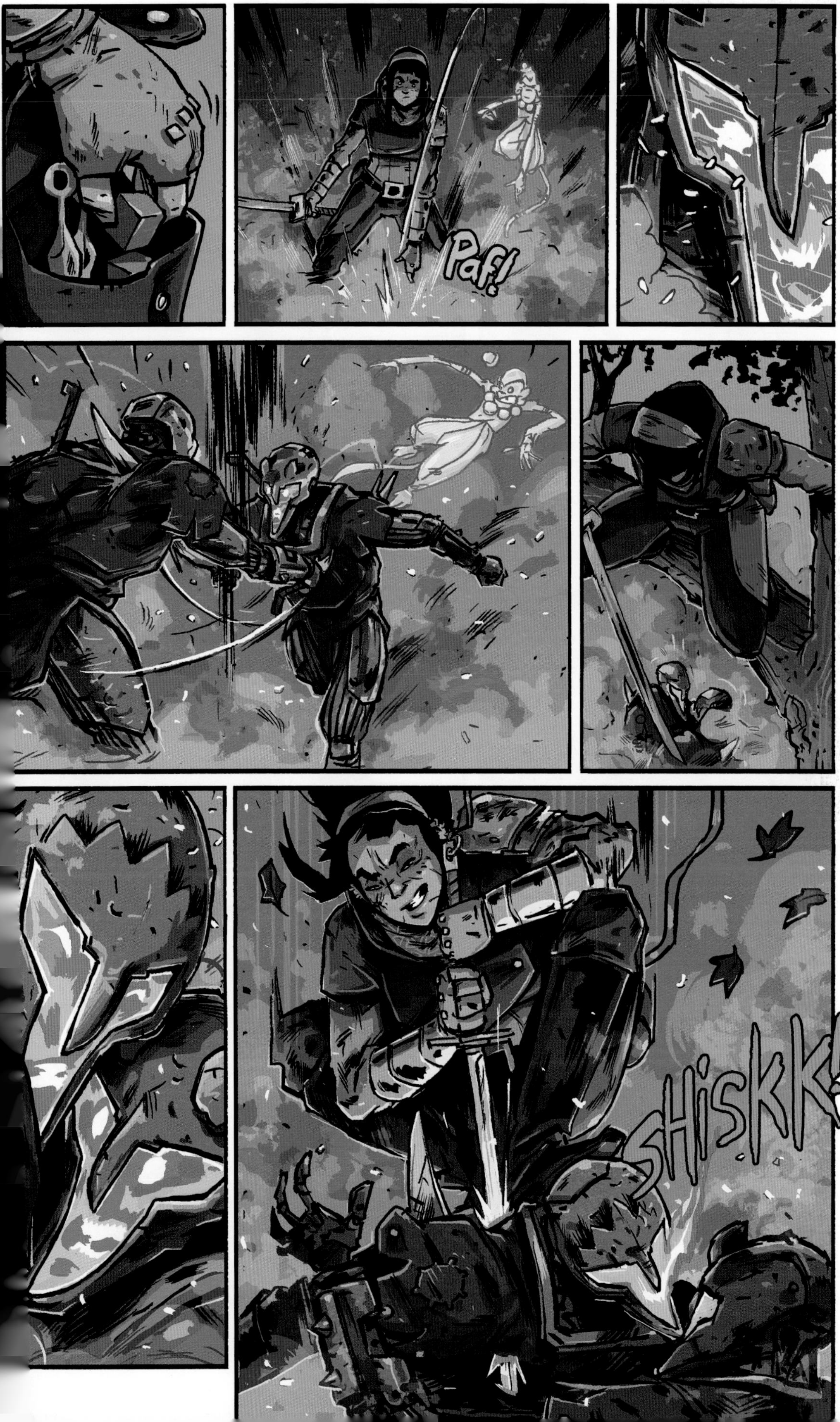
Paf!
SHISKK!

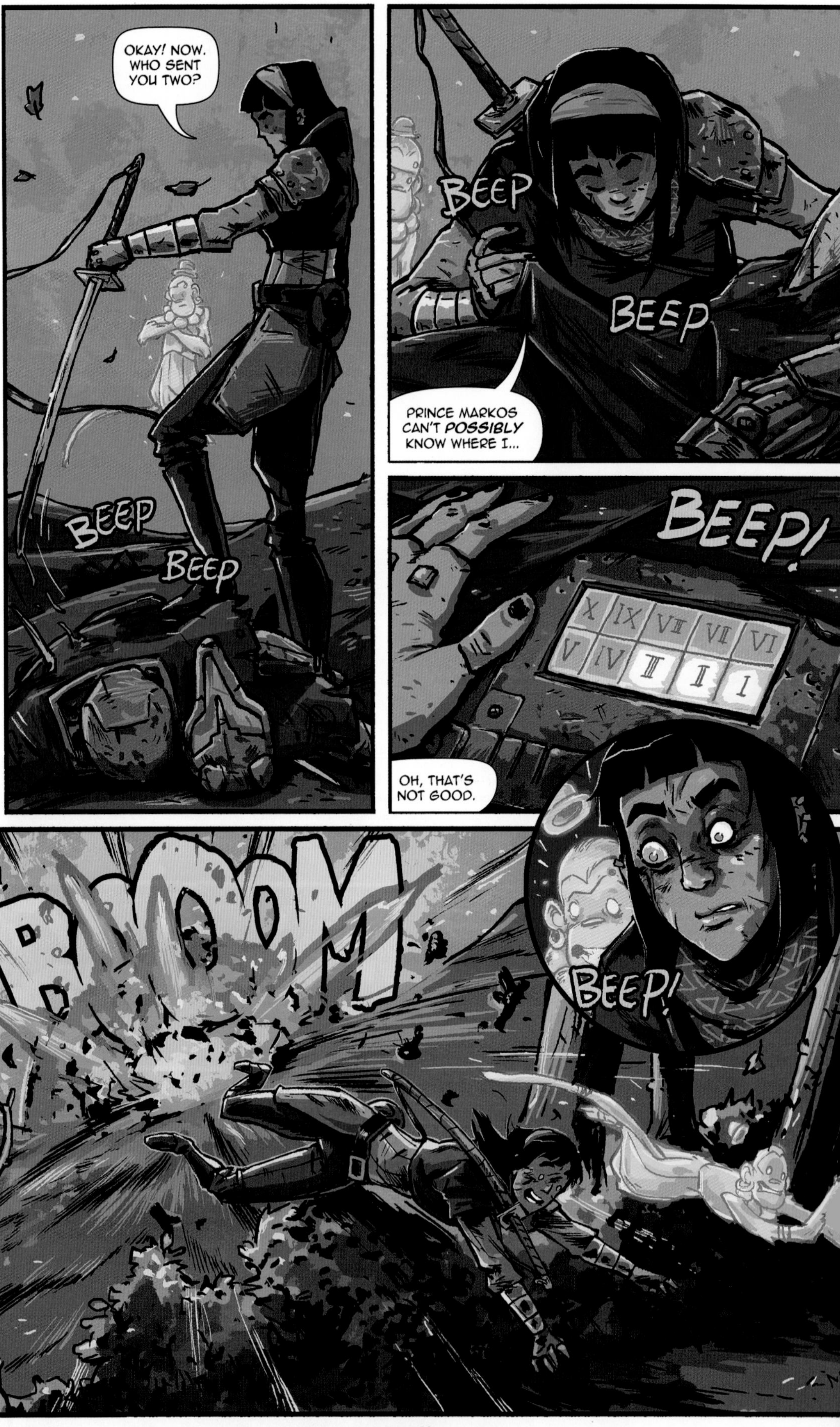
OKAY! NOW. WHO SENT YOU TWO?
BEEP
BEEP
BEEP
BEEP
PRINCE MARKOS CAN'T *POSSIBLY* KNOW WHERE I...
BEEP!
X IX VII VII VI
V IV III II I
OH, THAT'S NOT GOOD.
BEEP!
BOOOOM

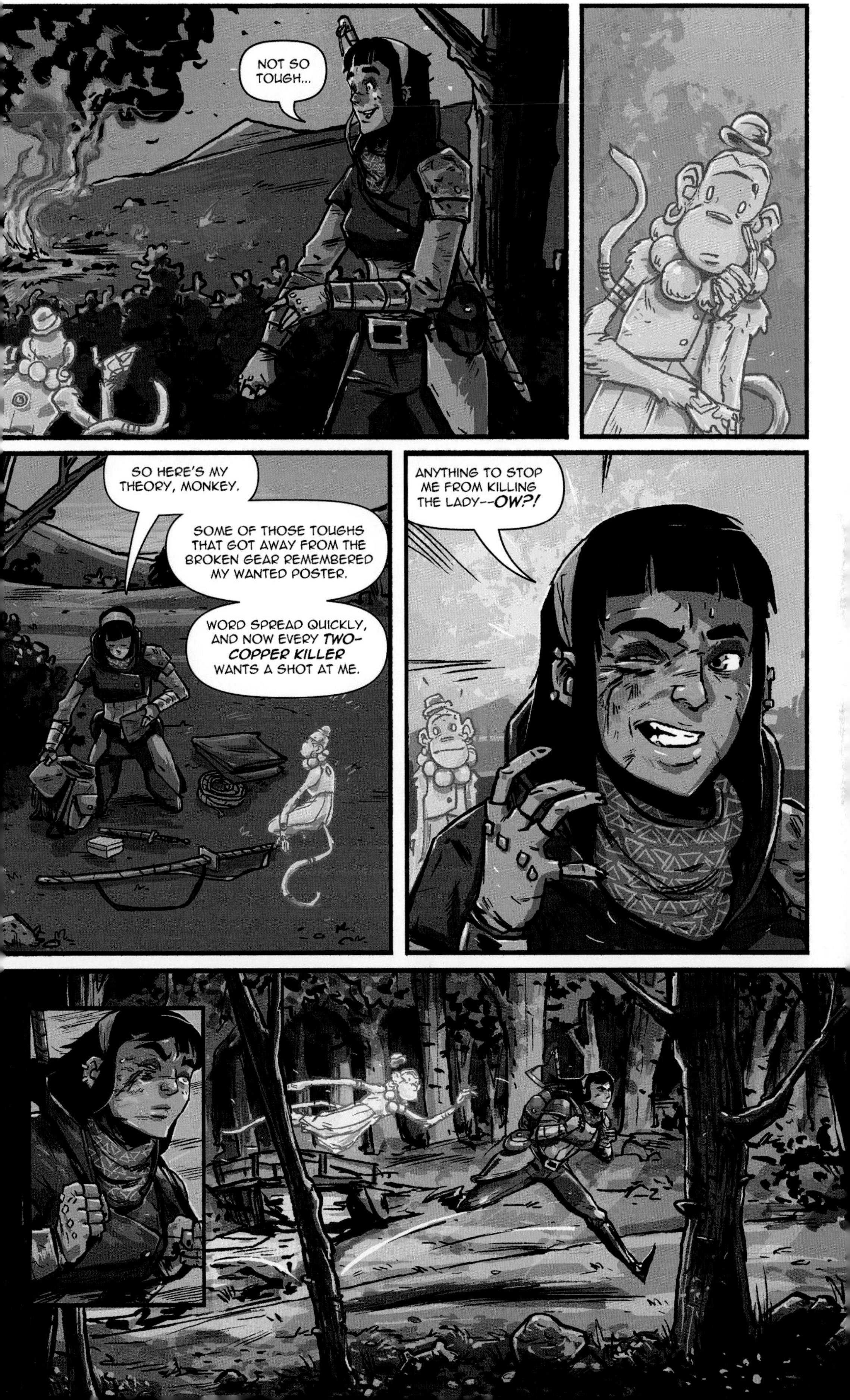
NOT SO TOUGH...
SO HERE'S MY THEORY, MONKEY.
SOME OF THOSE TOUGHS THAT GOT AWAY FROM THE BROKEN GEAR REMEMBERED MY WANTED POSTER.
WORD SPREAD QUICKLY, AND NOW EVERY TWO-COPPER KILLER WANTS A SHOT AT ME.
ANYTHING TO STOP ME FROM KILLING THE LADY--OW?!

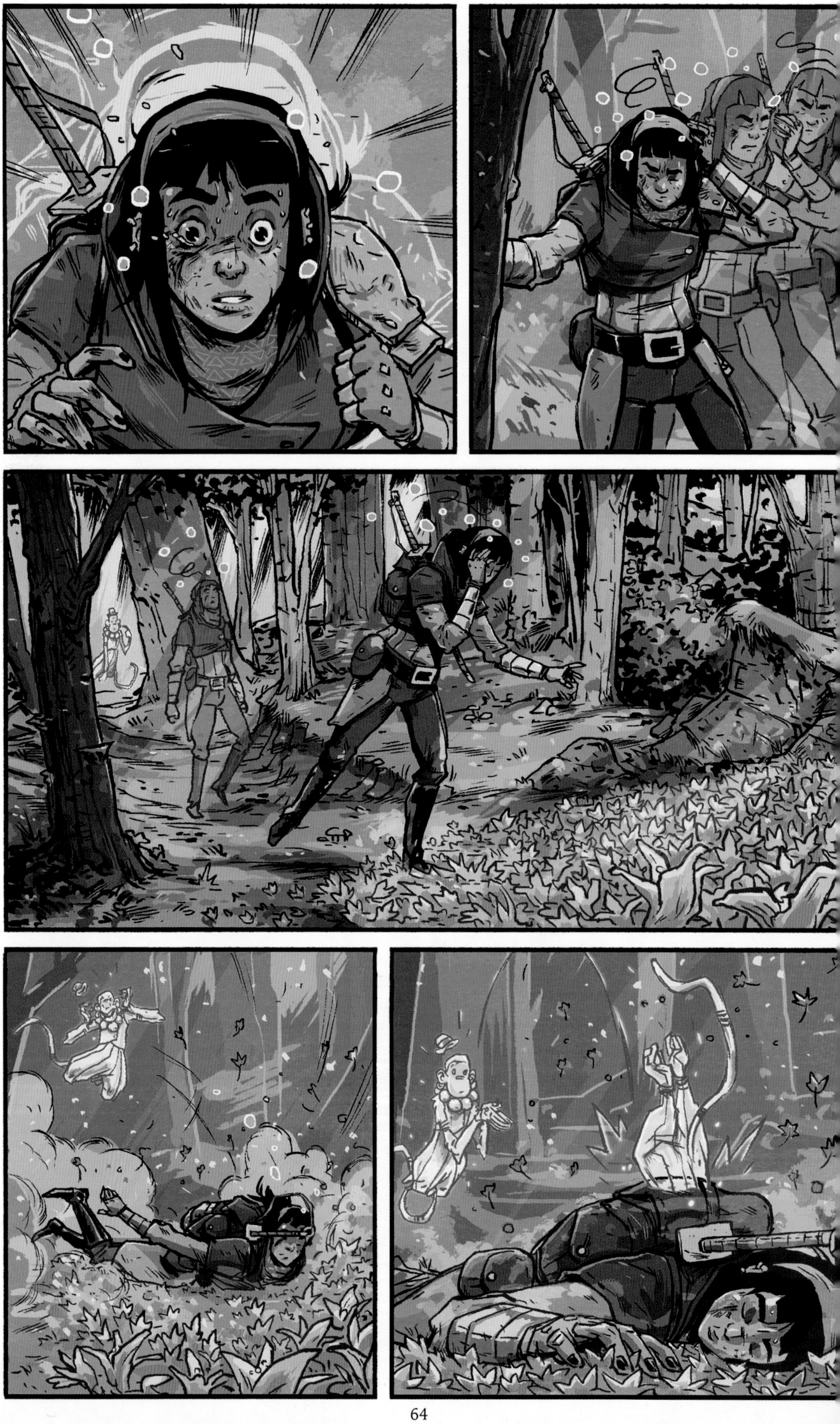

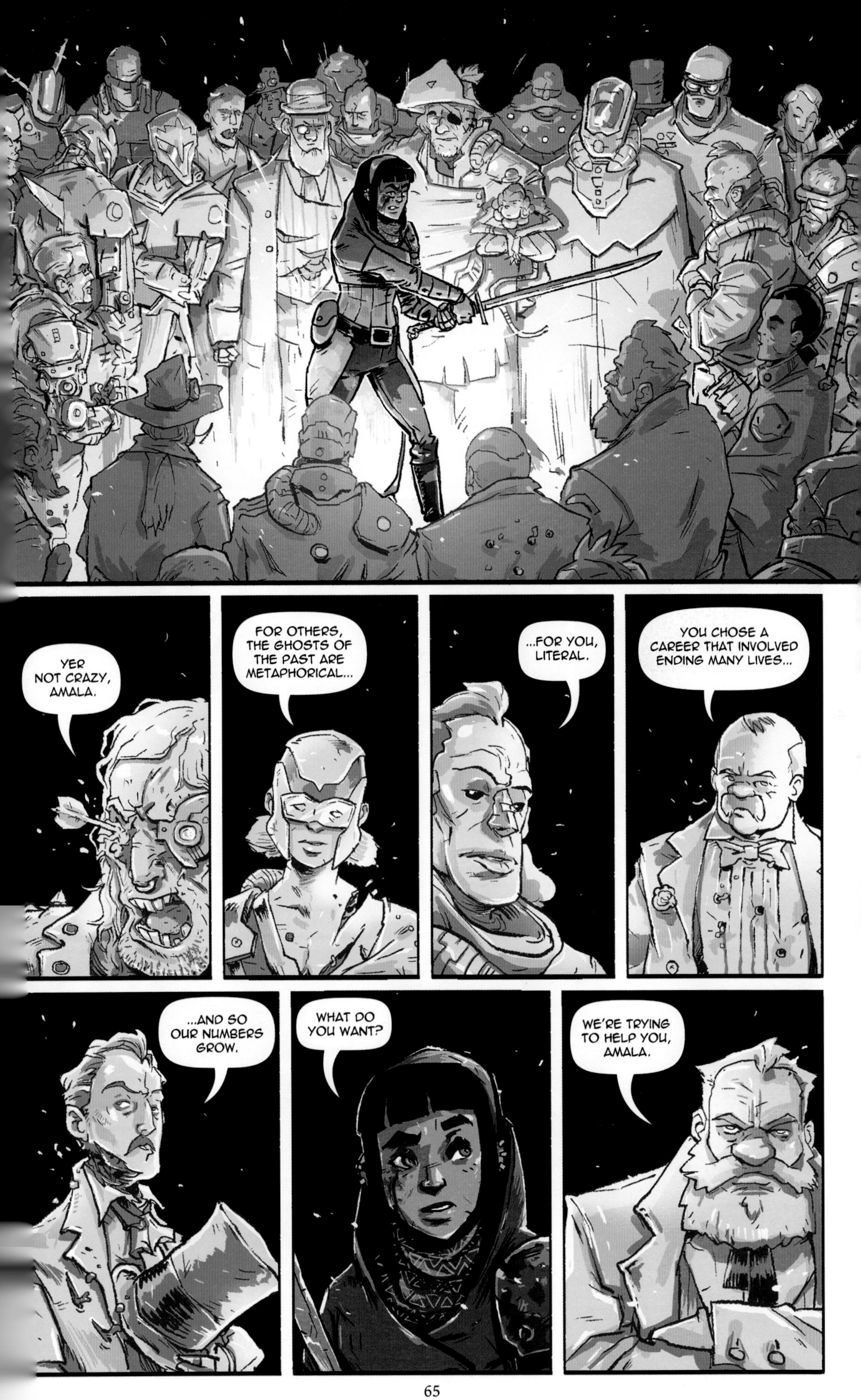

YER NOT CRAZY, AMALA.
FOR OTHERS, THE GHOSTS OF THE PAST ARE METAPHORICAL...
...FOR YOU, LITERAL.
YOU CHOSE A CAREER THAT INVOLVED ENDING MANY LIVES...
...AND SO OUR NUMBERS GROW.
WHAT DO YOU WANT?
WE'RE TRYING TO HELP YOU, AMALA.

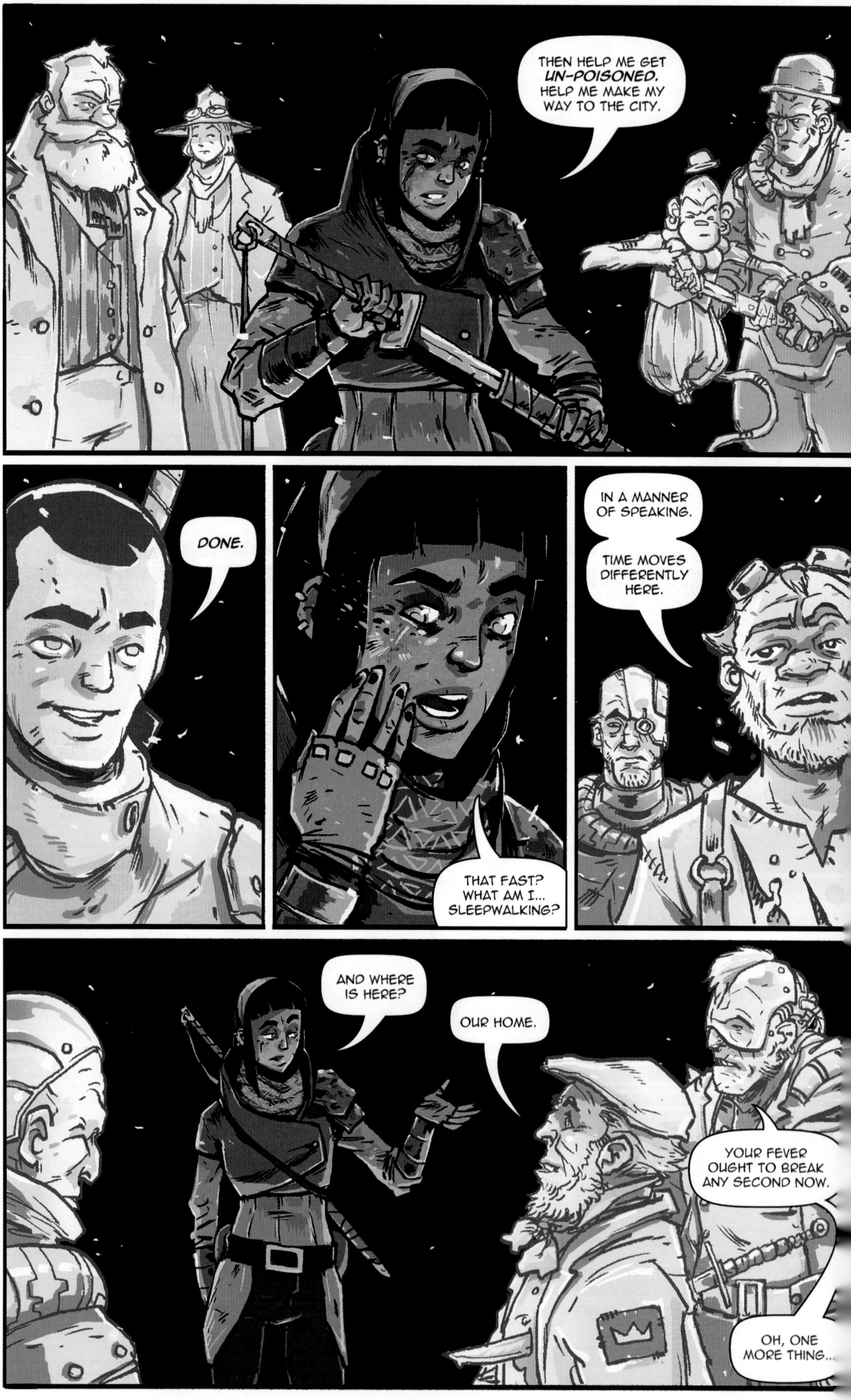
THEN HELP ME GET *UN-POISONED.* HELP ME MAKE MY WAY TO THE CITY.
DONE.
THAT FAST? WHAT AM I... SLEEPWALKING?
IN A MANNER OF SPEAKING.
TIME MOVES DIFFERENTLY HERE.
AND WHERE IS HERE?
OUR HOME.
YOUR FEVER OUGHT TO BREAK ANY SECOND NOW.
OH, ONE MORE THING...

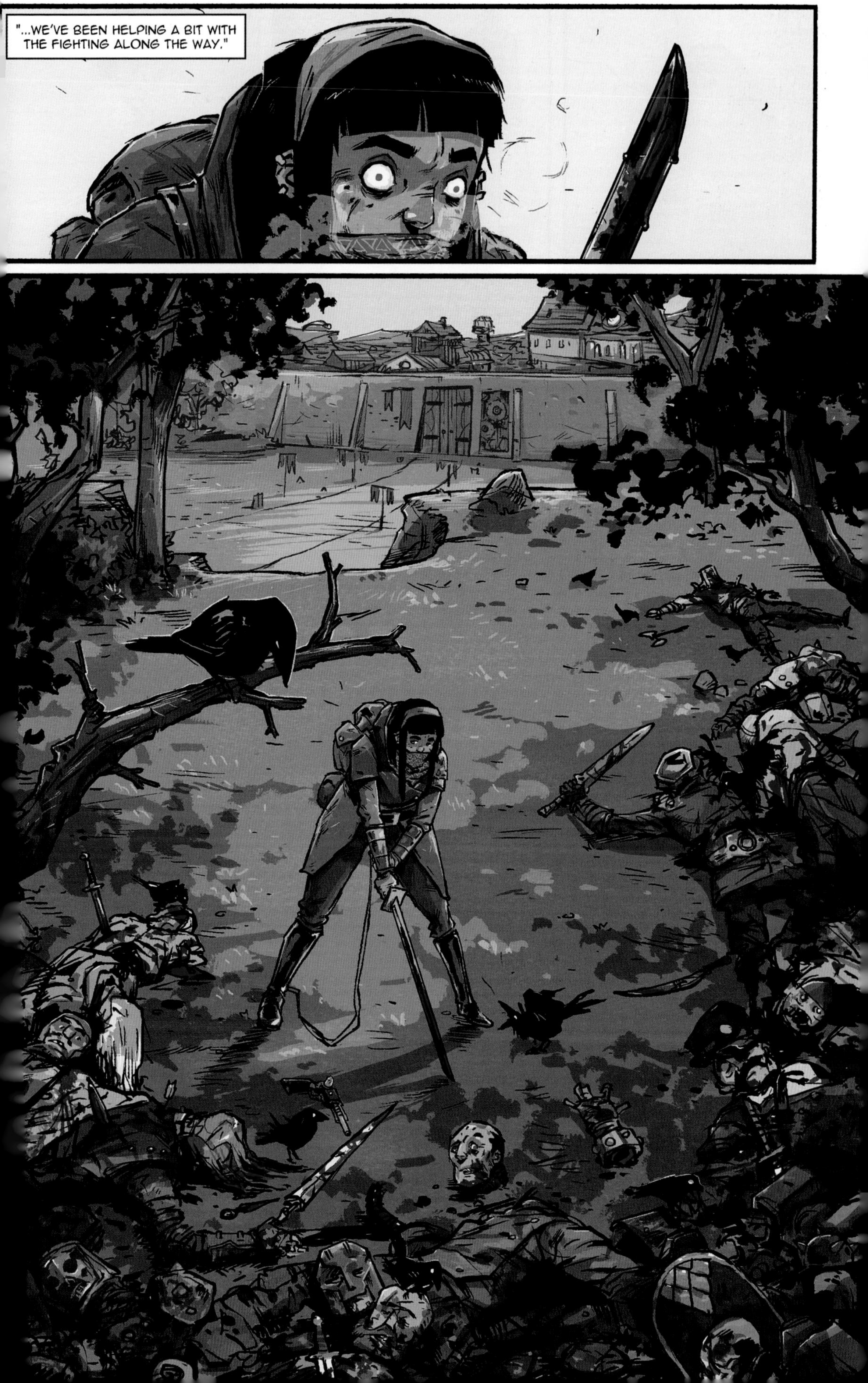
"...WE'VE BEEN HELPING A BIT WITH THE FIGHTING ALONG THE WAY."

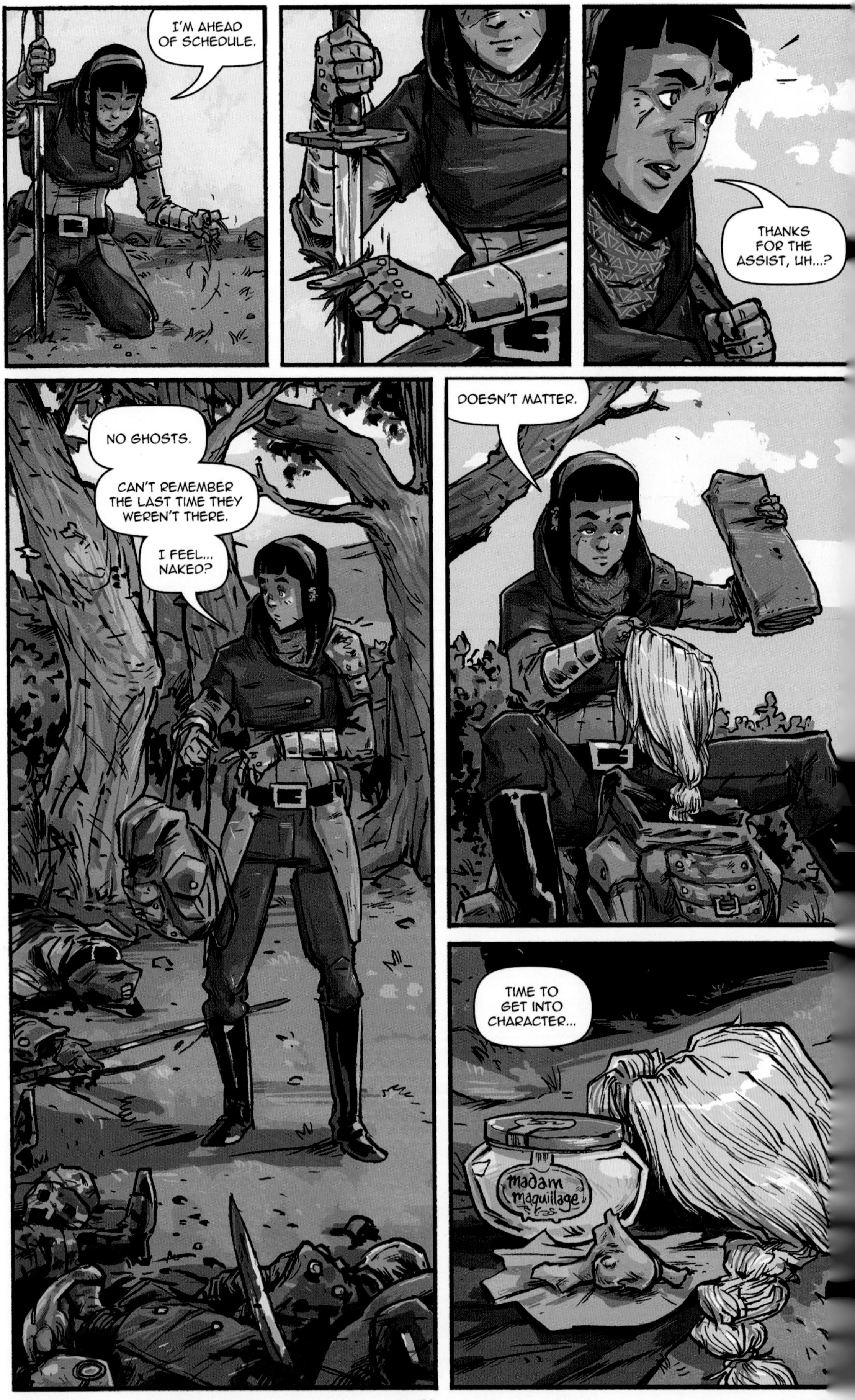
I'M AHEAD OF SCHEDULE.
THANKS FOR THE ASSIST, UH...?
NO GHOSTS.
CAN'T REMEMBER THE LAST TIME THEY WEREN'T THERE.
I FEEL... NAKED?
DOESN'T MATTER.
TIME TO GET INTO CHARACTER...
madam maquillage

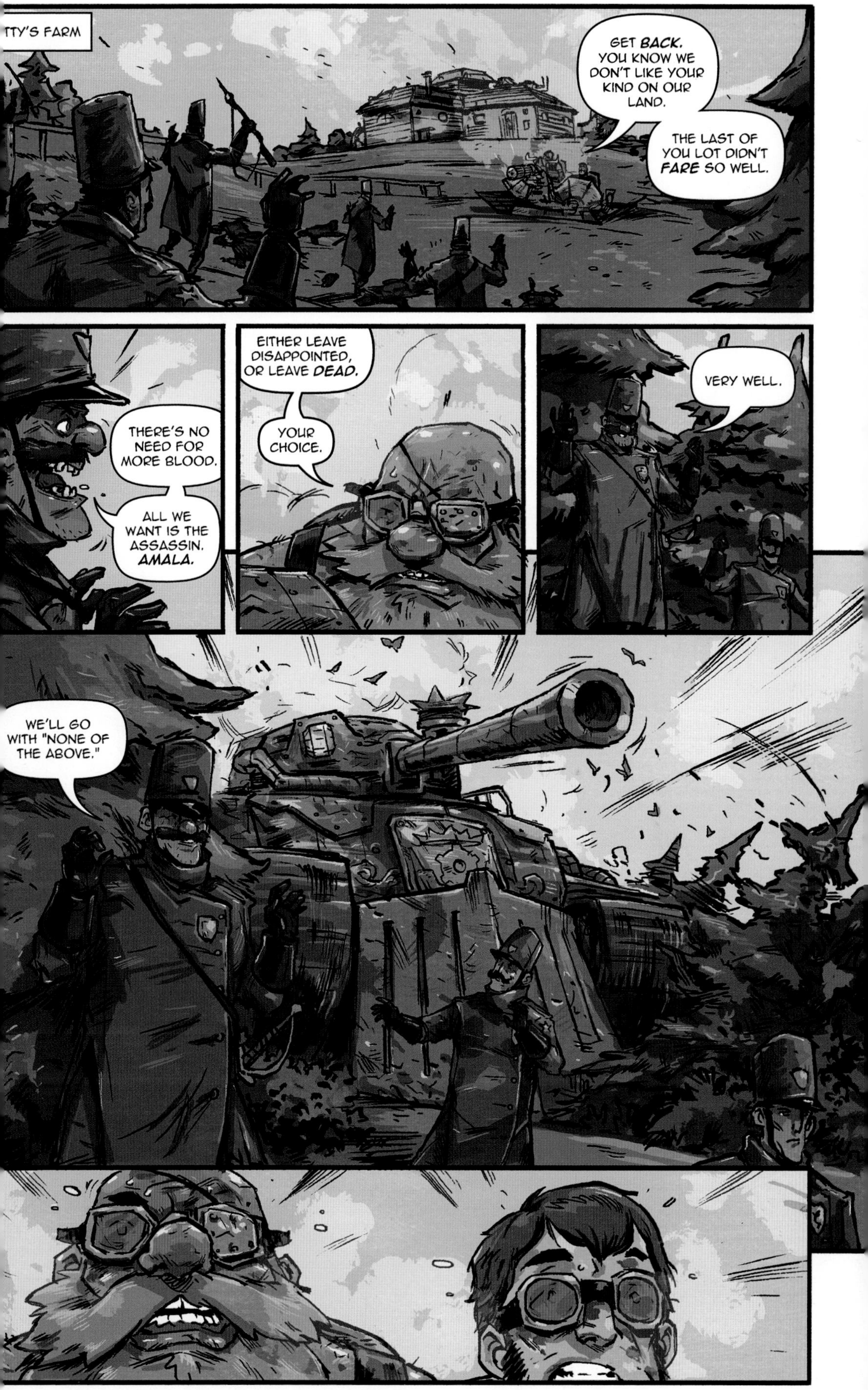
TTY'S FARM
GET BACK. YOU KNOW WE DON'T LIKE YOUR KIND ON OUR LAND.
THE LAST OF YOU LOT DIDN'T FARE SO WELL.
THERE'S NO NEED FOR MORE BLOOD.
ALL WE WANT IS THE ASSASSIN. AMALA.
EITHER LEAVE DISAPPOINTED, OR LEAVE DEAD.
YOUR CHOICE.
VERY WELL.
WE'LL GO WITH "NONE OF THE ABOVE."

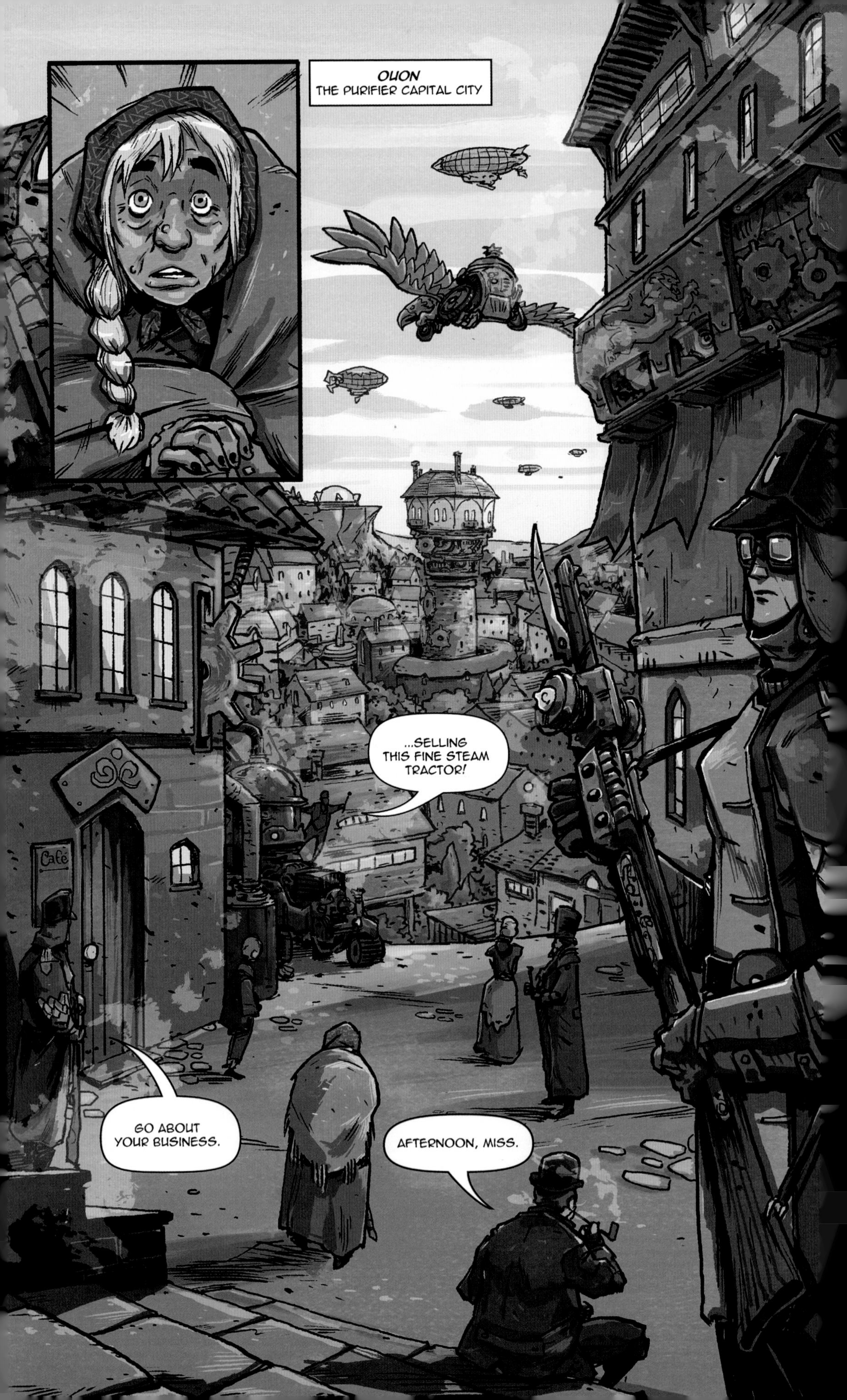
OUON
THE PURIFIER CAPITAL CITY
...SELLING THIS FINE STEAM TRACTOR!
Café
GO ABOUT YOUR BUSINESS.
AFTERNOON, MISS.

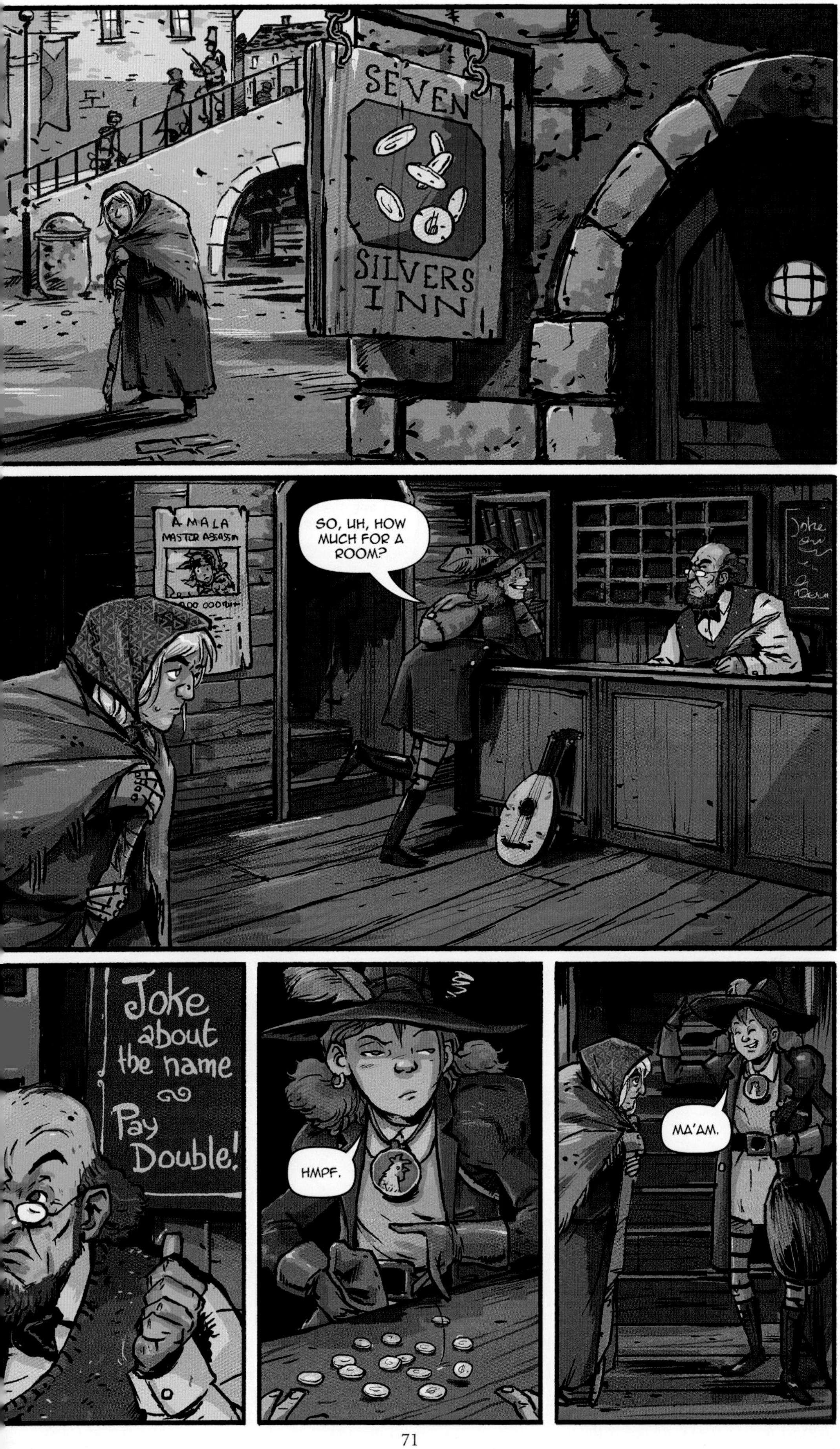

SEVEN
SILVERS INN
AMALA
MASTER ASSASSIN
SO, UH, HOW MUCH FOR A ROOM?
Joke about the name
Pay Double!
HMPF.
MA'AM.

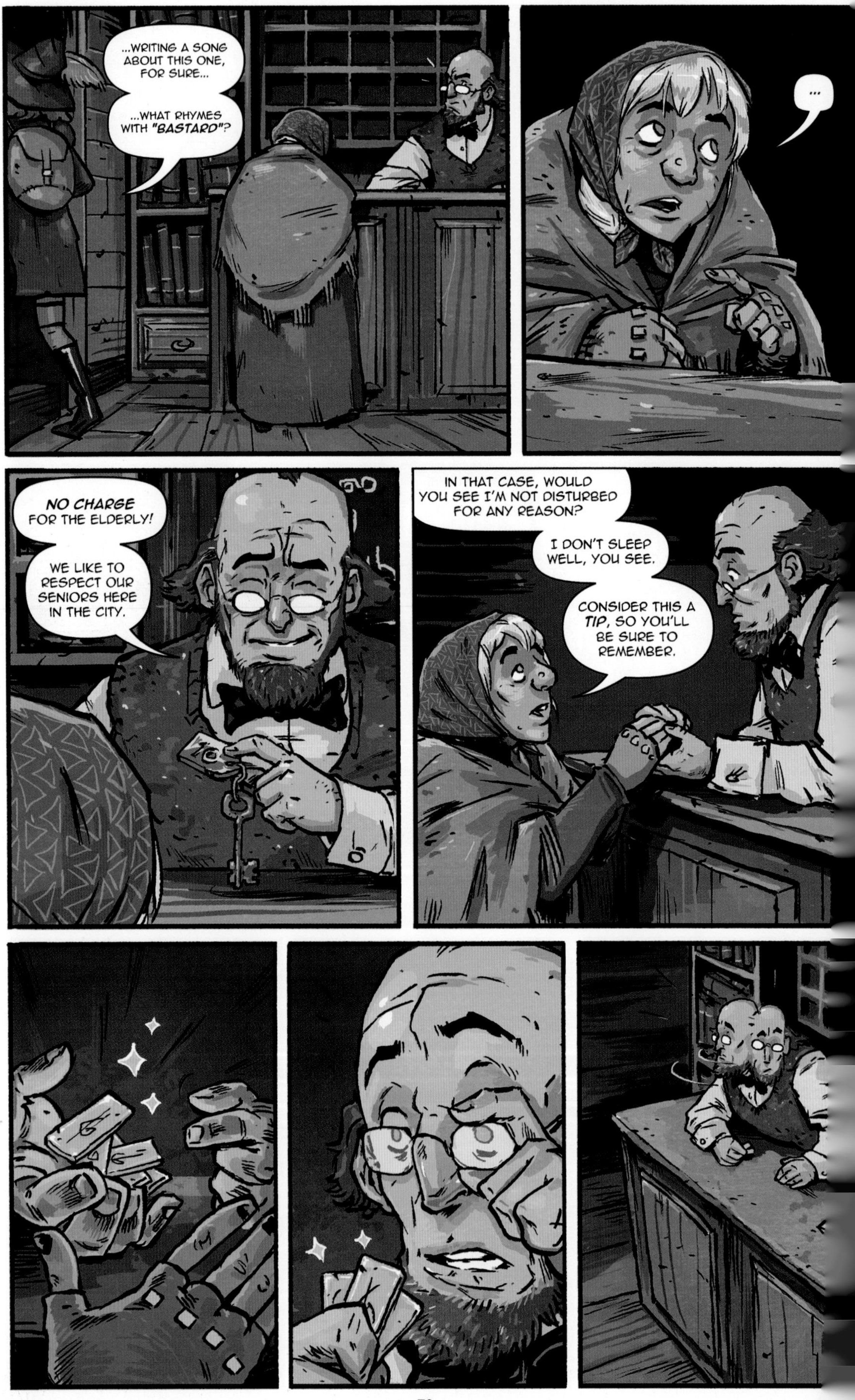
...WRITING A SONG ABOUT THIS ONE, FOR SURE...
...WHAT RHYMES WITH "BASTARD"?
...
NO CHARGE FOR THE ELDERLY!
WE LIKE TO RESPECT OUR SENIORS HERE IN THE CITY.
IN THAT CASE, WOULD YOU SEE I'M NOT DISTURBED FOR ANY REASON?
I DON'T SLEEP WELL, YOU SEE.
CONSIDER THIS A TIP, SO YOU'LL BE SURE TO REMEMBER.

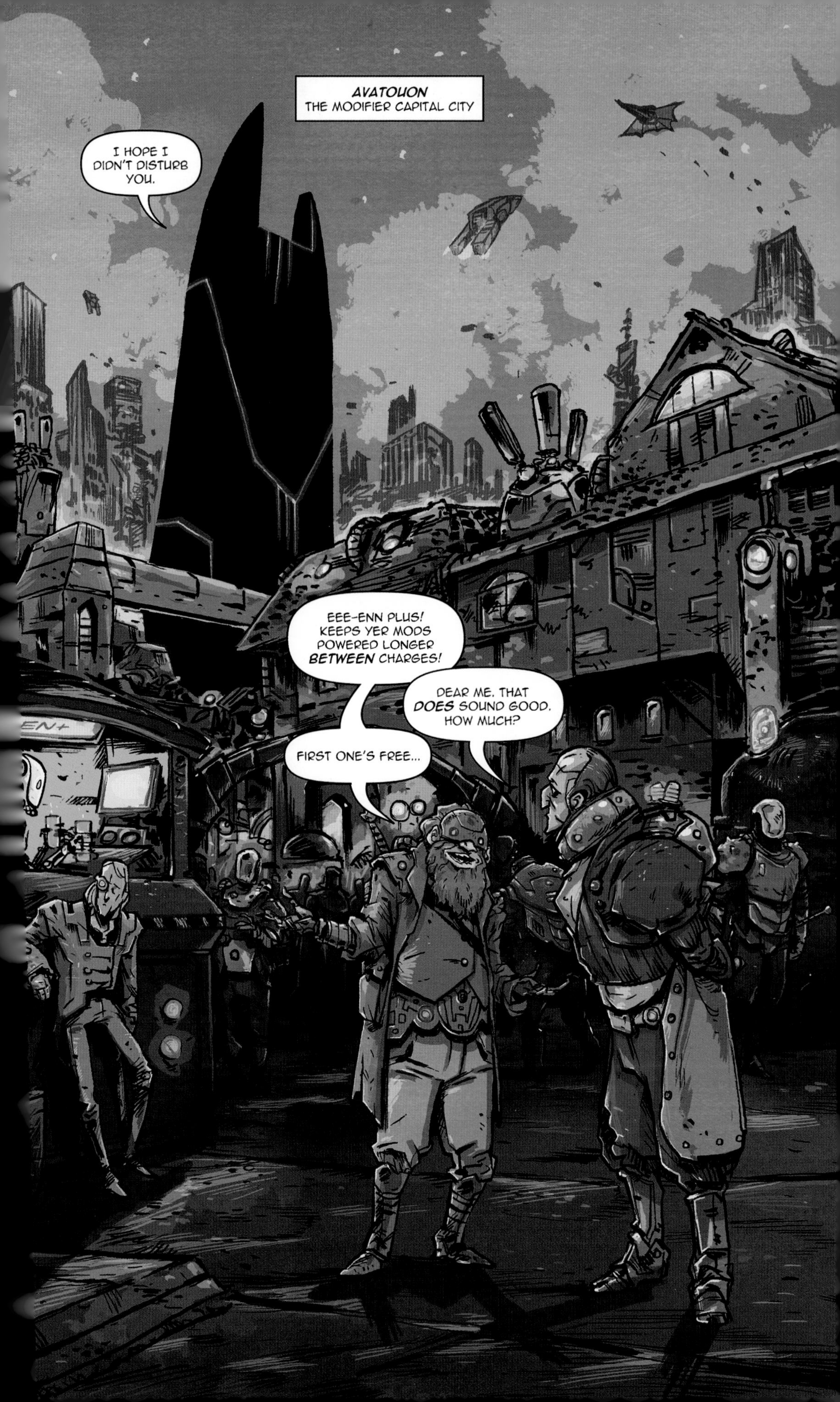
AVATOUON
THE MODIFIER CAPITAL CITY
I HOPE I DIDN'T DISTURB YOU.
EEE-ENN PLUS! KEEPS YER MODS POWERED LONGER BETWEEN CHARGES!
DEAR ME. THAT DOES SOUND GOOD. HOW MUCH?
FIRST ONE'S FREE...

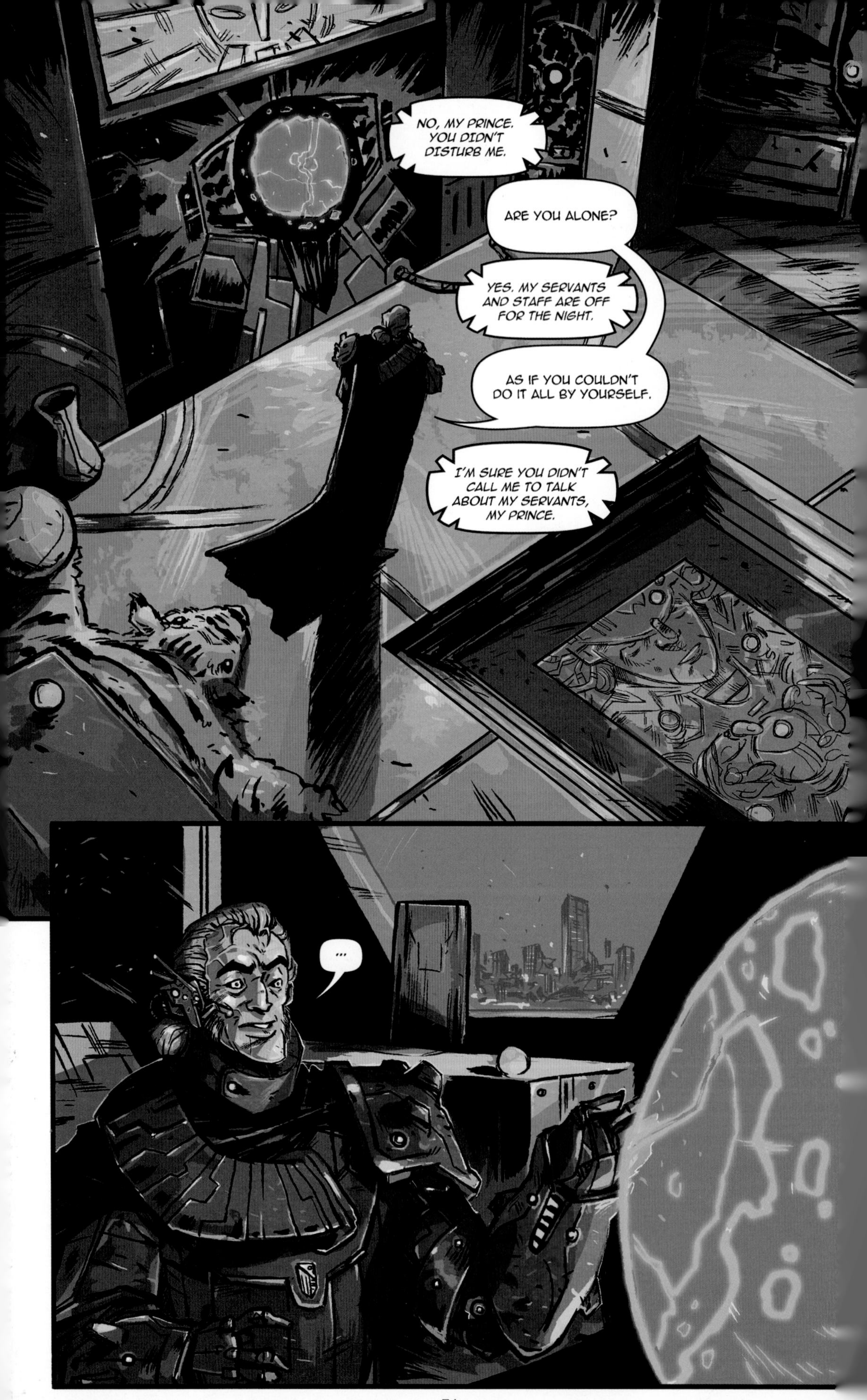
NO, MY PRINCE. YOU DIDN'T DISTURB ME.
ARE YOU ALONE?
YES. MY SERVANTS AND STAFF ARE OFF FOR THE NIGHT.
AS IF YOU COULDN'T DO IT ALL BY YOURSELF.
I'M SURE YOU DIDN'T CALL ME TO TALK ABOUT MY SERVANTS, MY PRINCE.
...

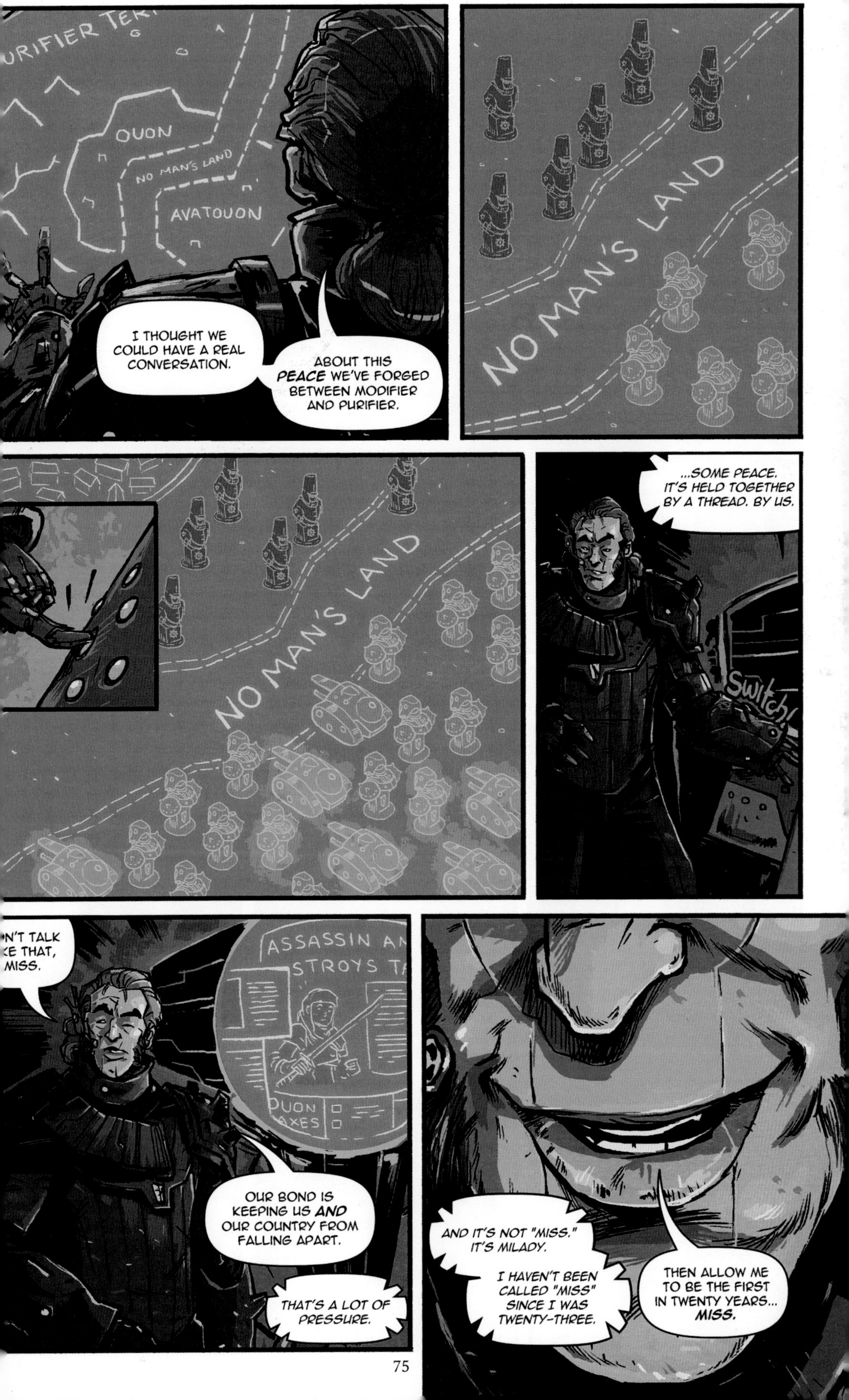
URIFIER TER
OUON
NO MAN'S LAND
AVATOUON
I THOUGHT WE COULD HAVE A REAL CONVERSATION.
ABOUT THIS PEACE WE'VE FORGED BETWEEN MODIFIER AND PURIFIER.
NO MAN'S LAND
NO MAN'S LAND
...SOME PEACE. IT'S HELD TOGETHER BY A THREAD. BY US.
SWITCH!
N'T TALK
E THAT,
MISS.
ASSASSIN AN
STROYS TA
UON
AXES
OUR BOND IS KEEPING US AND OUR COUNTRY FROM FALLING APART.
THAT'S A LOT OF PRESSURE.
AND IT'S NOT "MISS." IT'S MILADY.
I HAVEN'T BEEN CALLED "MISS" SINCE I WAS TWENTY-THREE.
THEN ALLOW ME TO BE THE FIRST IN TWENTY YEARS... MISS.

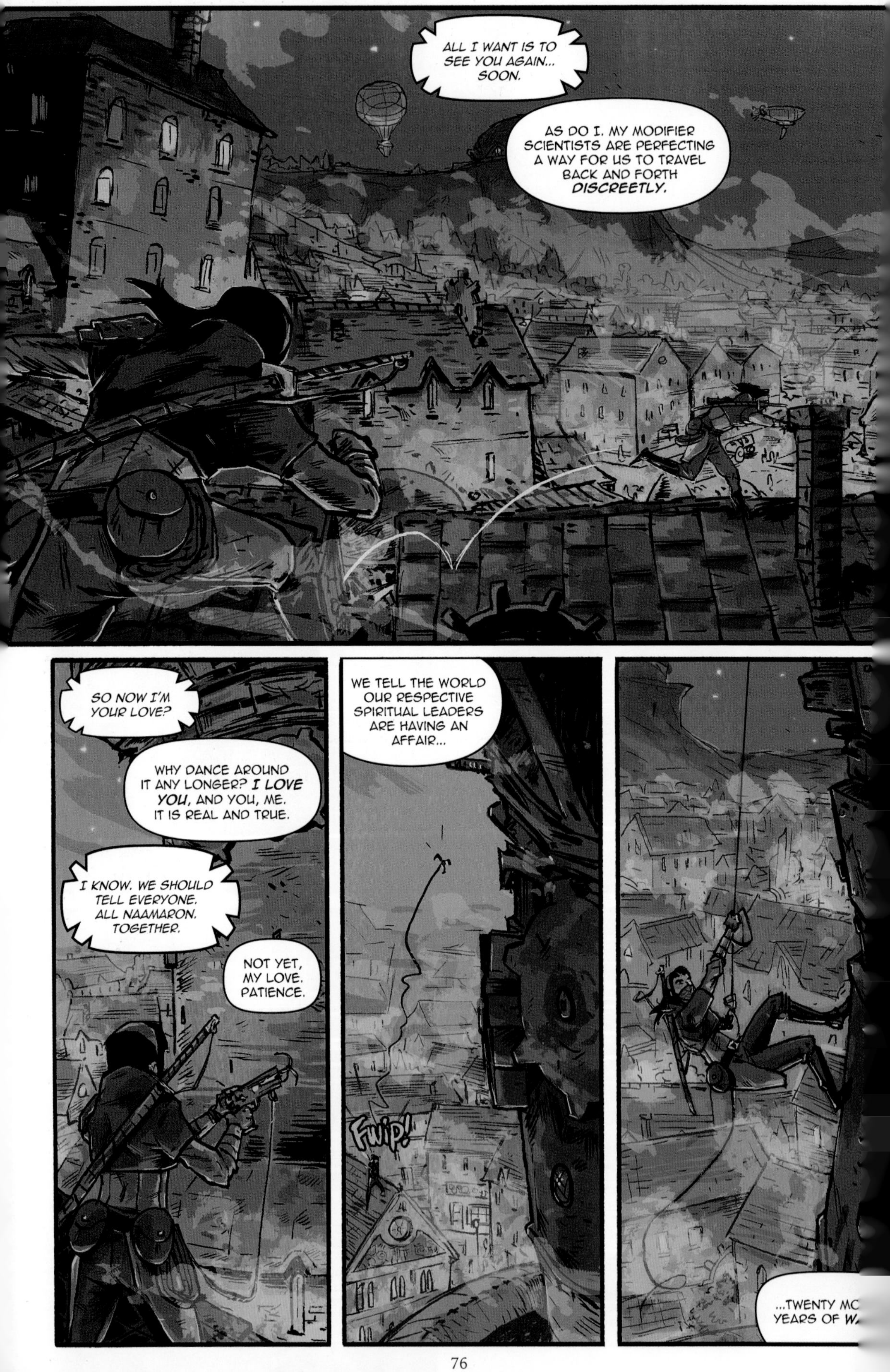
ALL I WANT IS TO SEE YOU AGAIN... SOON.
AS DO I. MY MODIFIER SCIENTISTS ARE PERFECTING A WAY FOR US TO TRAVEL BACK AND FORTH DISCREETLY.
SO NOW I'M YOUR LOVE?
WHY DANCE AROUND IT ANY LONGER? I LOVE YOU, AND YOU, ME. IT IS REAL AND TRUE.
I KNOW. WE SHOULD TELL EVERYONE. ALL NAAMARON. TOGETHER.
NOT YET, MY LOVE. PATIENCE.
WE TELL THE WORLD OUR RESPECTIVE SPIRITUAL LEADERS ARE HAVING AN AFFAIR...
FWIP!
...TWENTY MO
YEARS OF WA

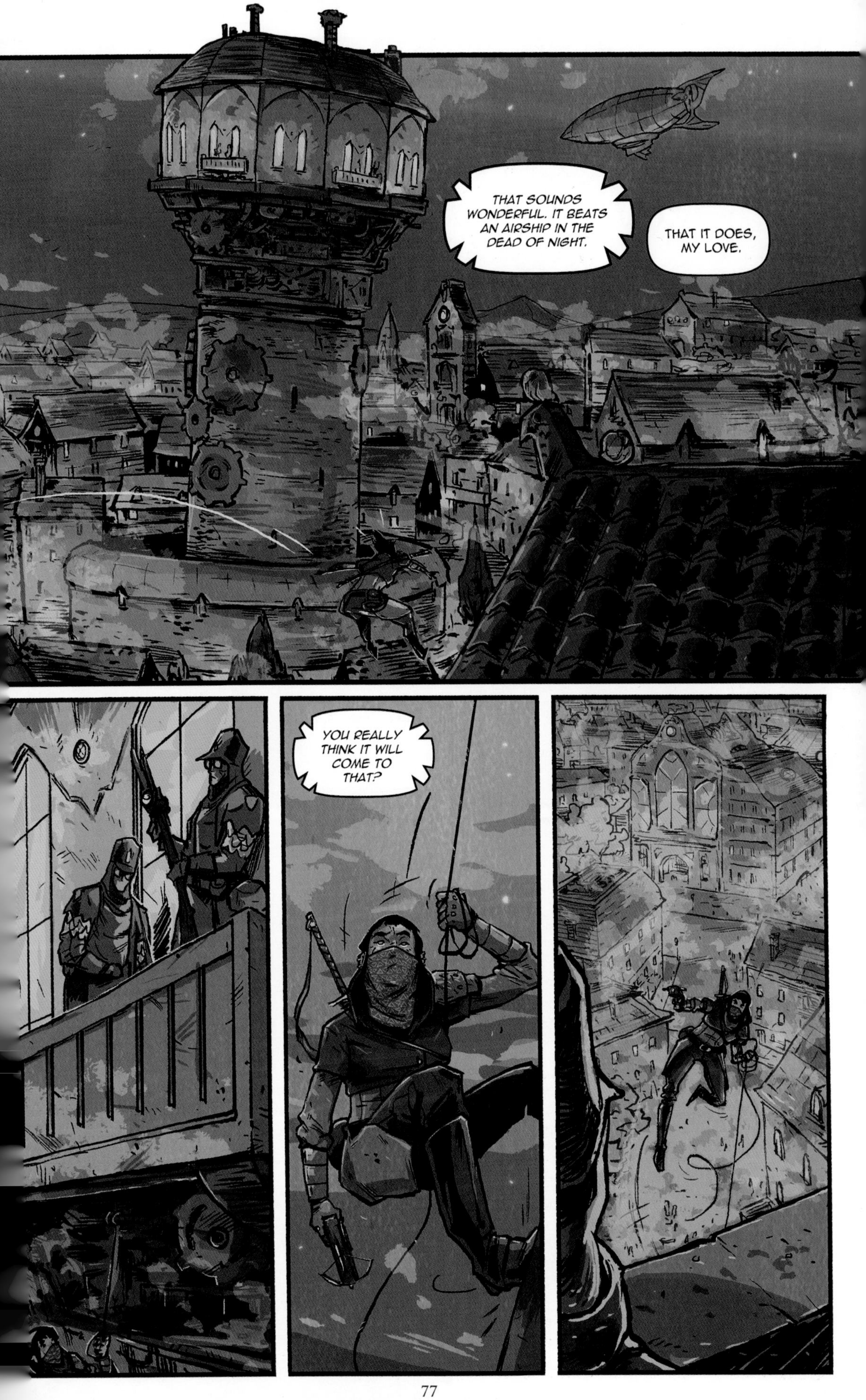
THAT SOUNDS WONDERFUL. IT BEATS AN AIRSHIP IN THE DEAD OF NIGHT.
THAT IT DOES, MY LOVE.
YOU REALLY THINK IT WILL COME TO THAT?

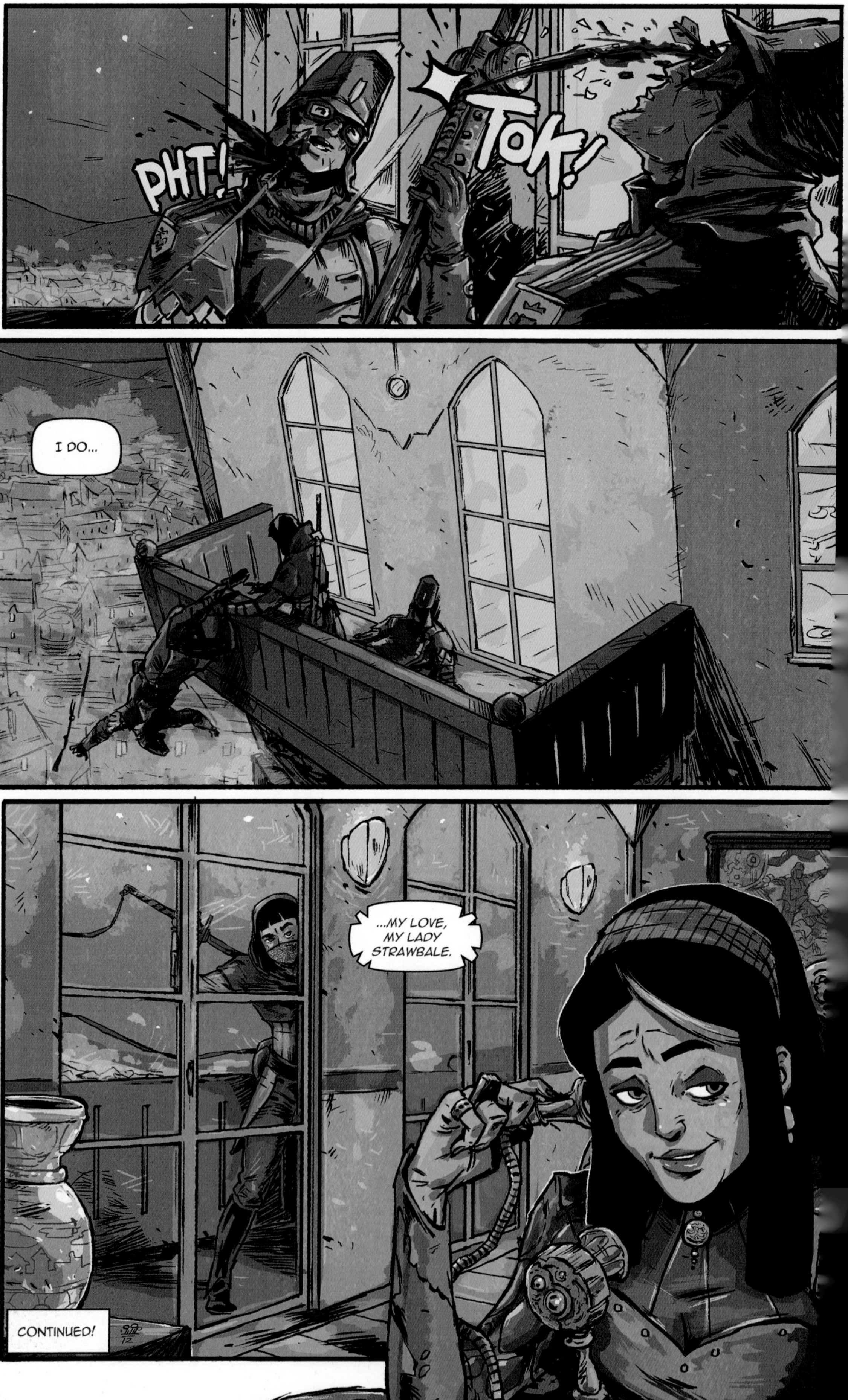
PHT!
TOK!
I DO...
...MY LOVE, MY LADY STRAWBALE.
CONTINUED!

SPIRITS OF NAAMARON
PART THREE

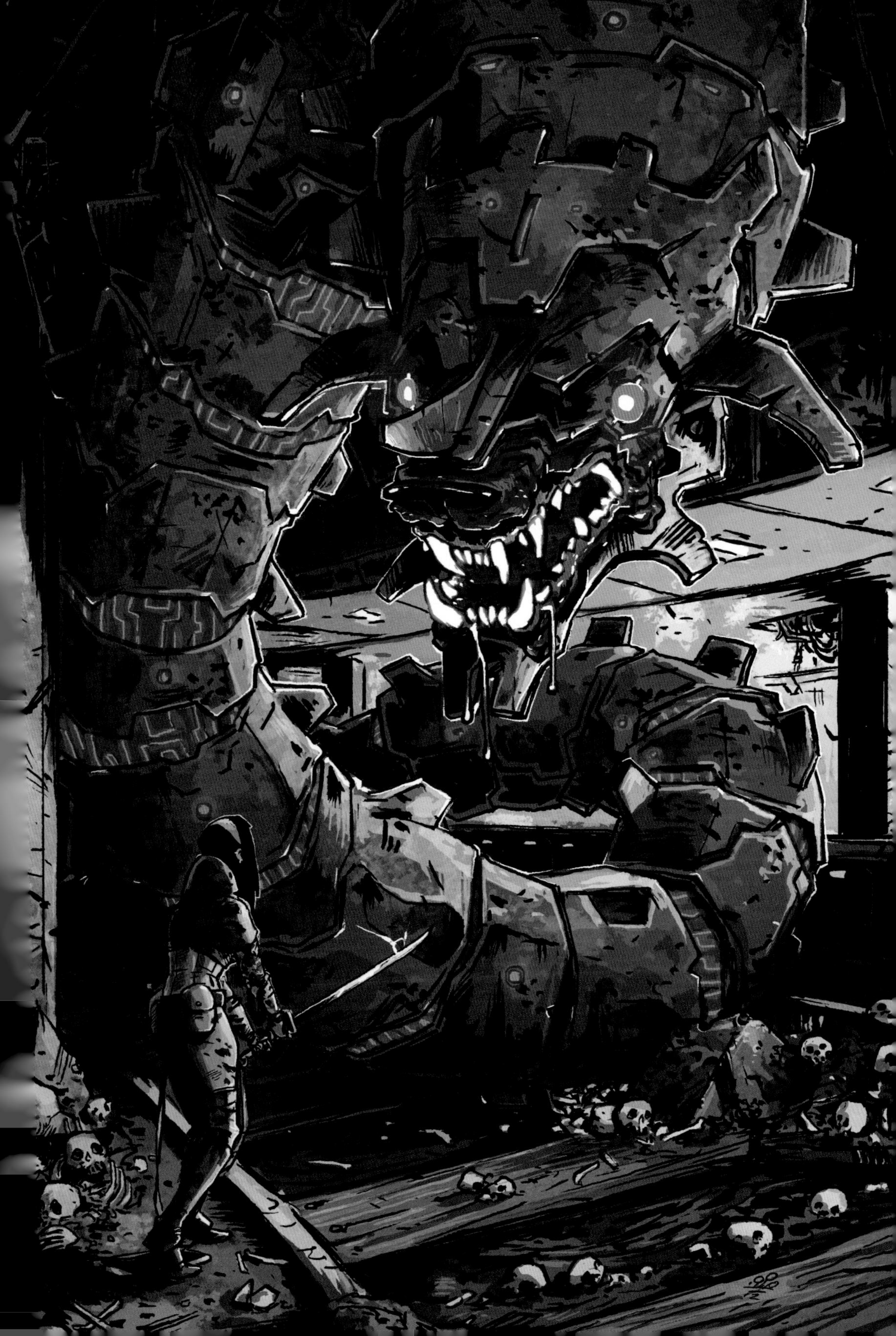

"THE ONLY WAY TO WIN IS NOT TO FIGHT . . ."

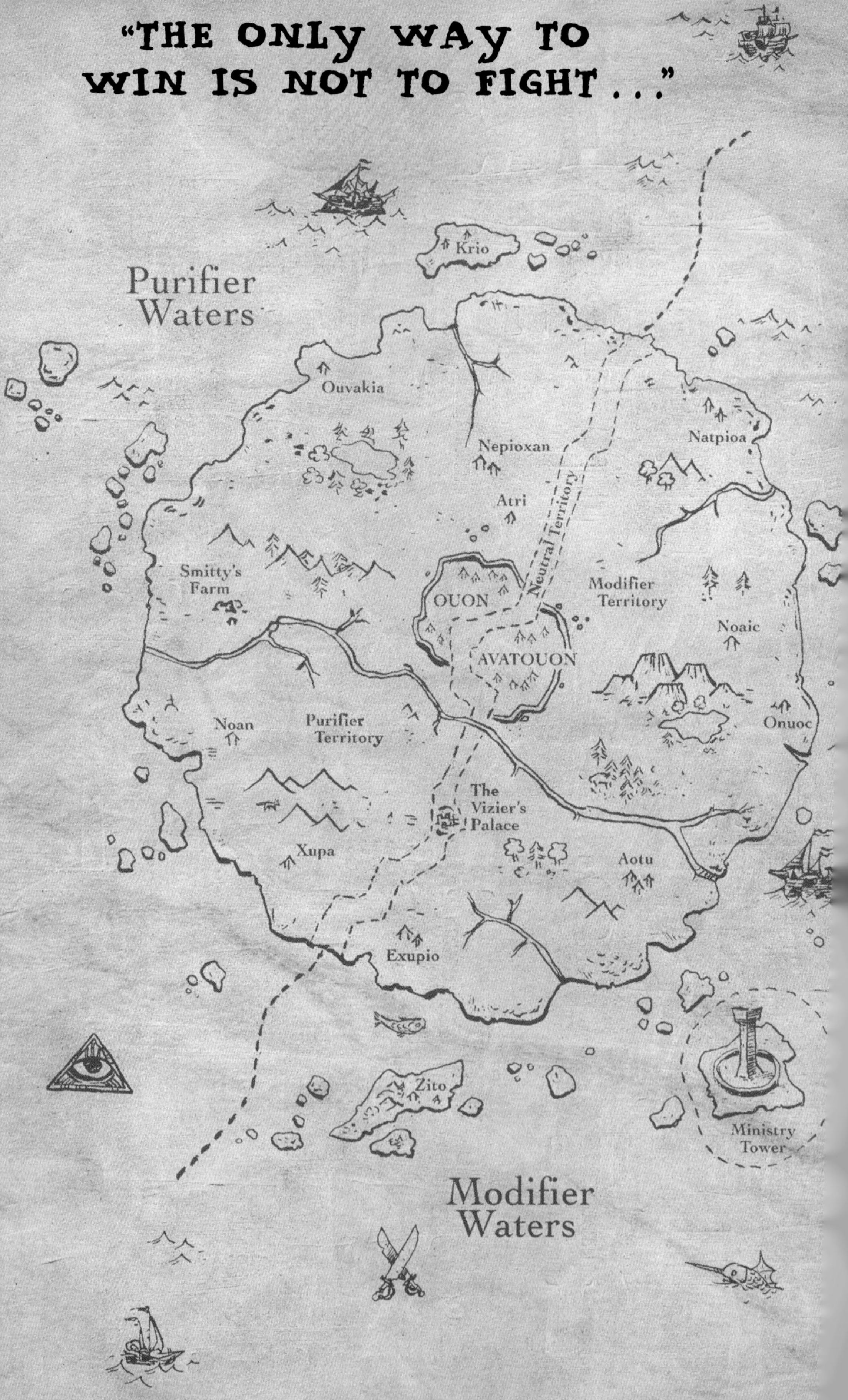
Purifier Waters
Krio
Ouvakia
Nepioxan
Natpioa
Atri
Neutral Territory
Smitty's Farm
OUON
AVATOUON
Modifier Territory
Noaic
Noan
Purifier Territory
Onuoc
The Vizier's Palace
Xupa
Aotu
Exupio
Zito
Ministry Tower
Modifier Waters

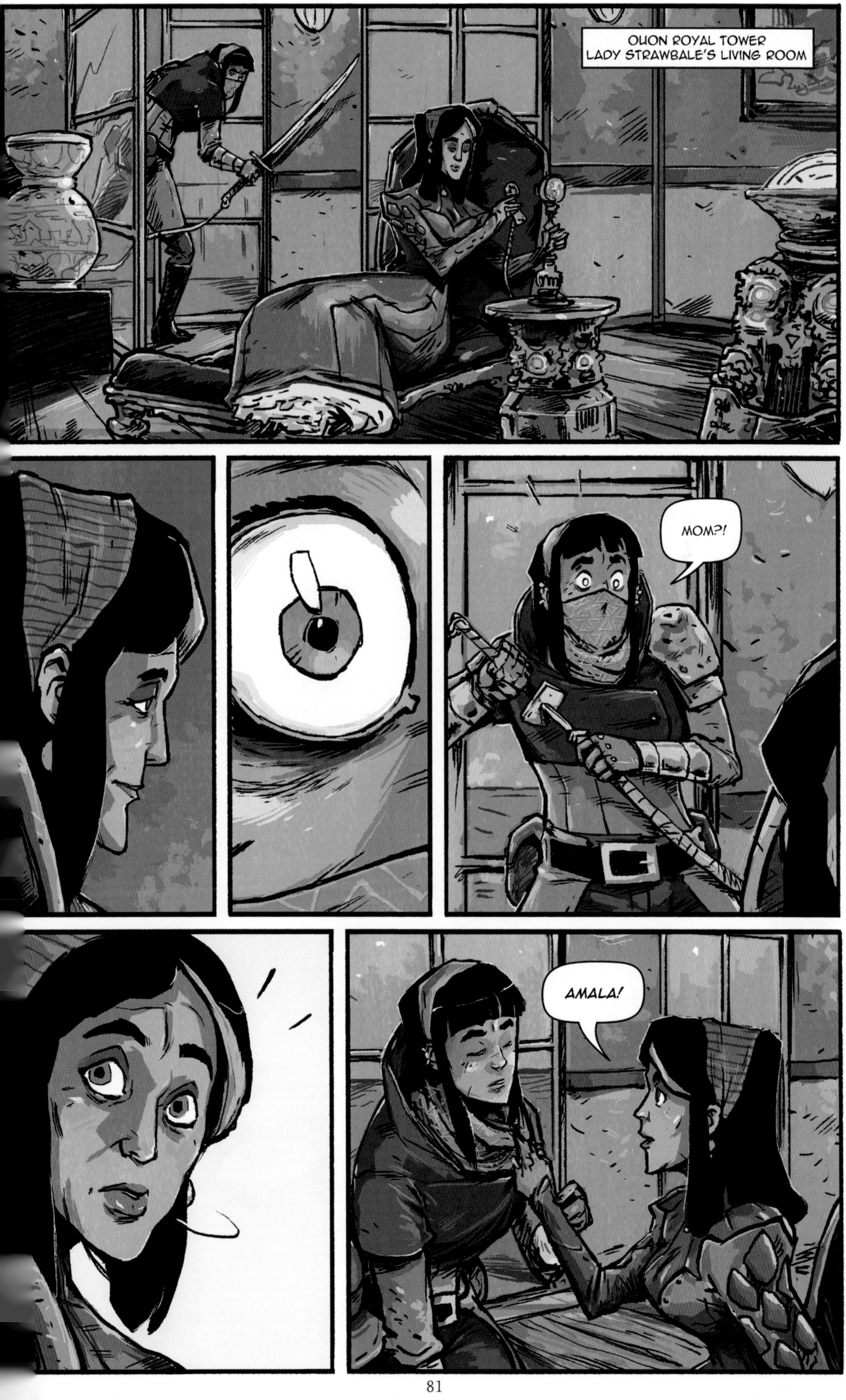
OUON ROYAL TOWER
LADY STRAWBALE'S LIVING ROOM
MOM?!
AMALA!

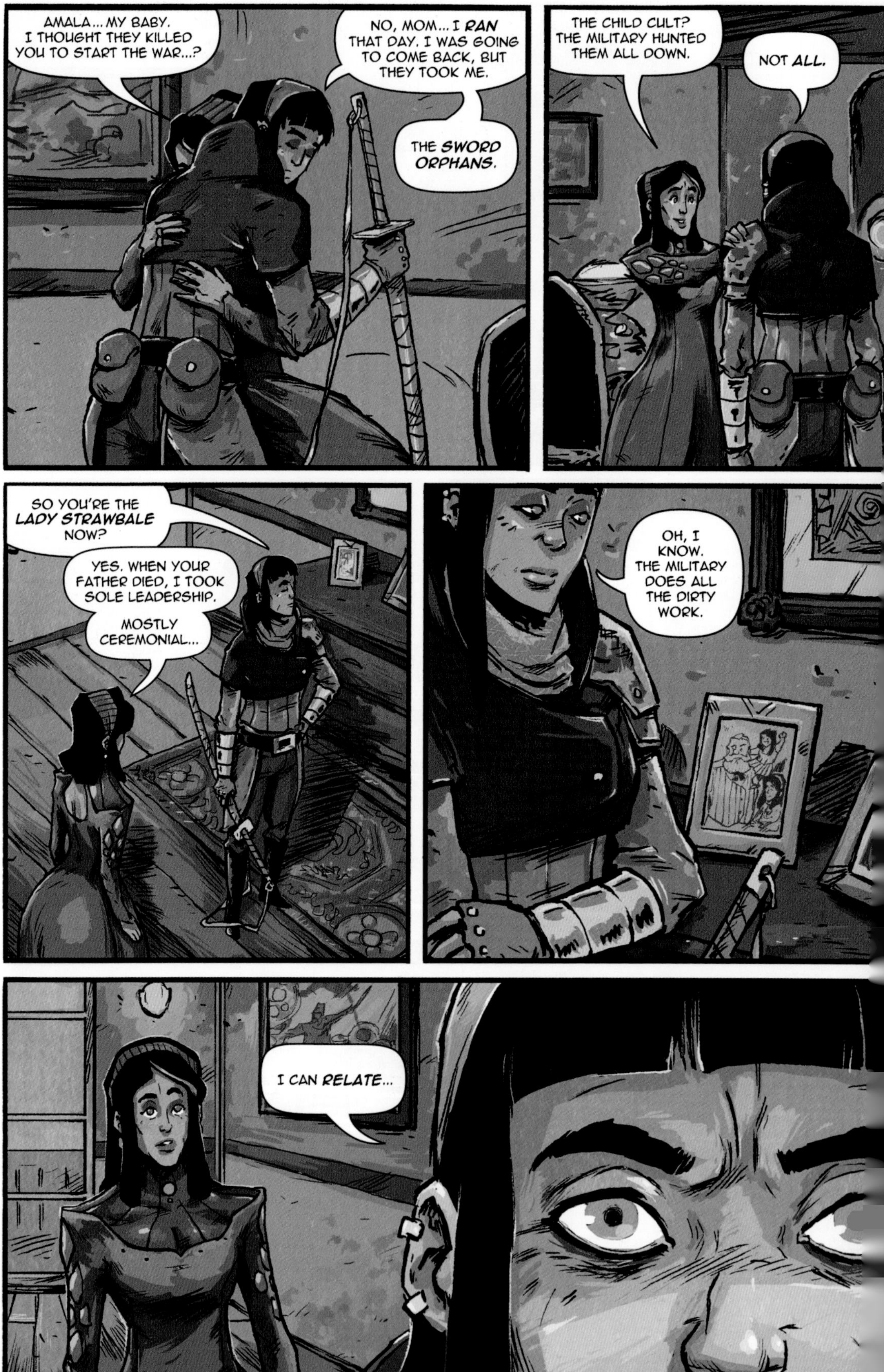
AMALA... MY BABY. I THOUGHT THEY KILLED YOU TO START THE WAR...?
NO, MOM... I RAN THAT DAY. I WAS GOING TO COME BACK, BUT THEY TOOK ME.
THE SWORD ORPHANS.
THE CHILD CULT? THE MILITARY HUNTED THEM ALL DOWN.
NOT ALL.
SO YOU'RE THE LADY STRAWBALE NOW?
YES. WHEN YOUR FATHER DIED, I TOOK SOLE LEADERSHIP.
MOSTLY CEREMONIAL...
OH, I KNOW. THE MILITARY DOES ALL THE DIRTY WORK.
I CAN RELATE...

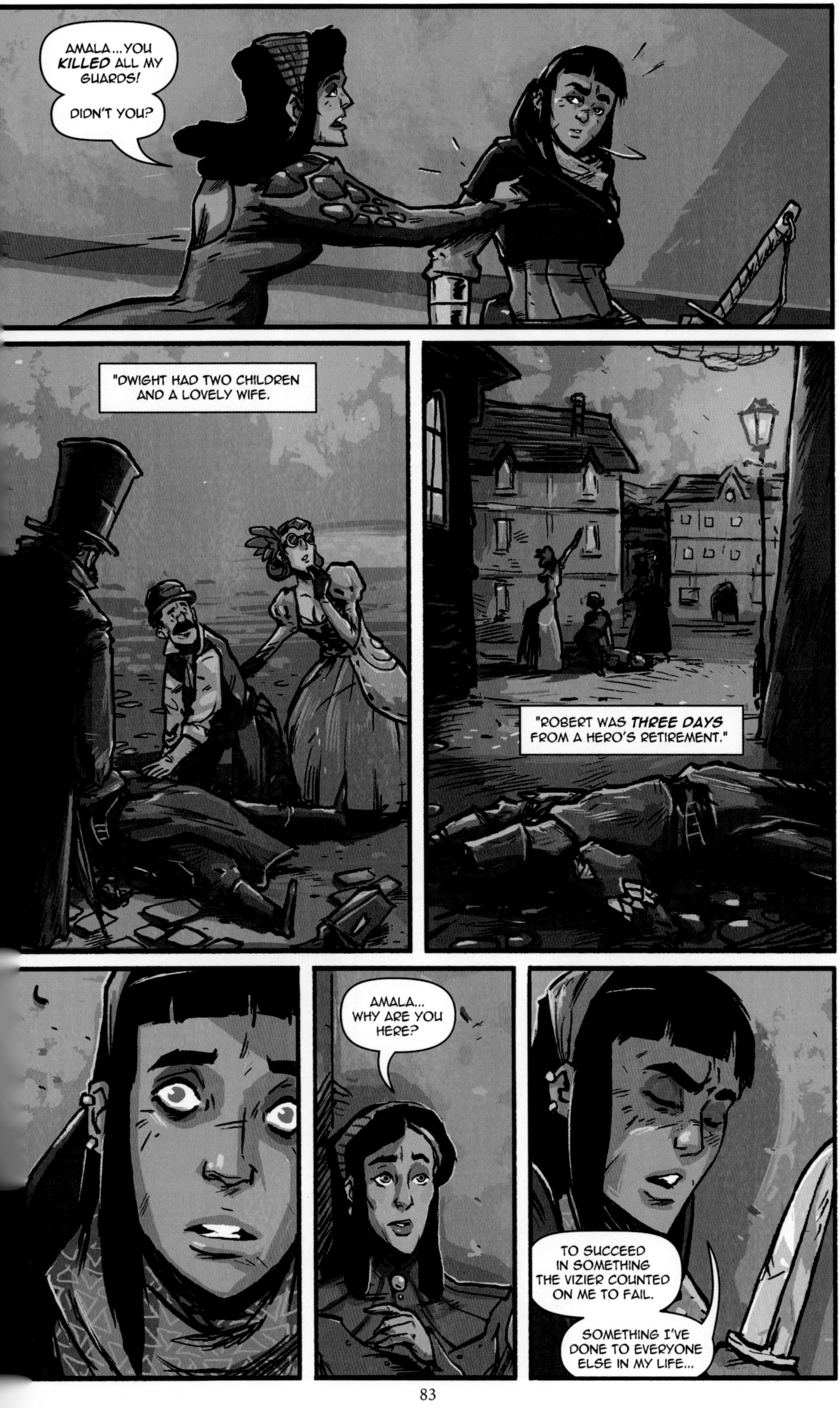
AMALA...YOU KILLED ALL MY GUARDS!
DIDN'T YOU?
"DWIGHT HAD TWO CHILDREN AND A LOVELY WIFE.
"ROBERT WAS THREE DAYS FROM A HERO'S RETIREMENT."
AMALA... WHY ARE YOU HERE?
TO SUCCEED IN SOMETHING THE VIZIER COUNTED ON ME TO FAIL.
SOMETHING I'VE DONE TO EVERYONE ELSE IN MY LIFE...

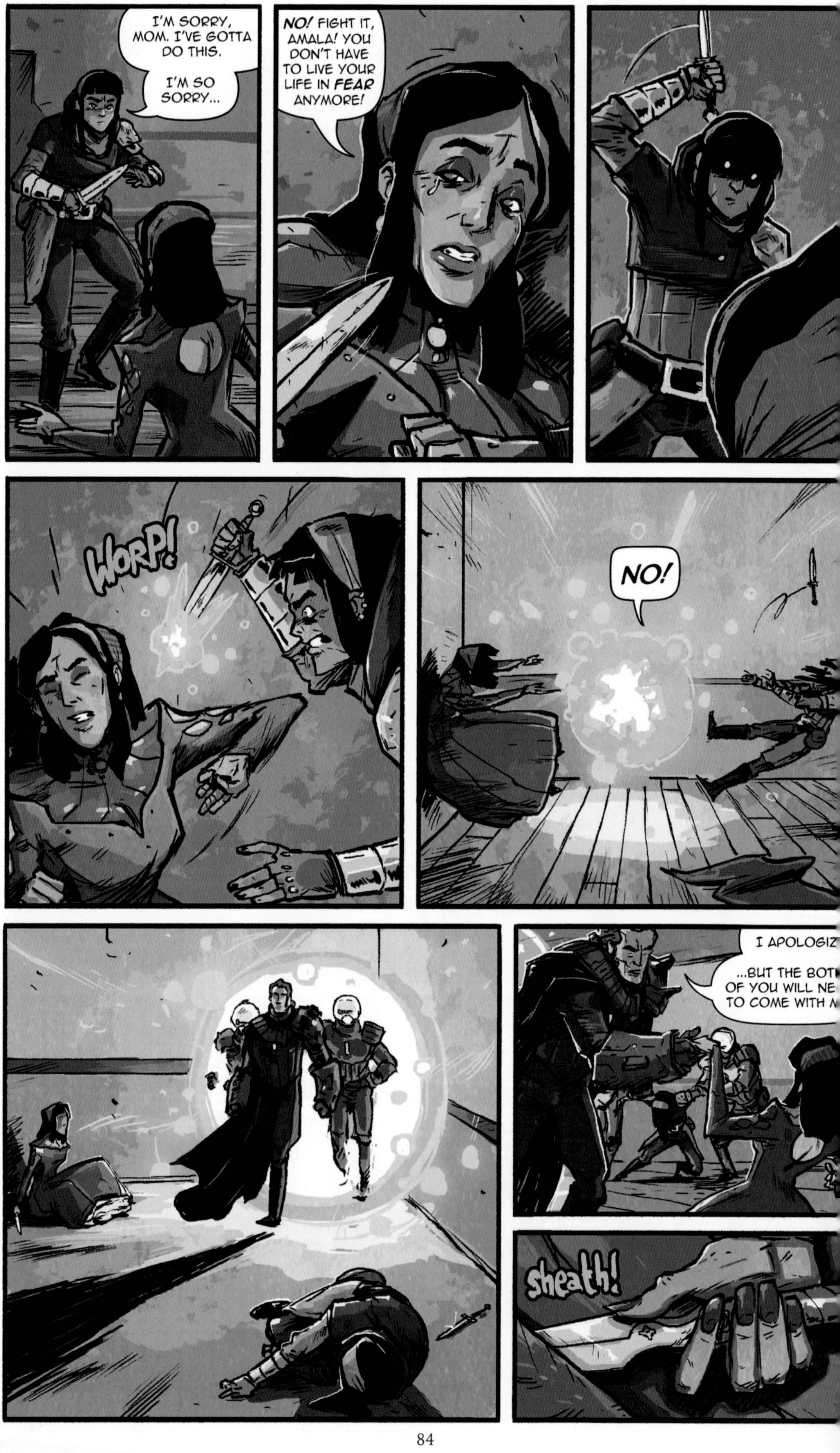
I'M SORRY, MOM. I'VE GOTTA DO THIS.
I'M SO SORRY...
NO! FIGHT IT, AMALA! YOU DON'T HAVE TO LIVE YOUR LIFE IN FEAR ANYMORE!
WORP!
NO!
I APOLOGIZ
...BUT THE BOT OF YOU WILL NE TO COME WITH M
sheath!

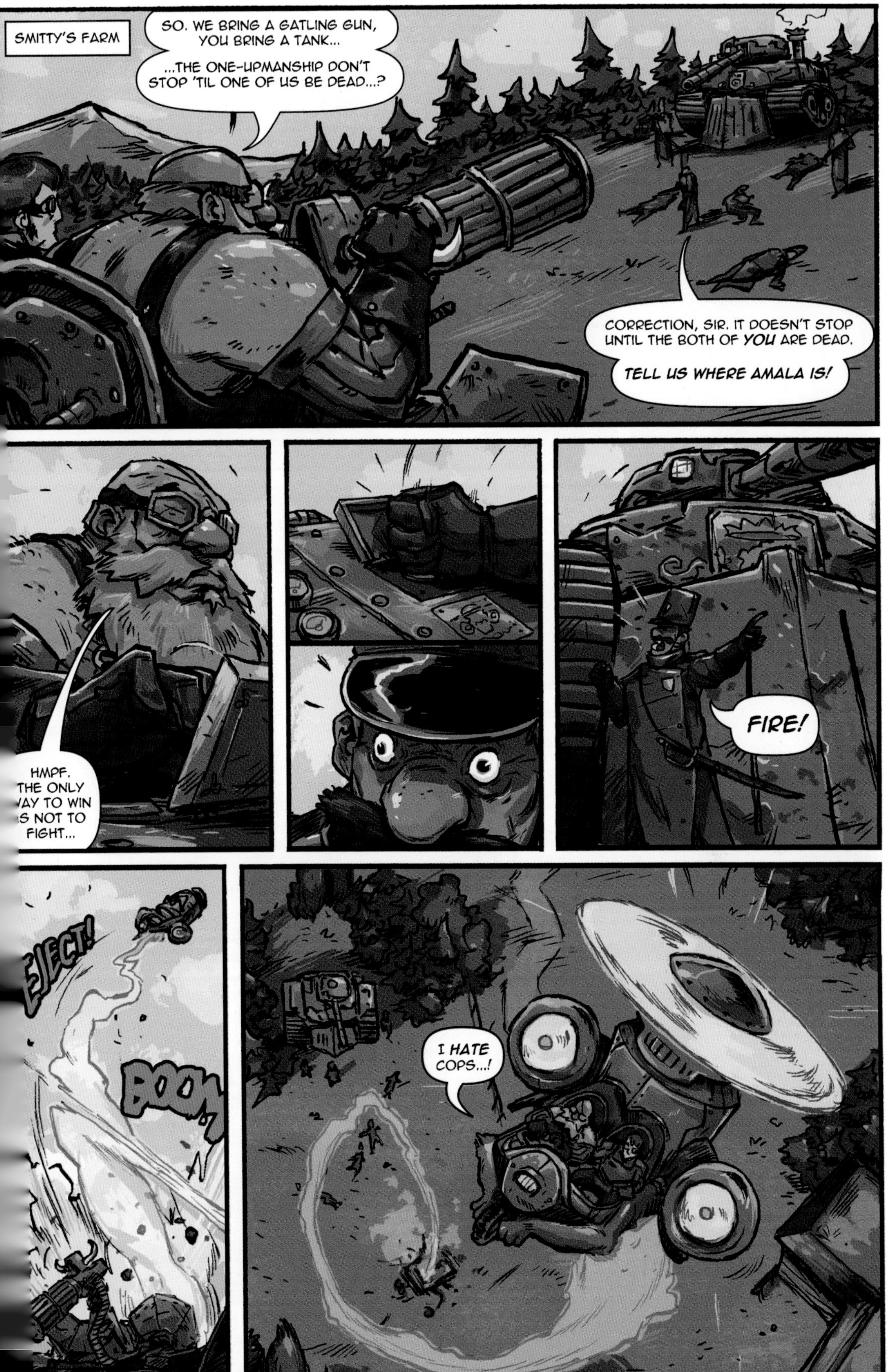
SMITTY'S FARM
SO. WE BRING A GATLING GUN, YOU BRING A TANK...
...THE ONE-UPMANSHIP DON'T STOP 'TIL ONE OF US BE DEAD...?
CORRECTION, SIR. IT DOESN'T STOP UNTIL THE BOTH OF *YOU* ARE DEAD.
TELL US WHERE AMALA IS!
HMPF. THE ONLY WAY TO WIN IS NOT TO FIGHT...
FIRE!
EJECT!
BOOM
I *HATE* COPS...!

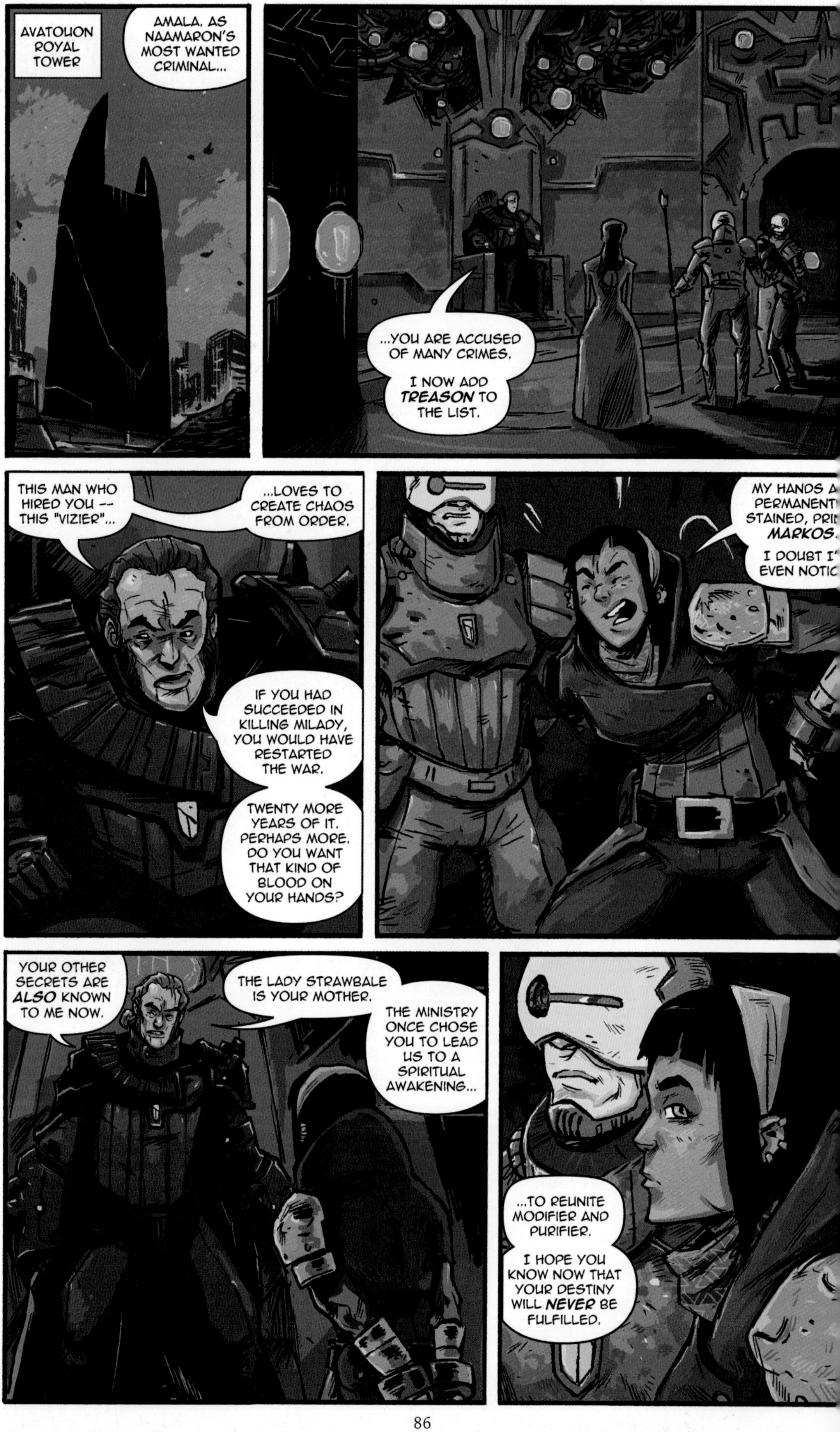
AVATOUON ROYAL TOWER
AMALA, AS NAAMARON'S MOST WANTED CRIMINAL...
...YOU ARE ACCUSED OF MANY CRIMES.
I NOW ADD *TREASON* TO THE LIST.
THIS MAN WHO HIRED YOU -- THIS "VIZIER"...
...LOVES TO CREATE CHAOS FROM ORDER.
IF YOU HAD SUCCEEDED IN KILLING MILADY, YOU WOULD HAVE RESTARTED THE WAR.
TWENTY MORE YEARS OF IT. PERHAPS MORE. DO YOU WANT THAT KIND OF BLOOD ON YOUR HANDS?
MY HANDS A PERMANENT STAINED, PRI *MARKOS.*
I DOUBT I' EVEN NOTIC
YOUR OTHER SECRETS ARE *ALSO* KNOWN TO ME NOW.
THE LADY STRAWBALE IS YOUR MOTHER.
THE MINISTRY ONCE CHOSE YOU TO LEAD US TO A SPIRITUAL AWAKENING...
...TO REUNITE MODIFIER AND PURIFIER.
I HOPE YOU KNOW NOW THAT YOUR DESTINY WILL *NEVER* BE FULFILLED.

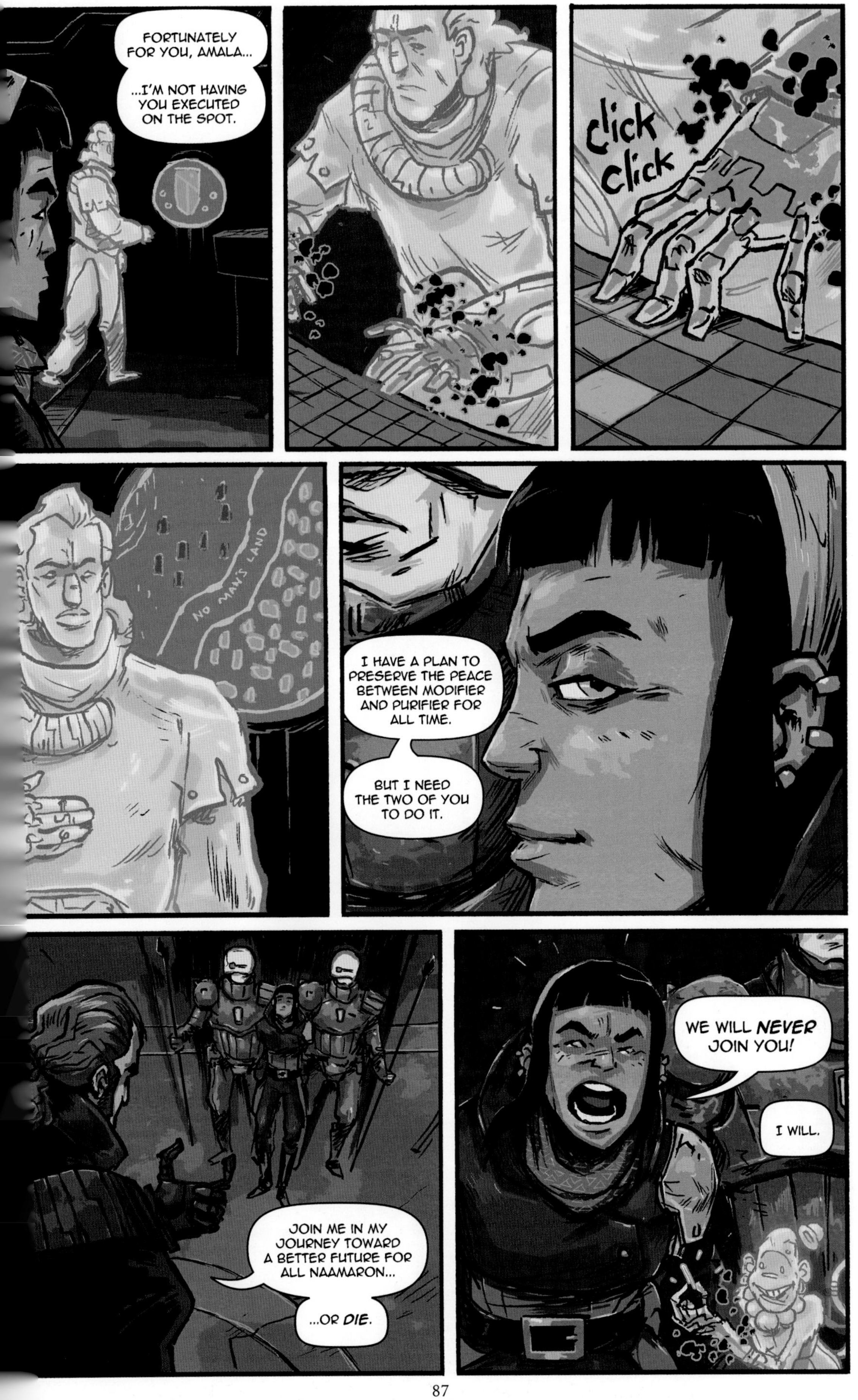
FORTUNATELY FOR YOU, AMALA...
...I'M NOT HAVING YOU EXECUTED ON THE SPOT.
CLICK CLICK
NO MAN'S LAND
I HAVE A PLAN TO PRESERVE THE PEACE BETWEEN MODIFIER AND PURIFIER FOR ALL TIME.
BUT I NEED THE TWO OF YOU TO DO IT.
JOIN ME IN MY JOURNEY TOWARD A BETTER FUTURE FOR ALL NAAMARON...
...OR *DIE*.
WE WILL ***NEVER*** JOIN YOU!
I WILL.

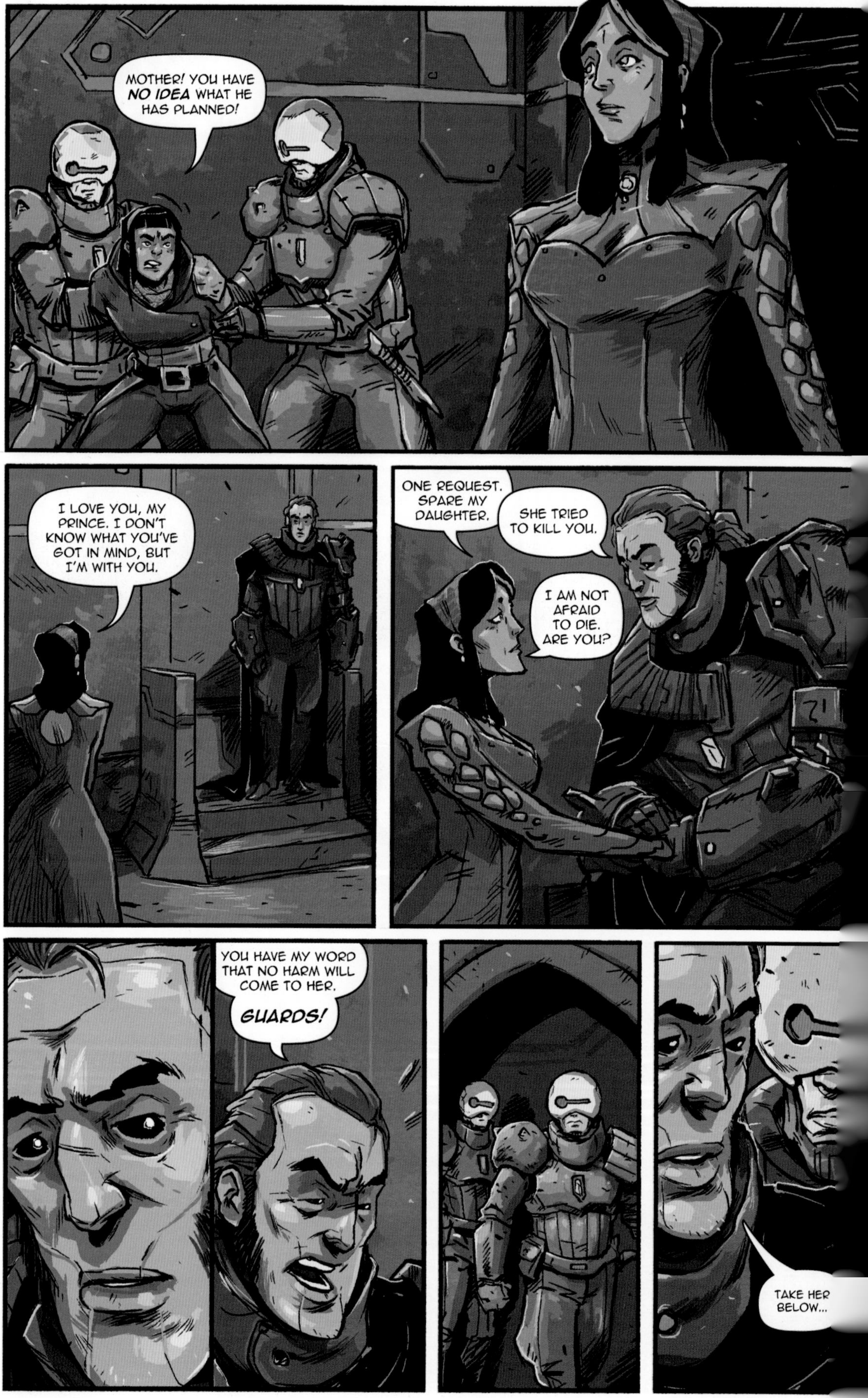
MOTHER! YOU HAVE NO IDEA WHAT HE HAS PLANNED!
I LOVE YOU, MY PRINCE. I DON'T KNOW WHAT YOU'VE GOT IN MIND, BUT I'M WITH YOU.
ONE REQUEST. SPARE MY DAUGHTER.
SHE TRIED TO KILL YOU.
I AM NOT AFRAID TO DIE. ARE YOU?
YOU HAVE MY WORD THAT NO HARM WILL COME TO HER.
GUARDS!
TAKE HER BELOW...

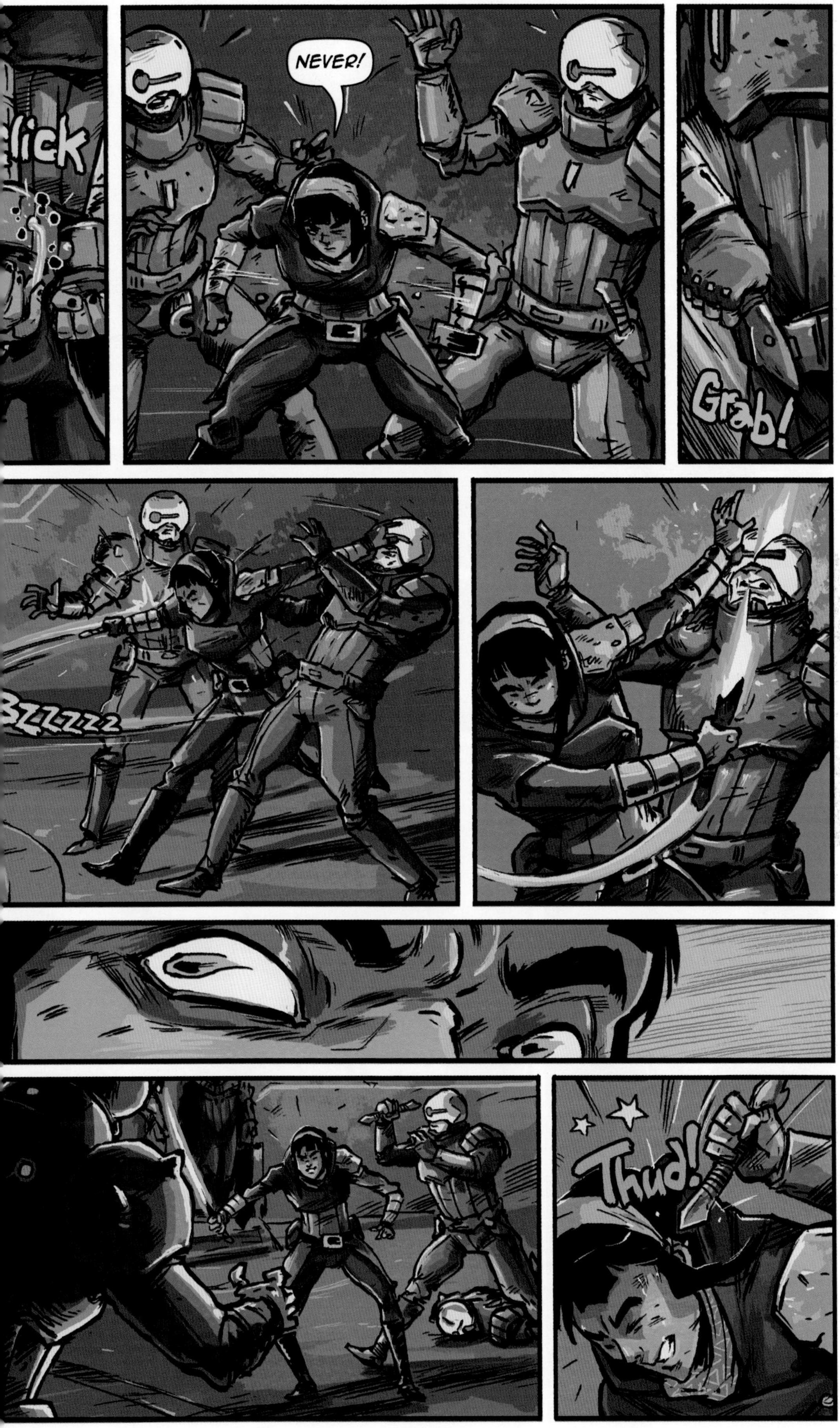
lick
NEVER!
Grab!
Bzzzzzz
Thud!

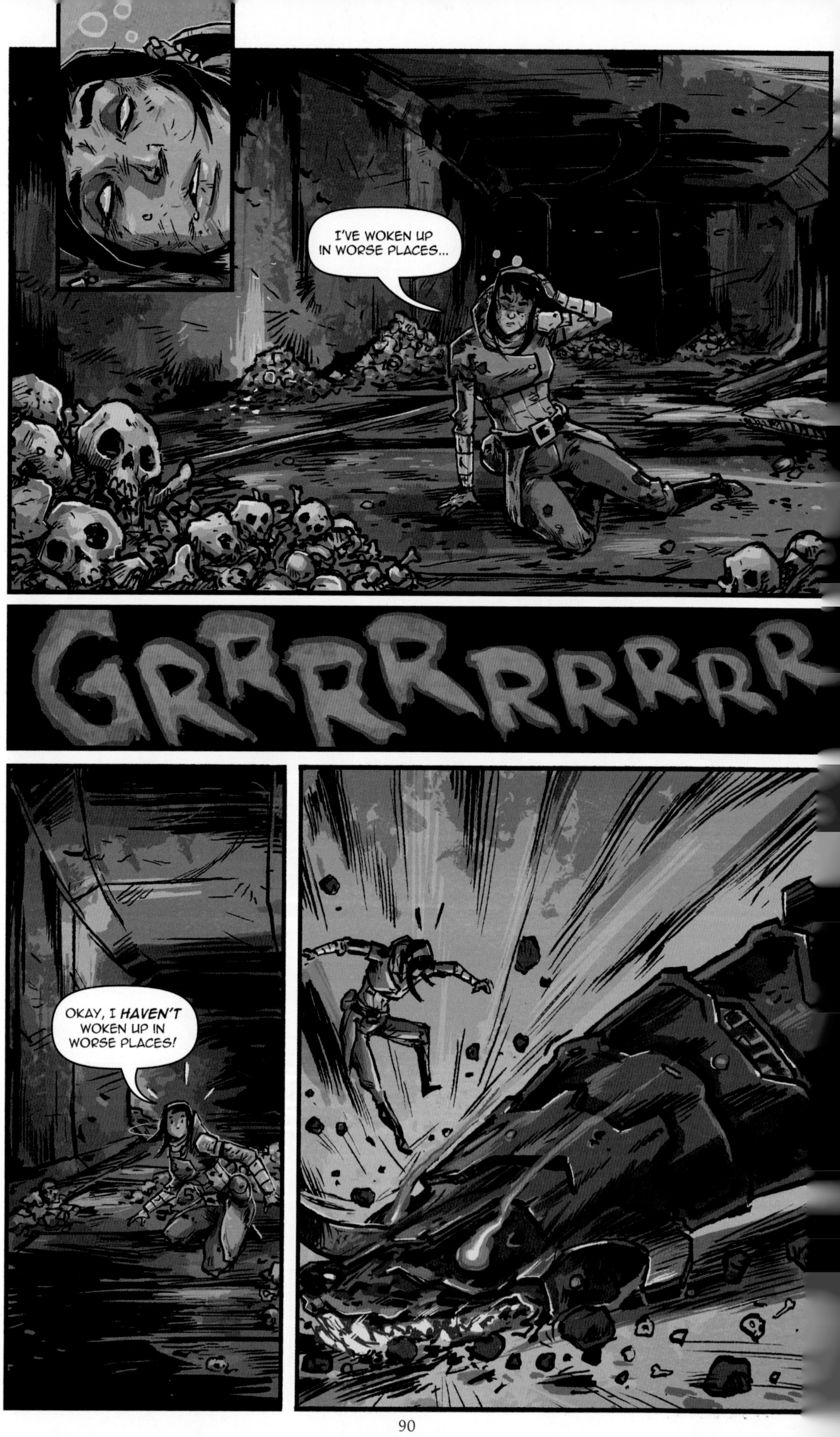
I'VE WOKEN UP IN WORSE PLACES...
GRRRRRRRRR
OKAY, I *HAVEN'T* WOKEN UP IN WORSE PLACES!

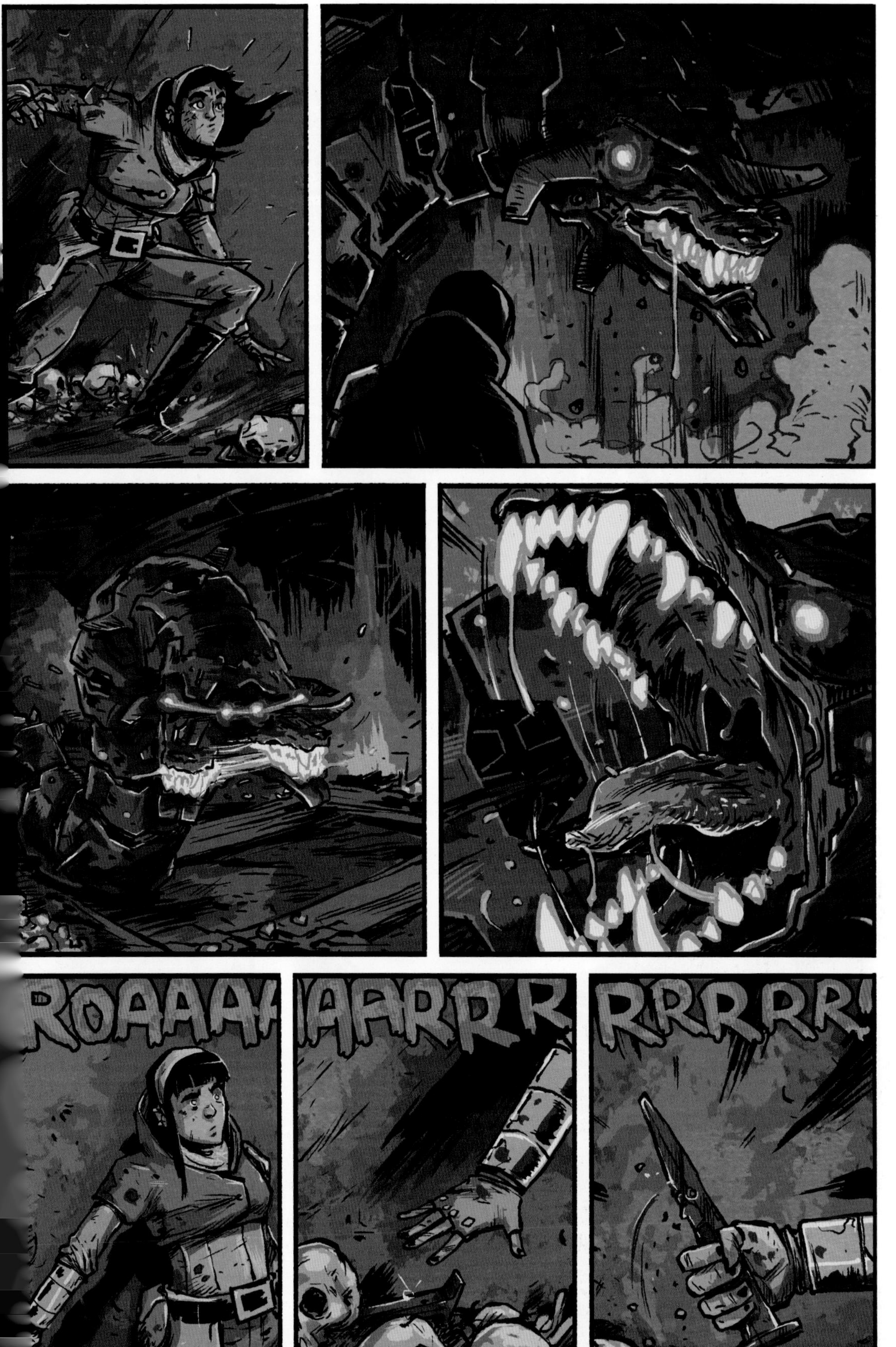
ROAAAAAARRRRRRR!

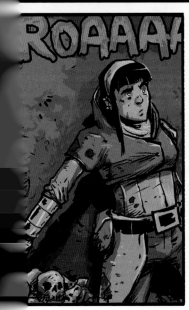

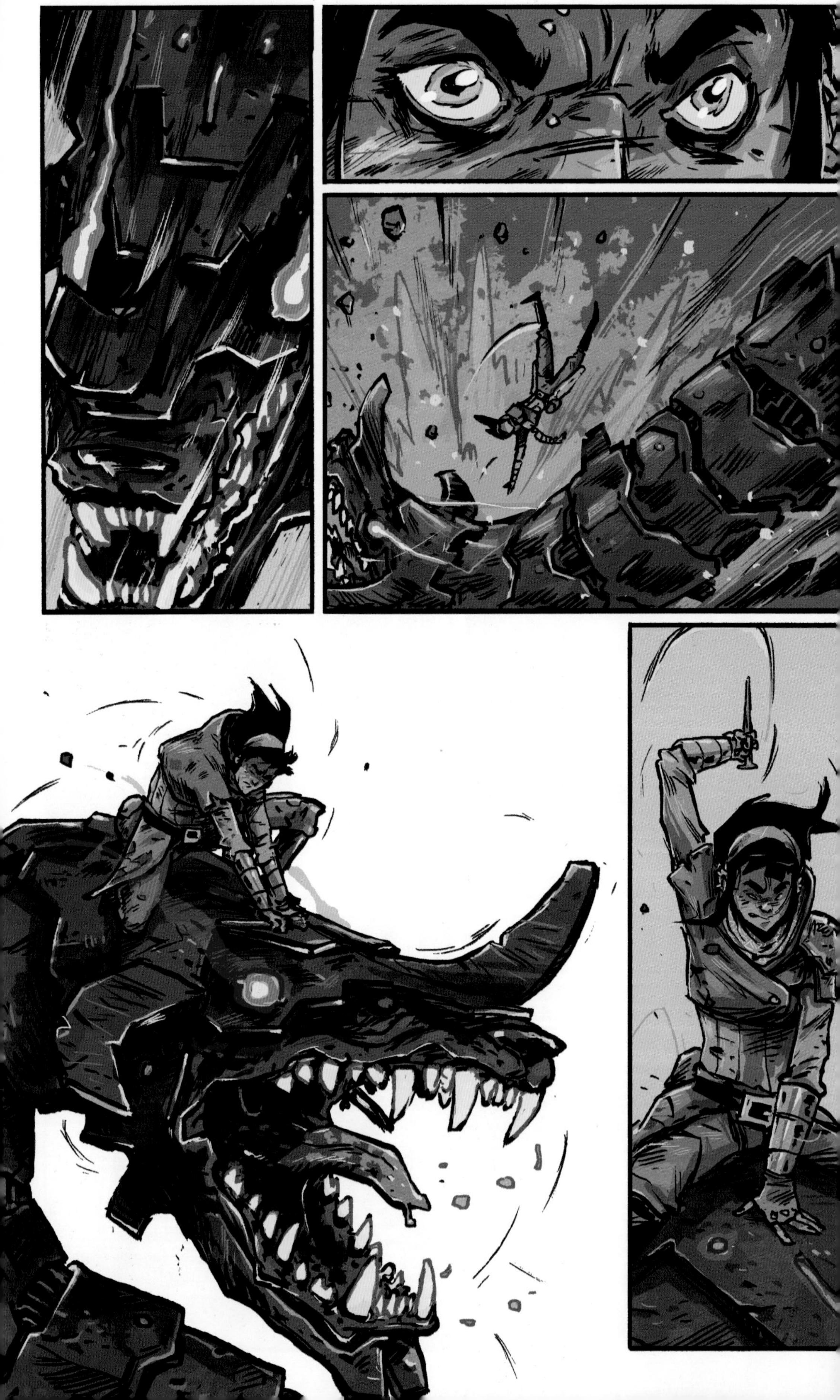

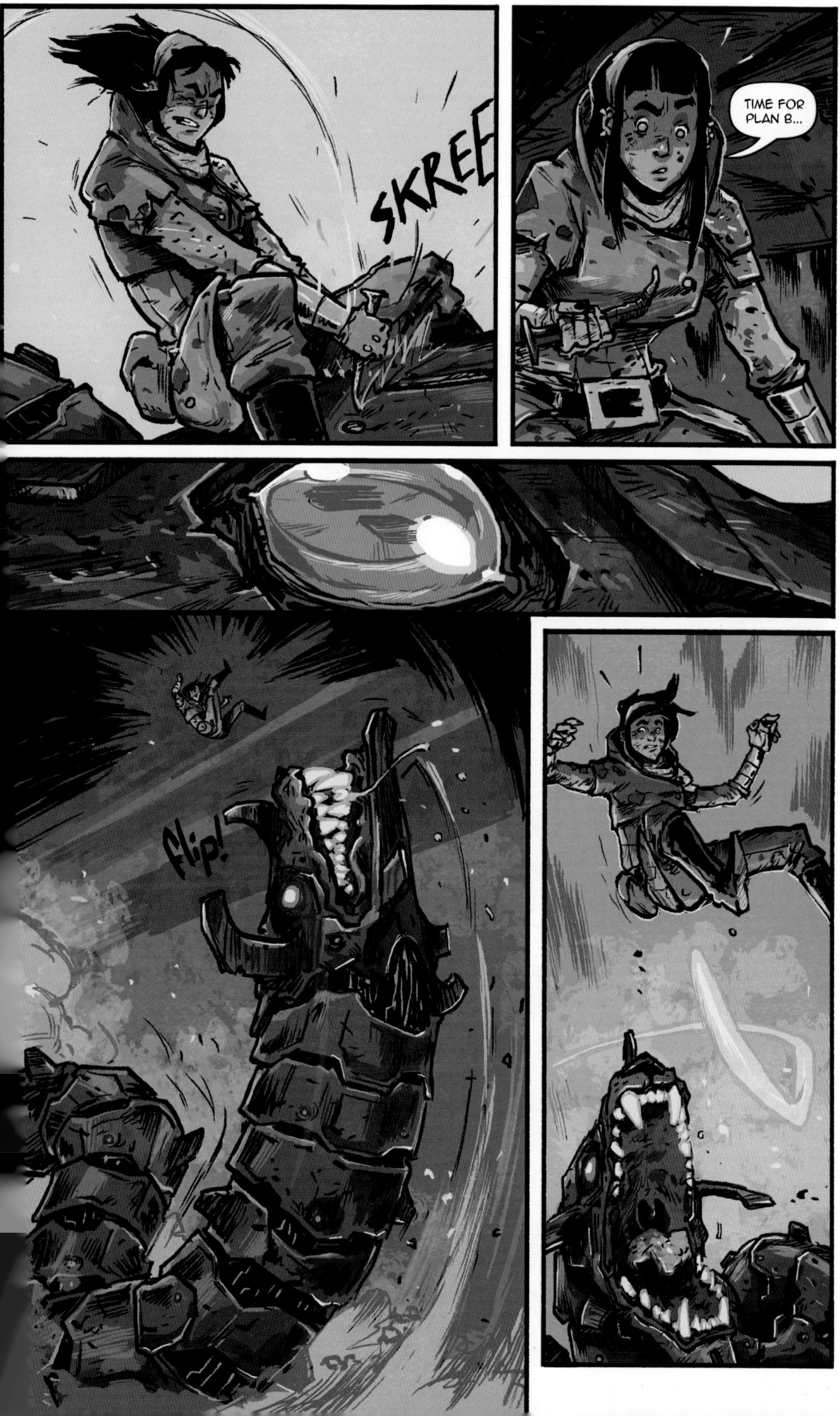
SKREE
TIME FOR PLAN B...
Flip!

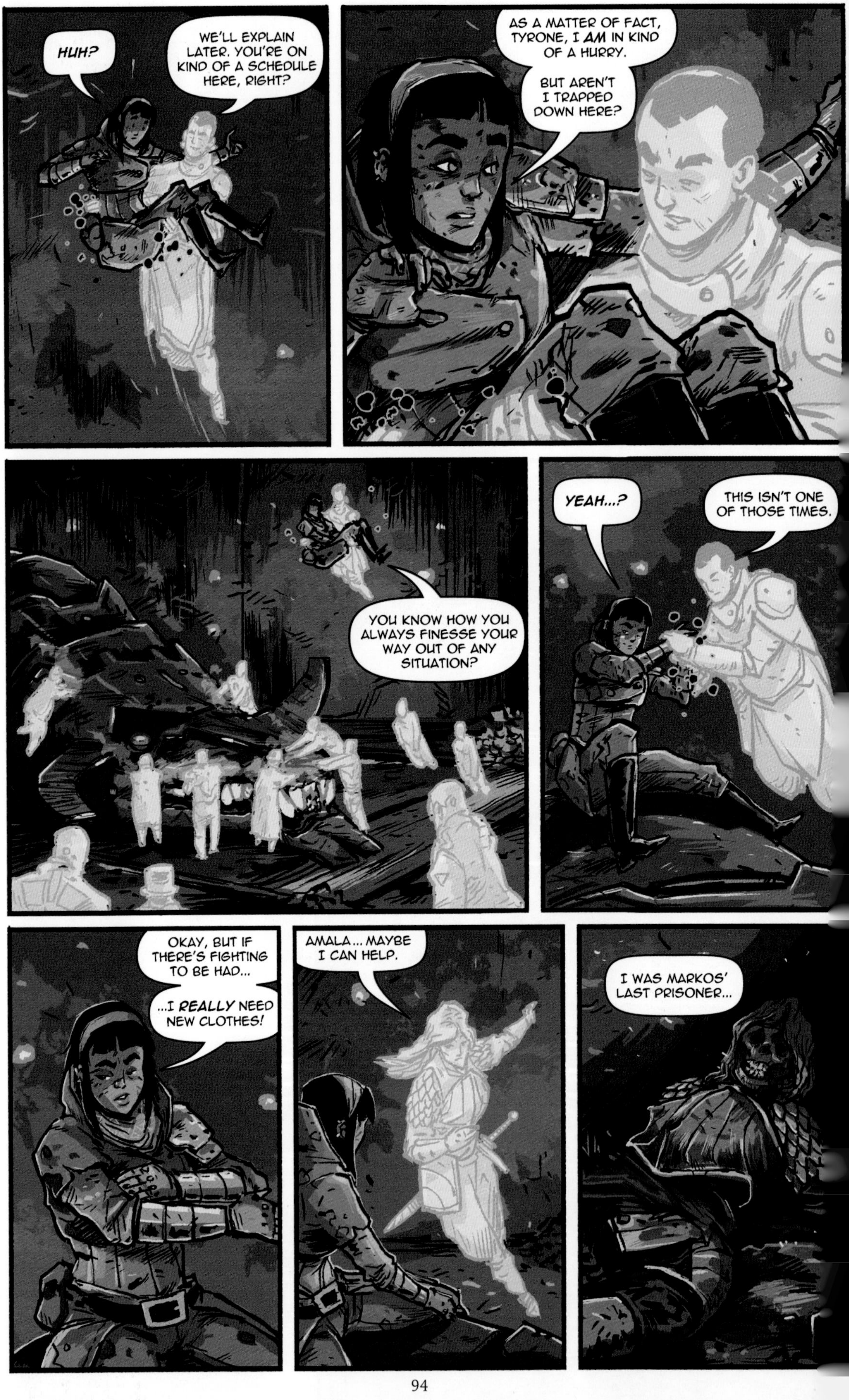
HUH?
WE'LL EXPLAIN LATER. YOU'RE ON KIND OF A SCHEDULE HERE, RIGHT?
AS A MATTER OF FACT, TYRONE, I AM IN KIND OF A HURRY.
BUT AREN'T I TRAPPED DOWN HERE?
YOU KNOW HOW YOU ALWAYS FINESSE YOUR WAY OUT OF ANY SITUATION?
YEAH...?
THIS ISN'T ONE OF THOSE TIMES.
OKAY, BUT IF THERE'S FIGHTING TO BE HAD...
...I REALLY NEED NEW CLOTHES!
AMALA... MAYBE I CAN HELP.
I WAS MARKOS' LAST PRISONER...

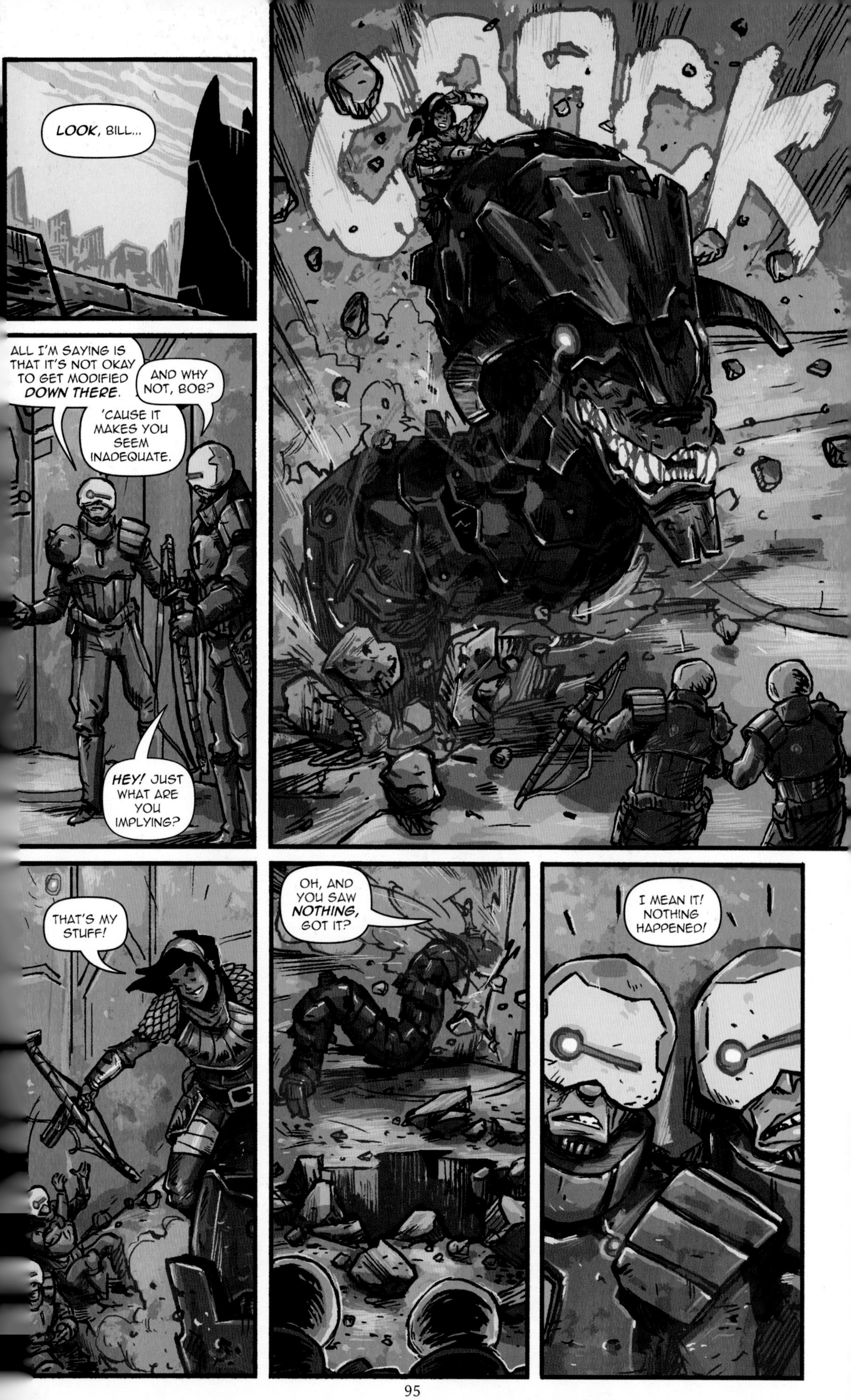
LOOK, BILL...
CRACK
ALL I'M SAYING IS THAT IT'S NOT OKAY TO GET MODIFIED DOWN THERE.
AND WHY NOT, BOB?
'CAUSE IT MAKES YOU SEEM INADEQUATE.
HEY! JUST WHAT ARE YOU IMPLYING?
THAT'S MY STUFF!
OH, AND YOU SAW NOTHING, GOT IT?
I MEAN IT! NOTHING HAPPENED!

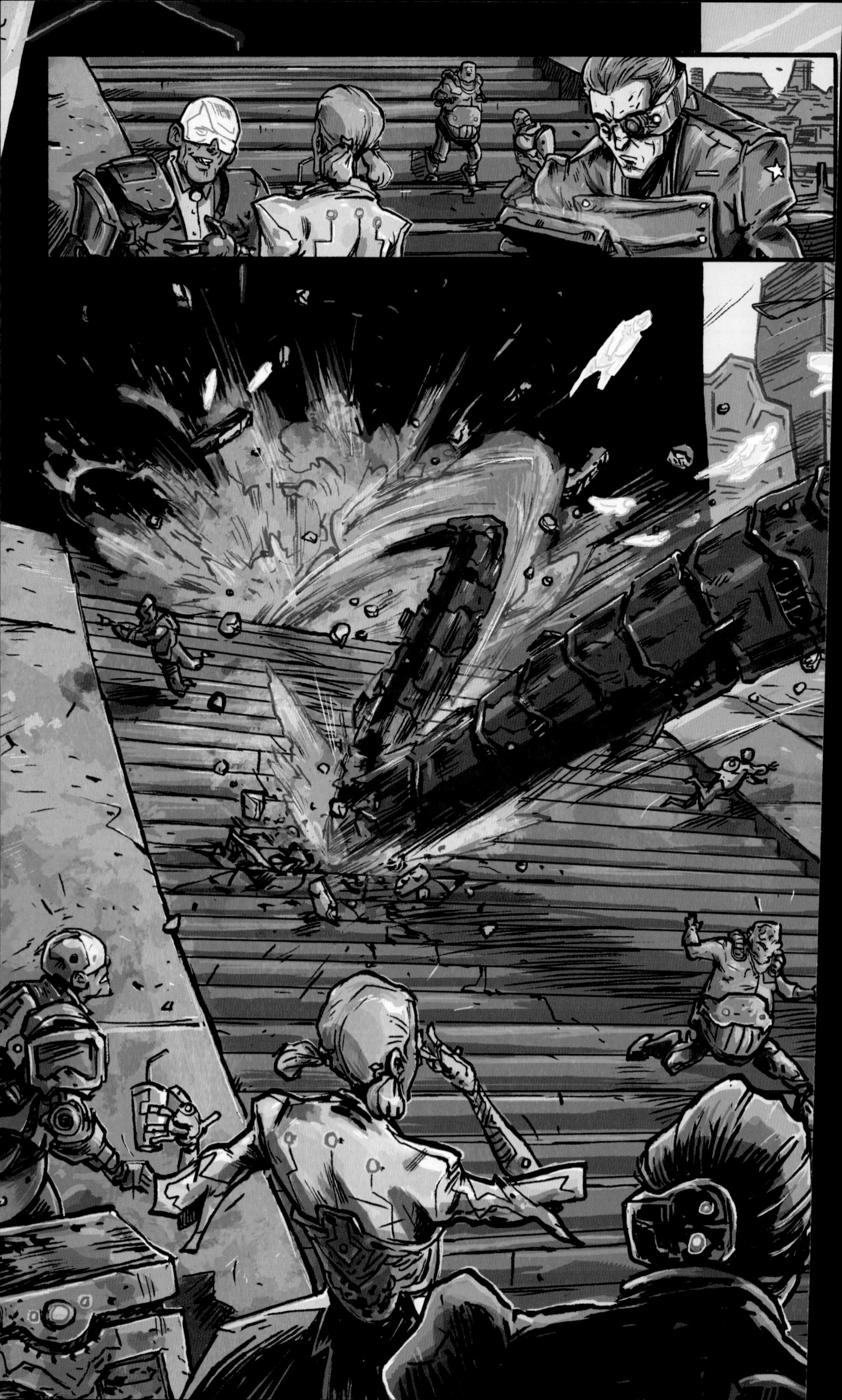

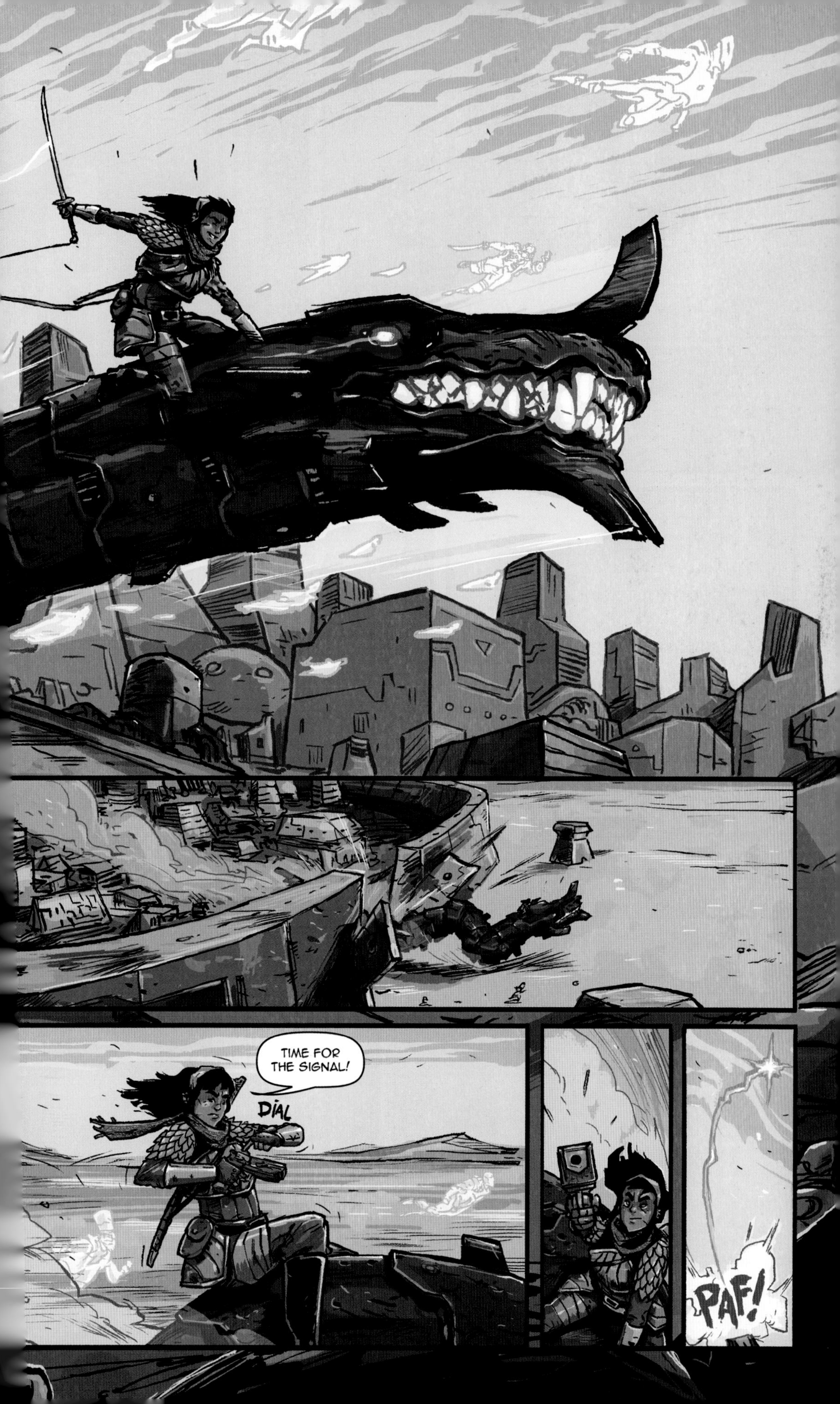
TIME FOR THE SIGNAL!
DIAL
PAF!

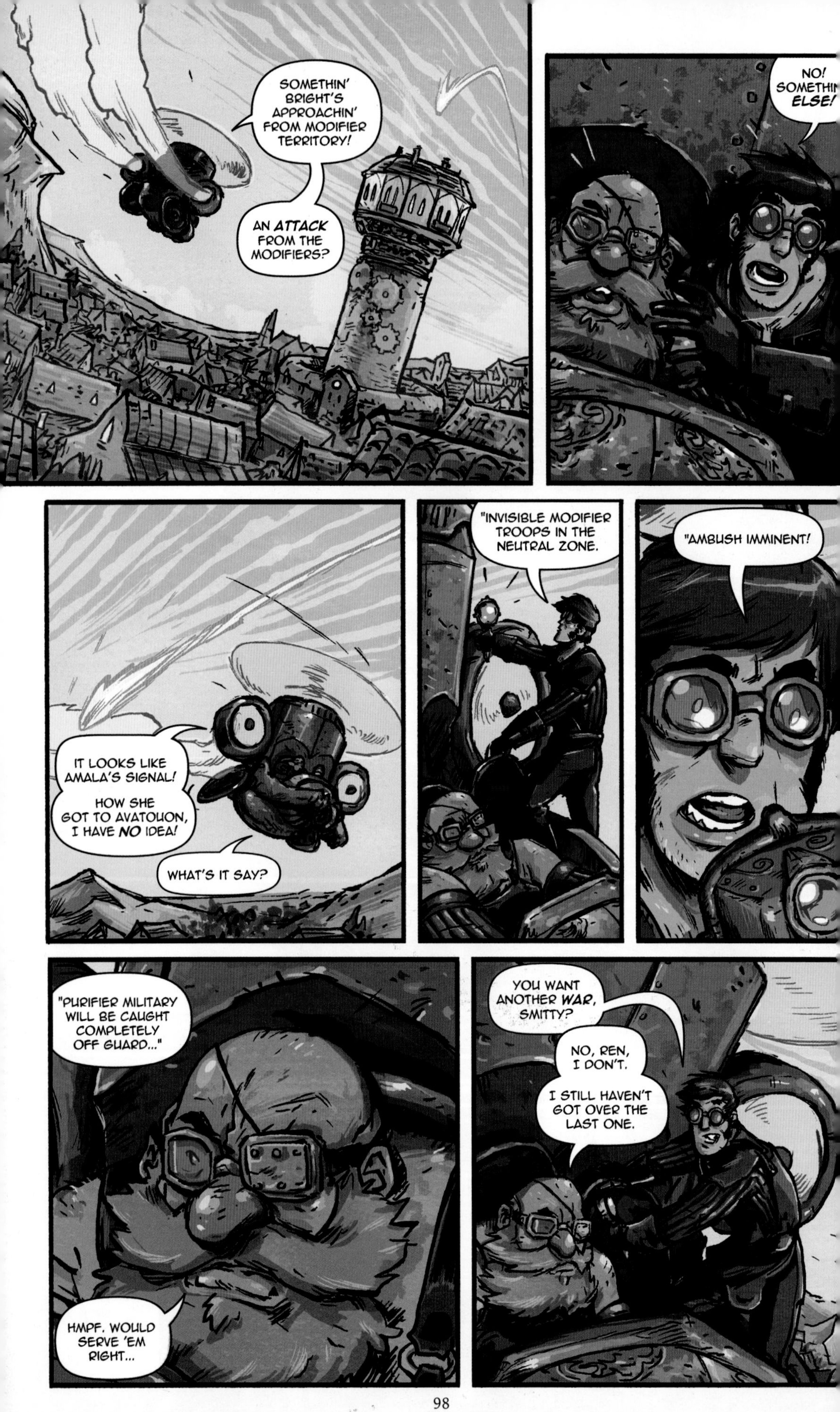
SOMETHIN' BRIGHT'S APPROACHIN' FROM MODIFIER TERRITORY!
AN ATTACK FROM THE MODIFIERS?
NO! SOMETHIN ELSE!
IT LOOKS LIKE AMALA'S SIGNAL!
HOW SHE GOT TO AVATOUON, I HAVE NO IDEA!
WHAT'S IT SAY?
"INVISIBLE MODIFIER TROOPS IN THE NEUTRAL ZONE.
"AMBUSH IMMINENT!
"PURIFIER MILITARY WILL BE CAUGHT COMPLETELY OFF GUARD..."
HMPF. WOULD SERVE 'EM RIGHT...
YOU WANT ANOTHER WAR, SMITTY?
NO, REN, I DON'T.
I STILL HAVEN'T GOT OVER THE LAST ONE.

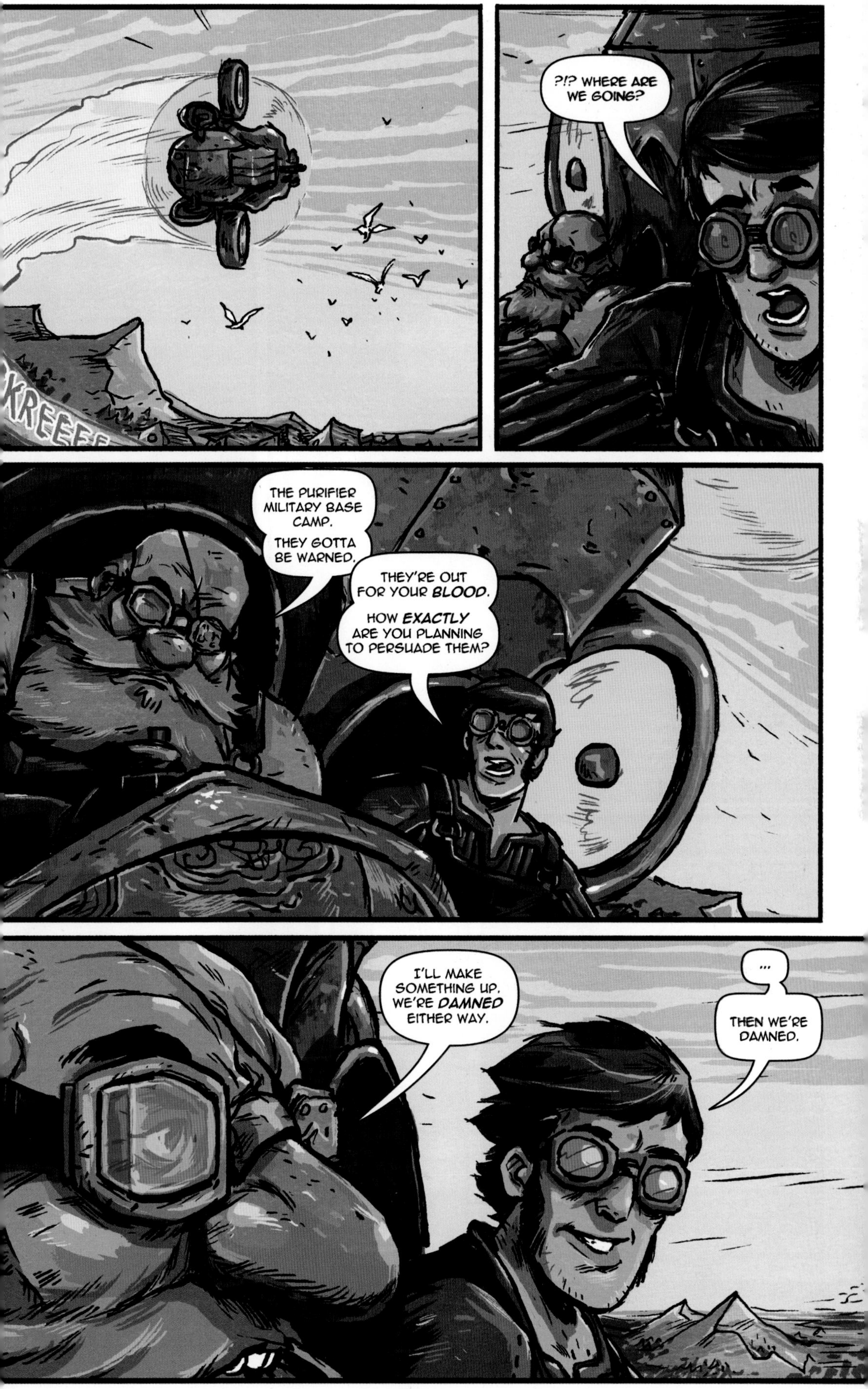
KREEEEE
?!? WHERE ARE WE GOING?
THE PURIFIER MILITARY BASE CAMP.
THEY GOTTA BE WARNED.
THEY'RE OUT FOR YOUR BLOOD.
HOW EXACTLY ARE YOU PLANNING TO PERSUADE THEM?
I'LL MAKE SOMETHING UP. WE'RE DAMNED EITHER WAY.
...
THEN WE'RE DAMNED.

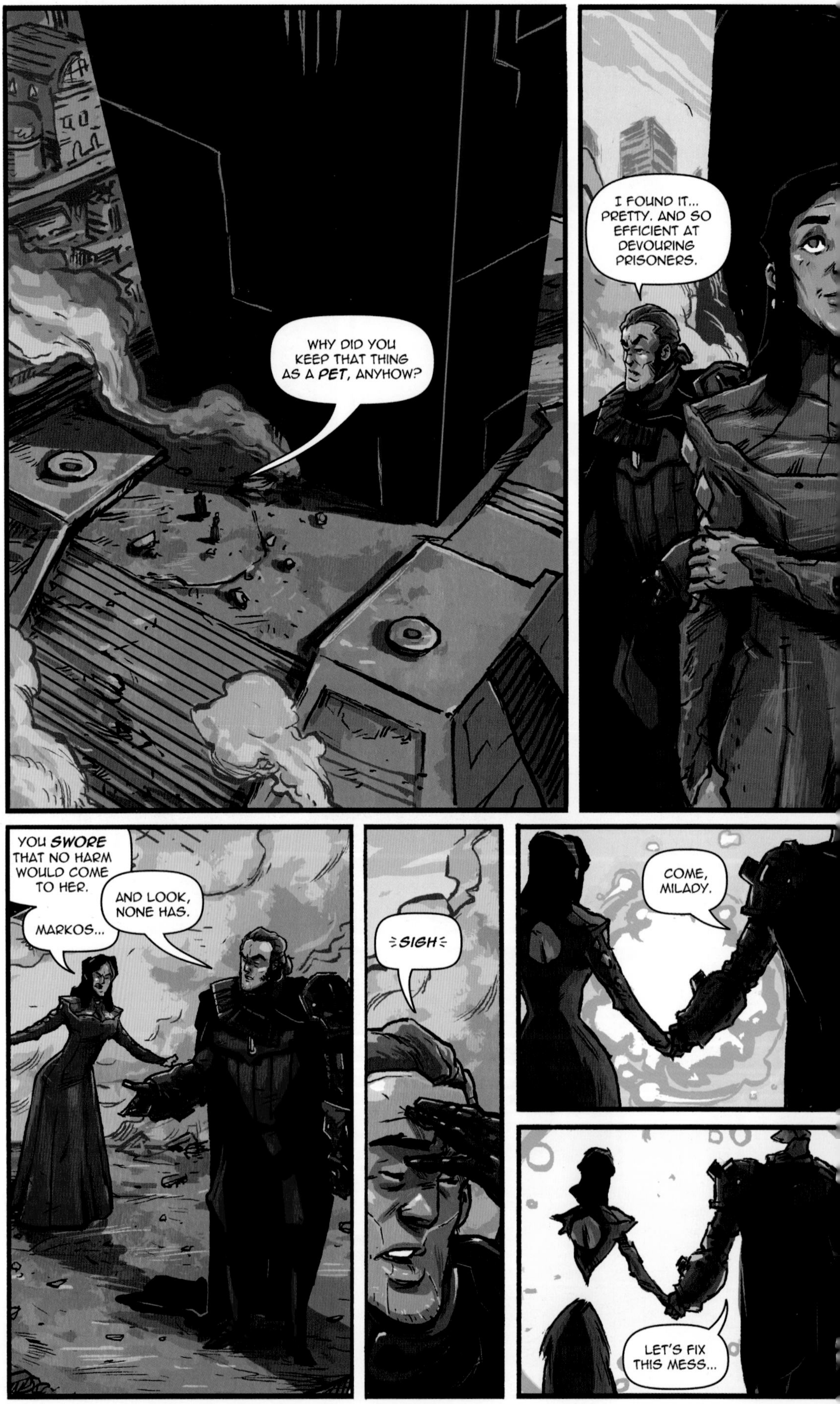
WHY DID YOU KEEP THAT THING AS A *PET*, ANYHOW?
I FOUND IT... PRETTY. AND SO EFFICIENT AT DEVOURING PRISONERS.
YOU *SWORE* THAT NO HARM WOULD COME TO HER.
MARKOS...
AND LOOK, NONE HAS.
SIGH
COME, MILADY.
LET'S FIX THIS MESS...

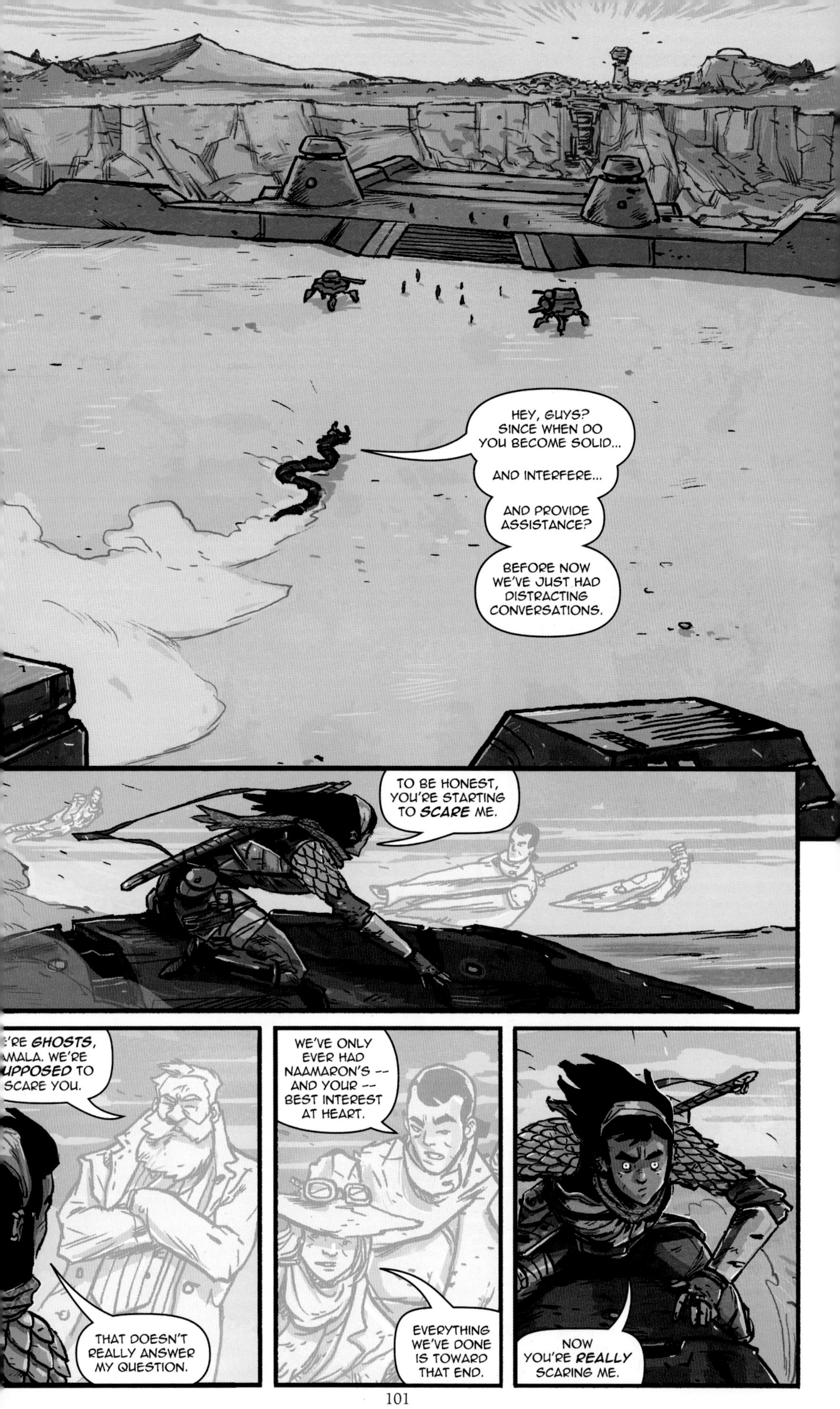
HEY, GUYS? SINCE WHEN DO YOU BECOME SOLID...
AND INTERFERE...
AND PROVIDE ASSISTANCE?
BEFORE NOW WE'VE JUST HAD DISTRACTING CONVERSATIONS.
TO BE HONEST, YOU'RE STARTING TO SCARE ME.
'RE GHOSTS, MALA. WE'RE UPPOSED TO SCARE YOU.
THAT DOESN'T REALLY ANSWER MY QUESTION.
WE'VE ONLY EVER HAD NAAMARON'S -- AND YOUR -- BEST INTEREST AT HEART.
EVERYTHING WE'VE DONE IS TOWARD THAT END.
NOW YOU'RE REALLY SCARING ME.

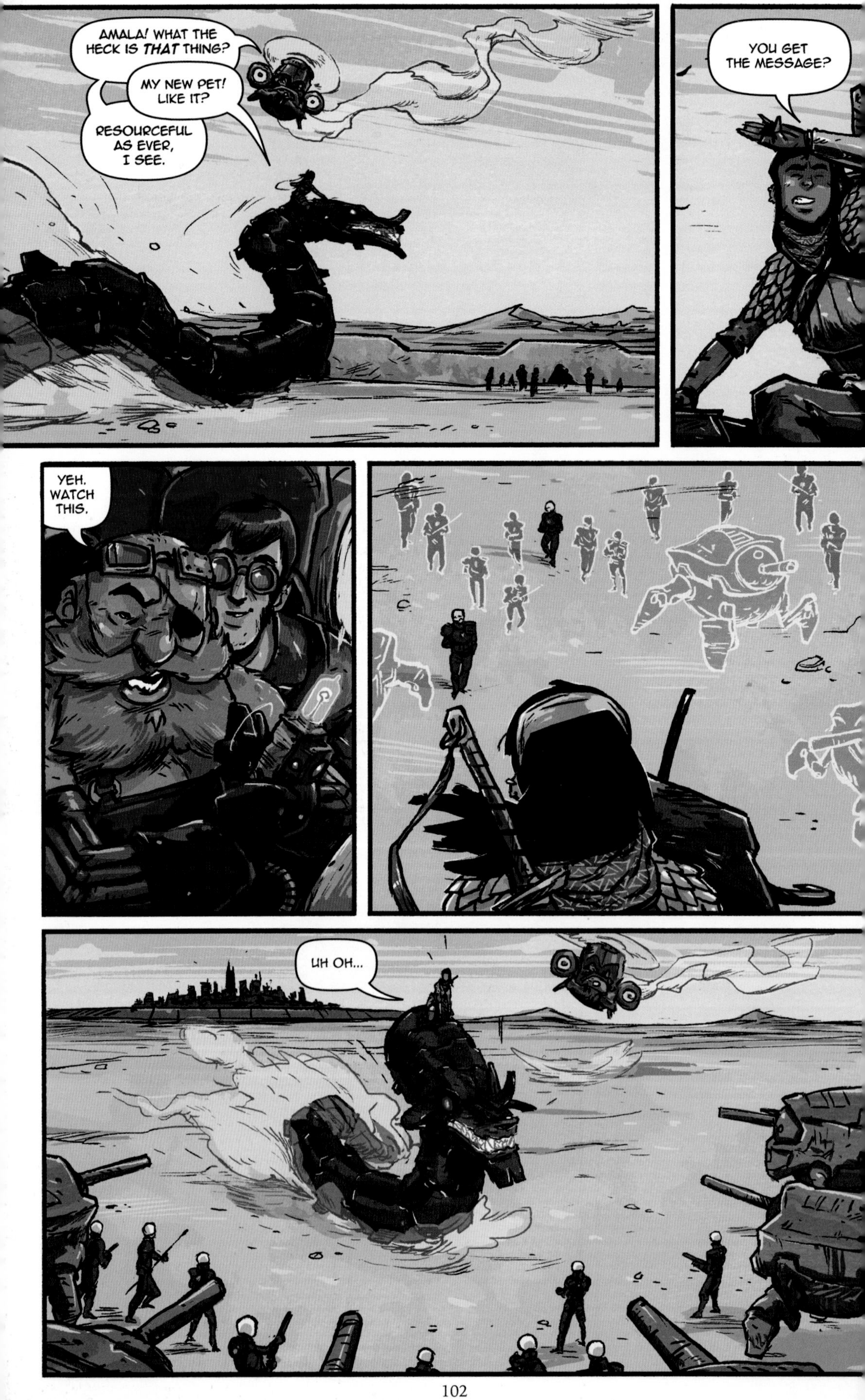
AMALA! WHAT THE HECK IS *THAT* THING?
MY NEW PET! LIKE IT?
RESOURCEFUL AS EVER, I SEE.
YOU GET THE MESSAGE?
YEH. WATCH THIS.
UH OH...

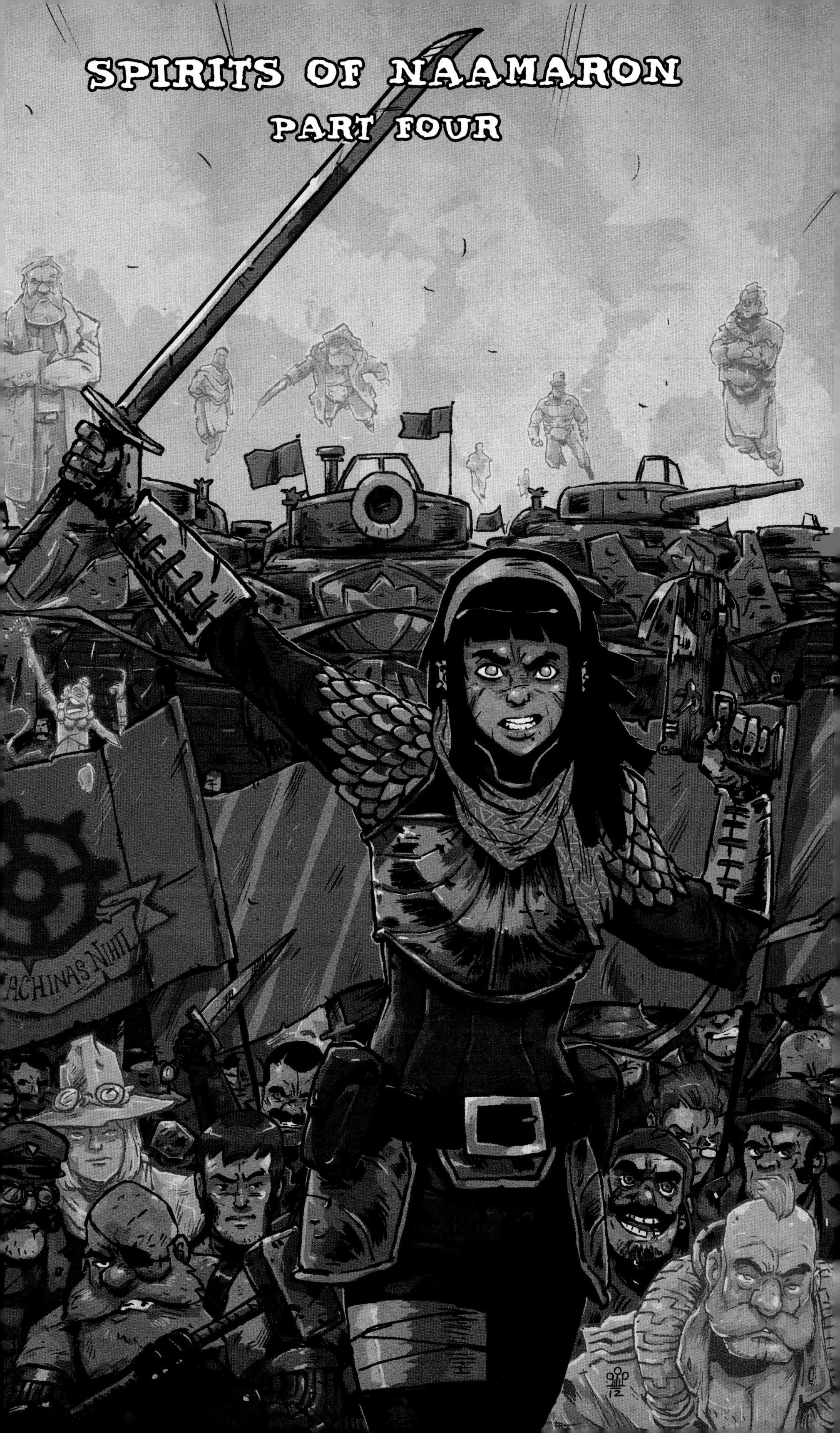
SPIRITS OF NAAMARON
PART FOUR

"SURVIVE THIS BLOODBATH AND WE'LL TALK."

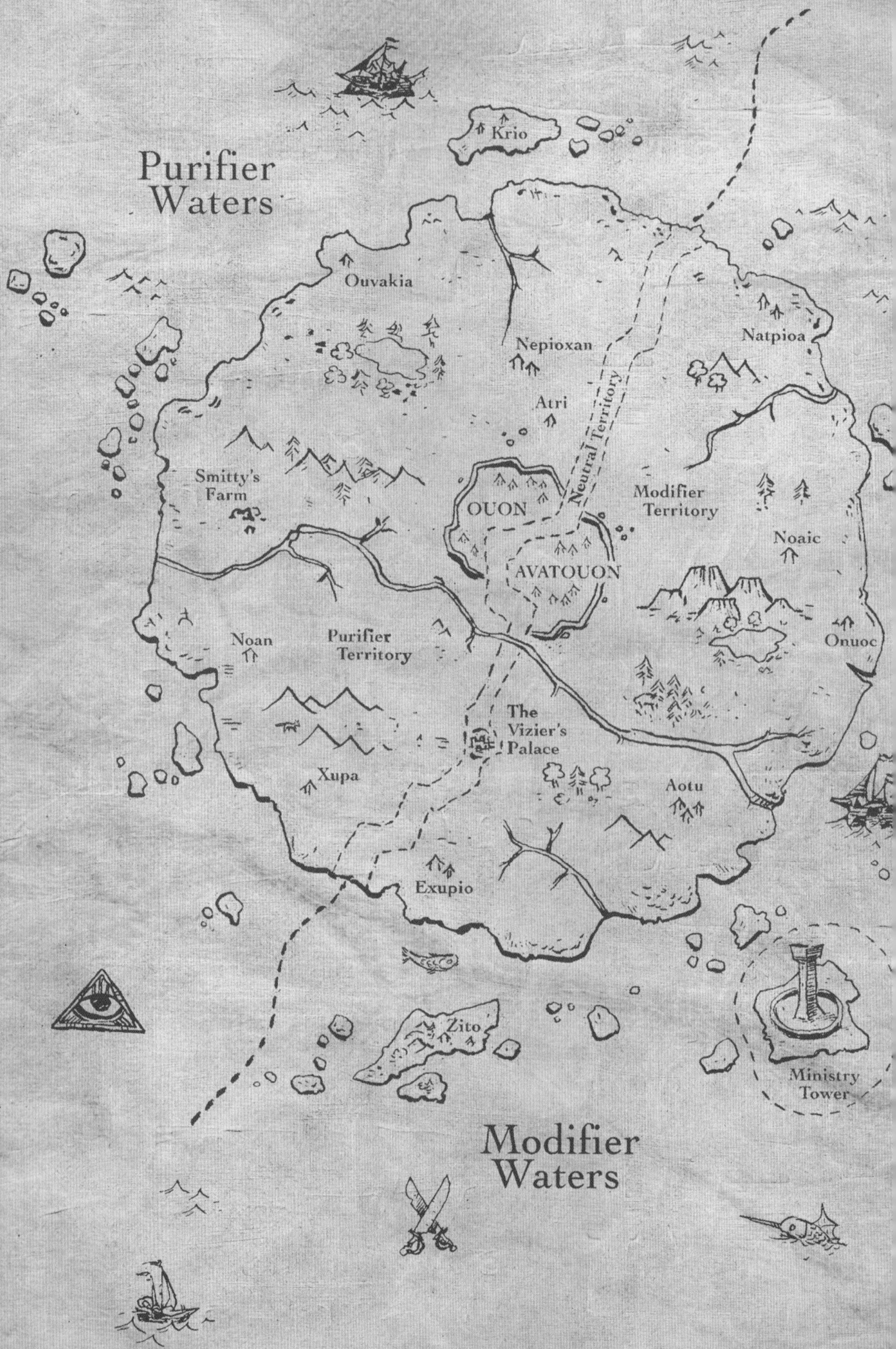

Purifier Waters
Krio
Ouvakia
Nepioxan
Natpioa
Atri
Neutral Territory
Smitty's Farm
OUON
Modifier Territory
Noaic
AVATOUON
Noan
Purifier Territory
Onuoc
The Vizier's Palace
Xupa
Aotu
Exupio
Zito
Ministry Tower
Modifier Waters

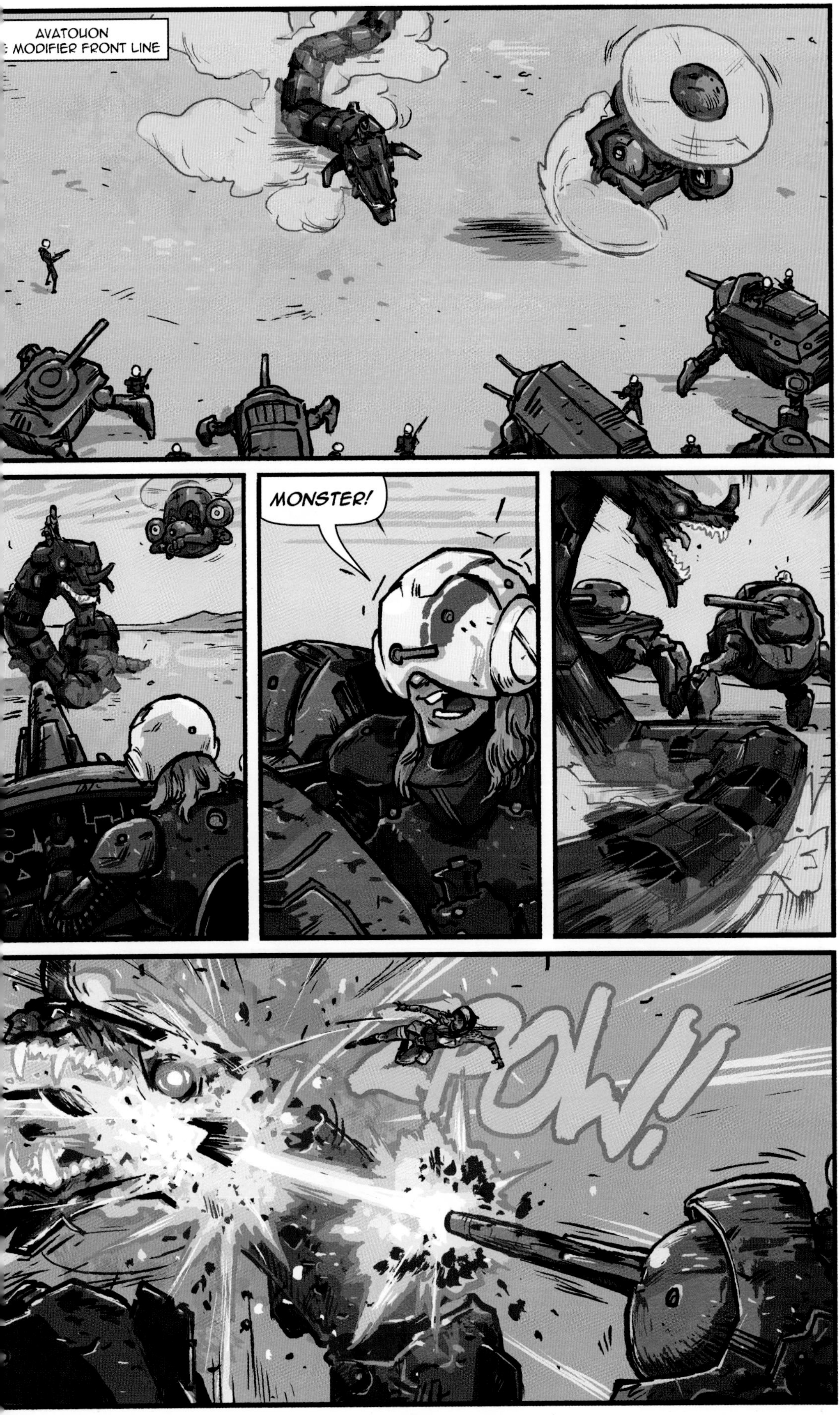
AVATOUON
E MODIFIER FRONT LINE
MONSTER!
POW!

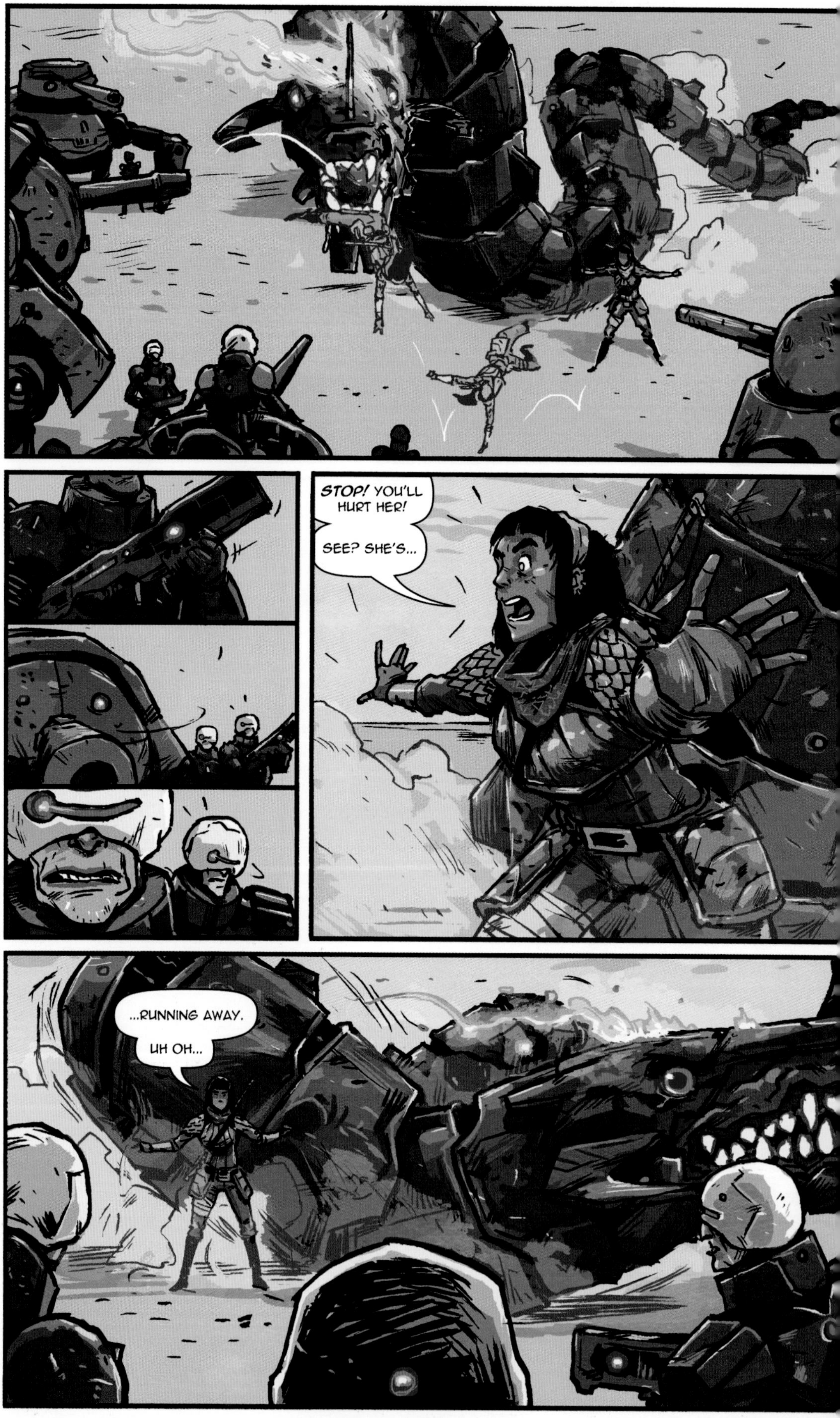
STOP! YOU'LL HURT HER!
SEE? SHE'S...
...RUNNING AWAY.
UH OH...

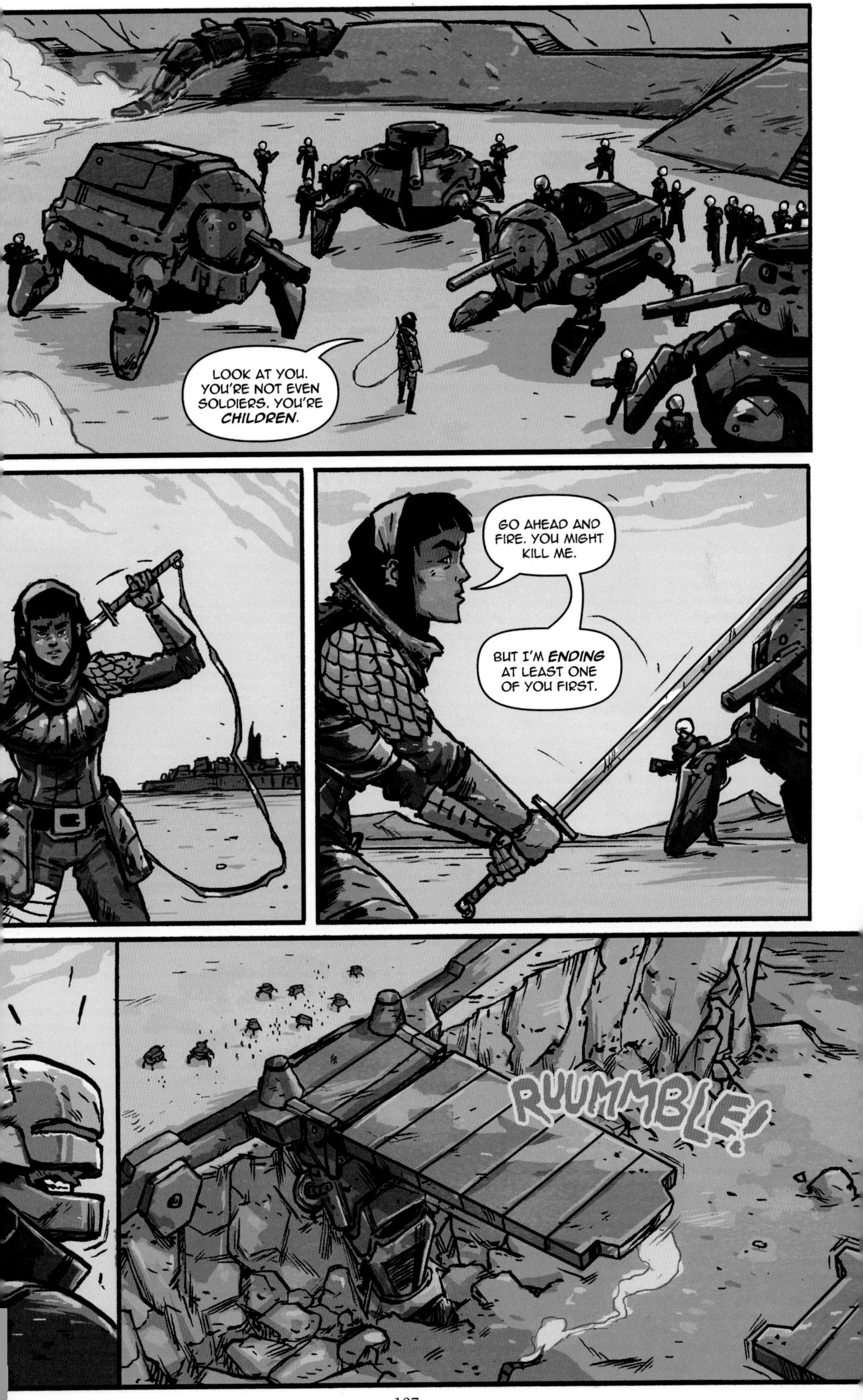

LOOK AT YOU. YOU'RE NOT EVEN SOLDIERS. YOU'RE CHILDREN.
GO AHEAD AND FIRE. YOU MIGHT KILL ME.
BUT I'M ENDING AT LEAST ONE OF YOU FIRST.
RUUMMBLE!

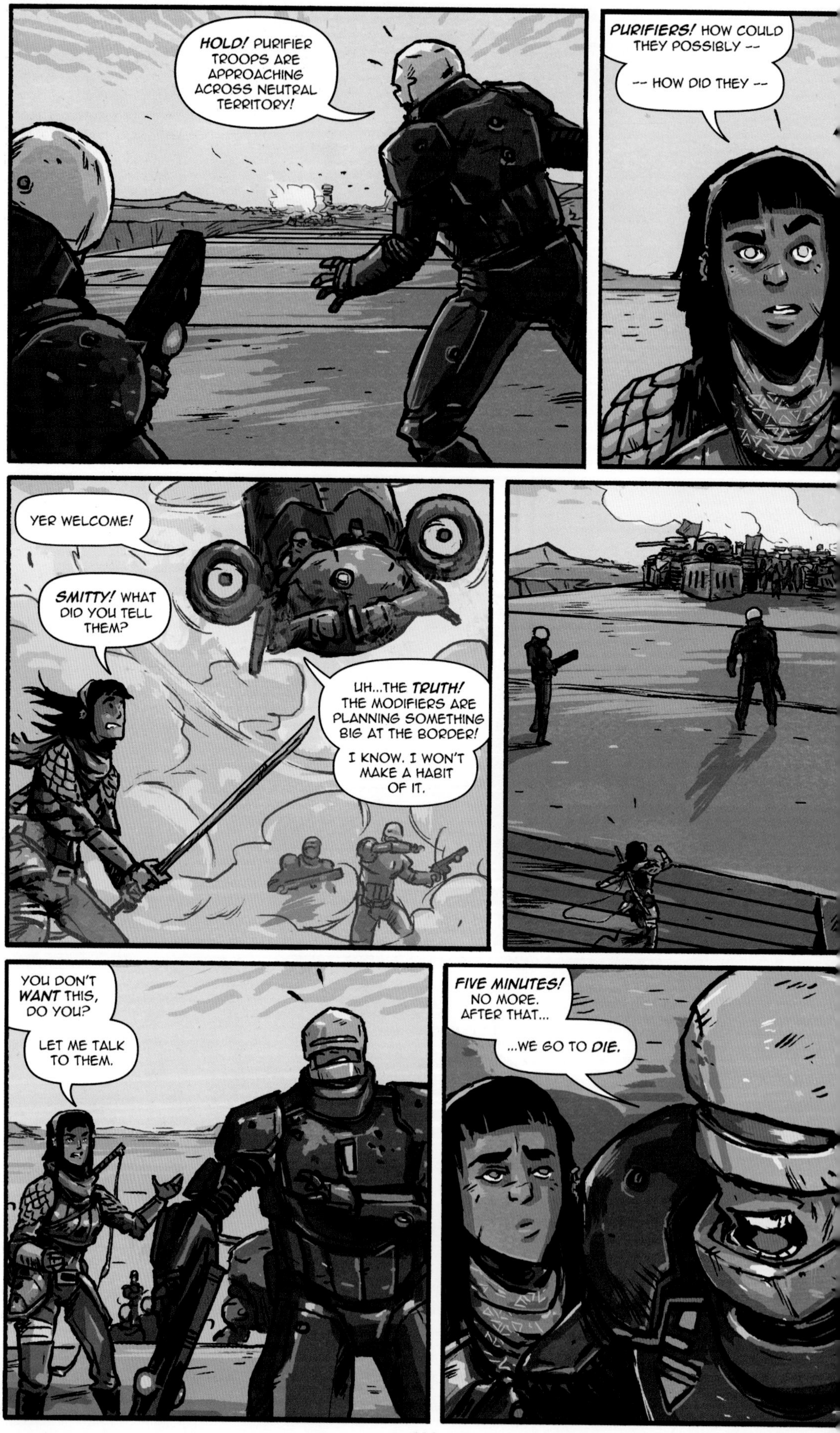
HOLD! PURIFIER TROOPS ARE APPROACHING ACROSS NEUTRAL TERRITORY!
PURIFIERS! HOW COULD THEY POSSIBLY --
-- HOW DID THEY --
YER WELCOME!
SMITTY! WHAT DID YOU TELL THEM?
UH...THE TRUTH! THE MODIFIERS ARE PLANNING SOMETHING BIG AT THE BORDER!
I KNOW. I WON'T MAKE A HABIT OF IT.
YOU DON'T WANT THIS, DO YOU?
LET ME TALK TO THEM.
FIVE MINUTES! NO MORE. AFTER THAT...
...WE GO TO DIE.

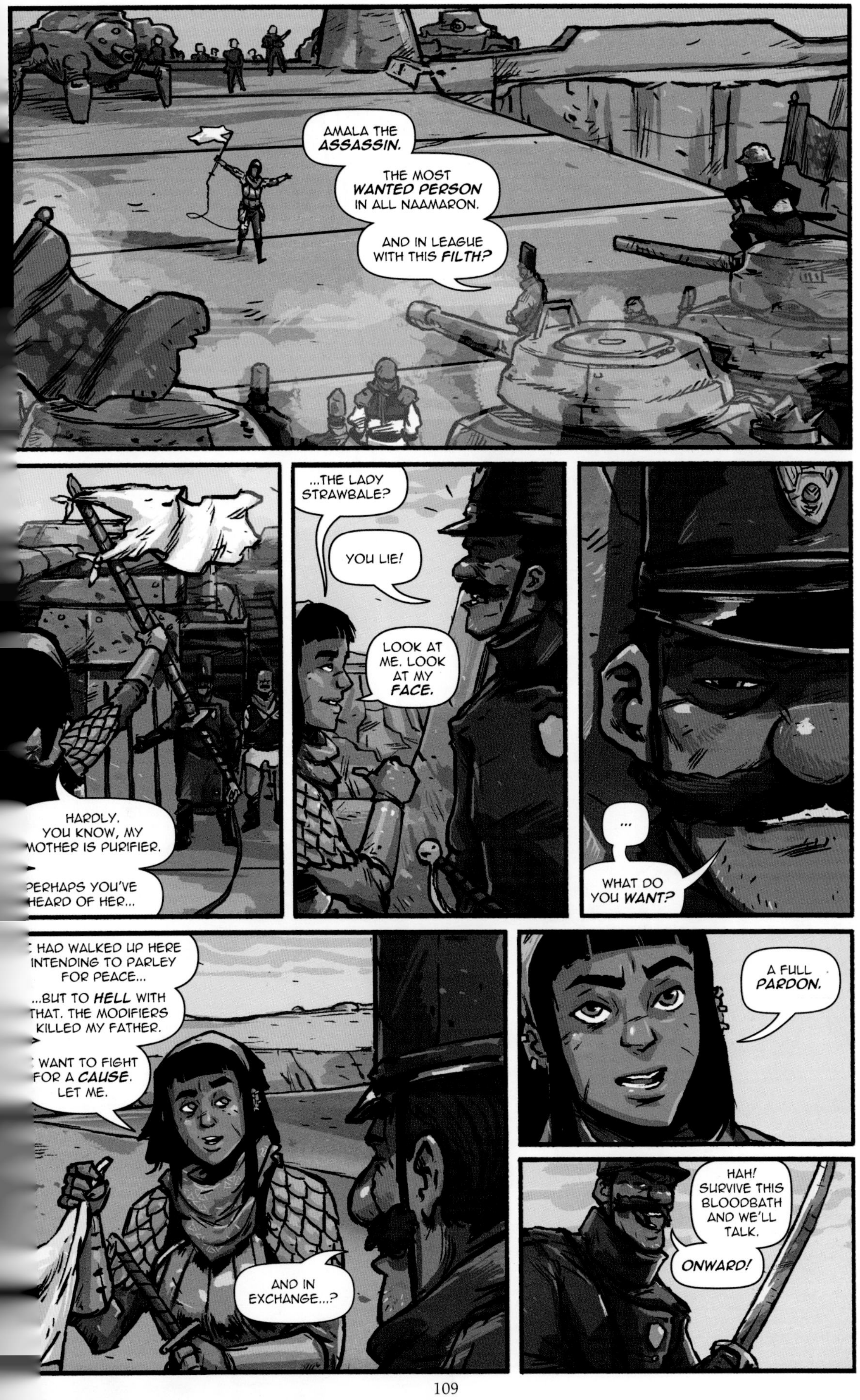
AMALA THE ASSASSIN.
THE MOST WANTED PERSON IN ALL NAAMARON.
AND IN LEAGUE WITH THIS FILTH?
HARDLY. YOU KNOW, MY MOTHER IS PURIFIER.
PERHAPS YOU'VE HEARD OF HER...
...THE LADY STRAWBALE?
YOU LIE!
LOOK AT ME. LOOK AT MY FACE.
...
WHAT DO YOU WANT?
HAD WALKED UP HERE INTENDING TO PARLEY FOR PEACE...
...BUT TO HELL WITH THAT. THE MODIFIERS KILLED MY FATHER.
WANT TO FIGHT FOR A CAUSE. LET ME.
AND IN EXCHANGE...?
A FULL PARDON.
HAH! SURVIVE THIS BLOODBATH AND WE'LL TALK.
ONWARD!

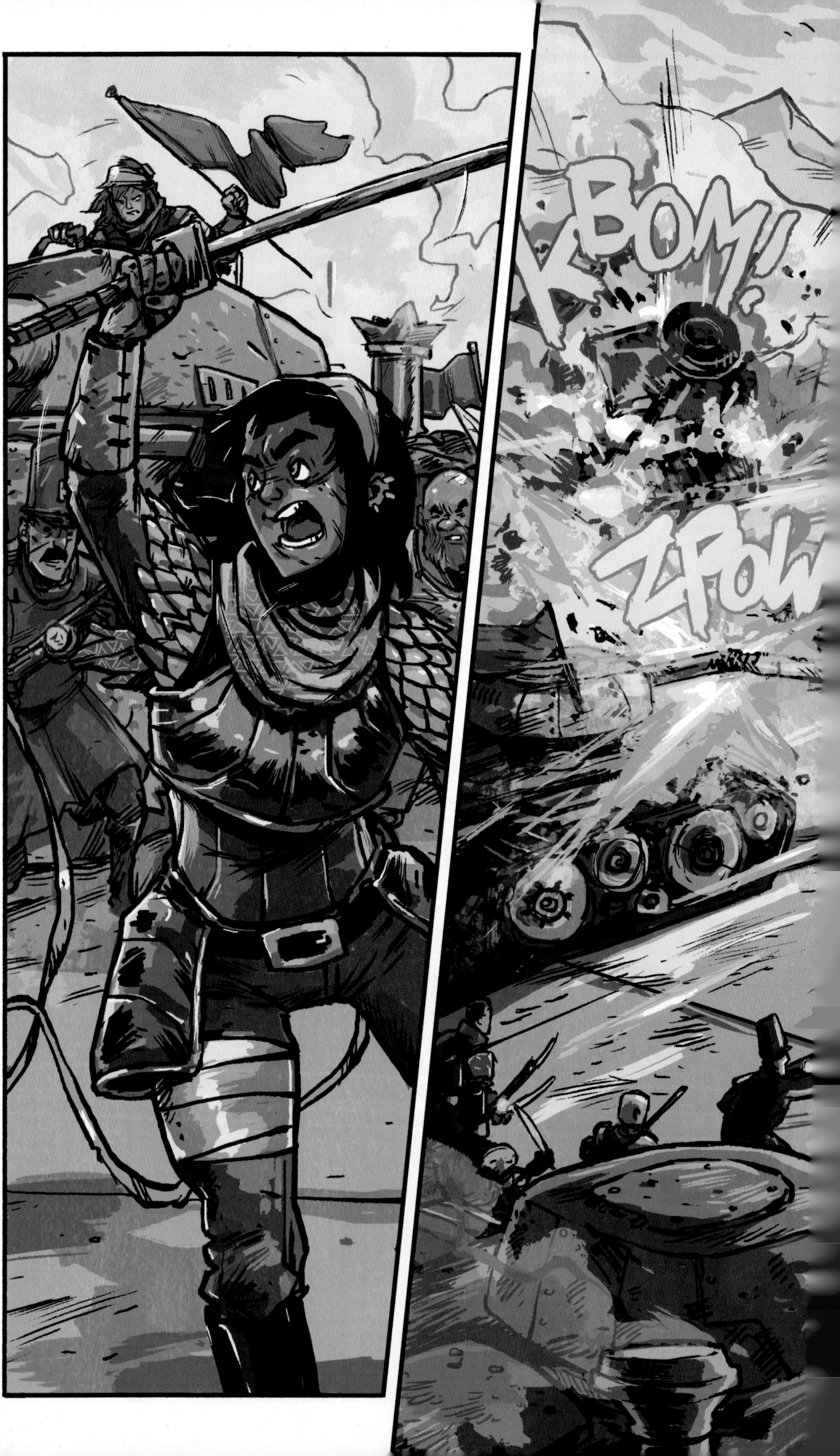
BOM!!
ZPOW

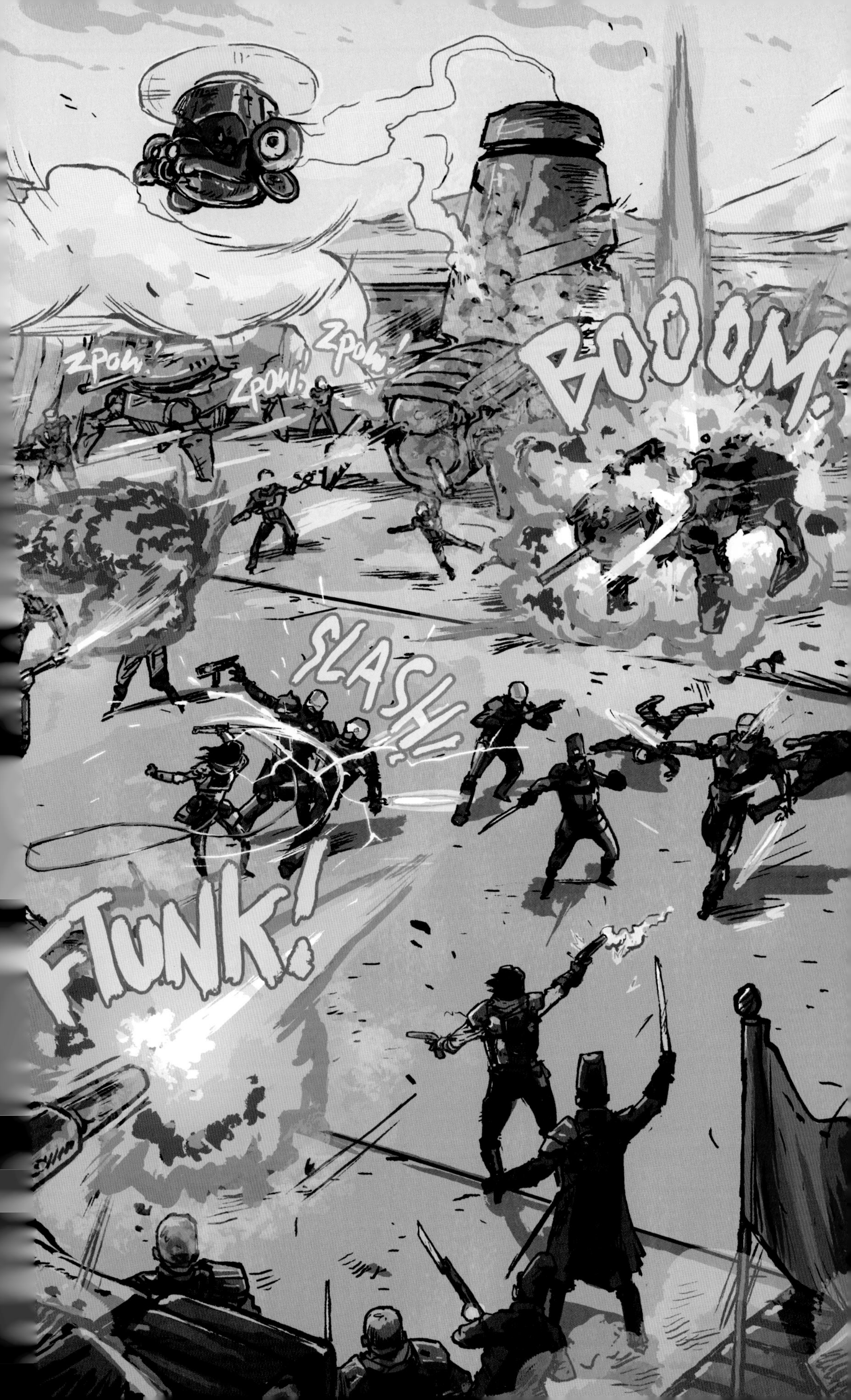
ZPOW!
ZPOW!
ZPOW!
BOOOM!
SLASH!
FTUNK!

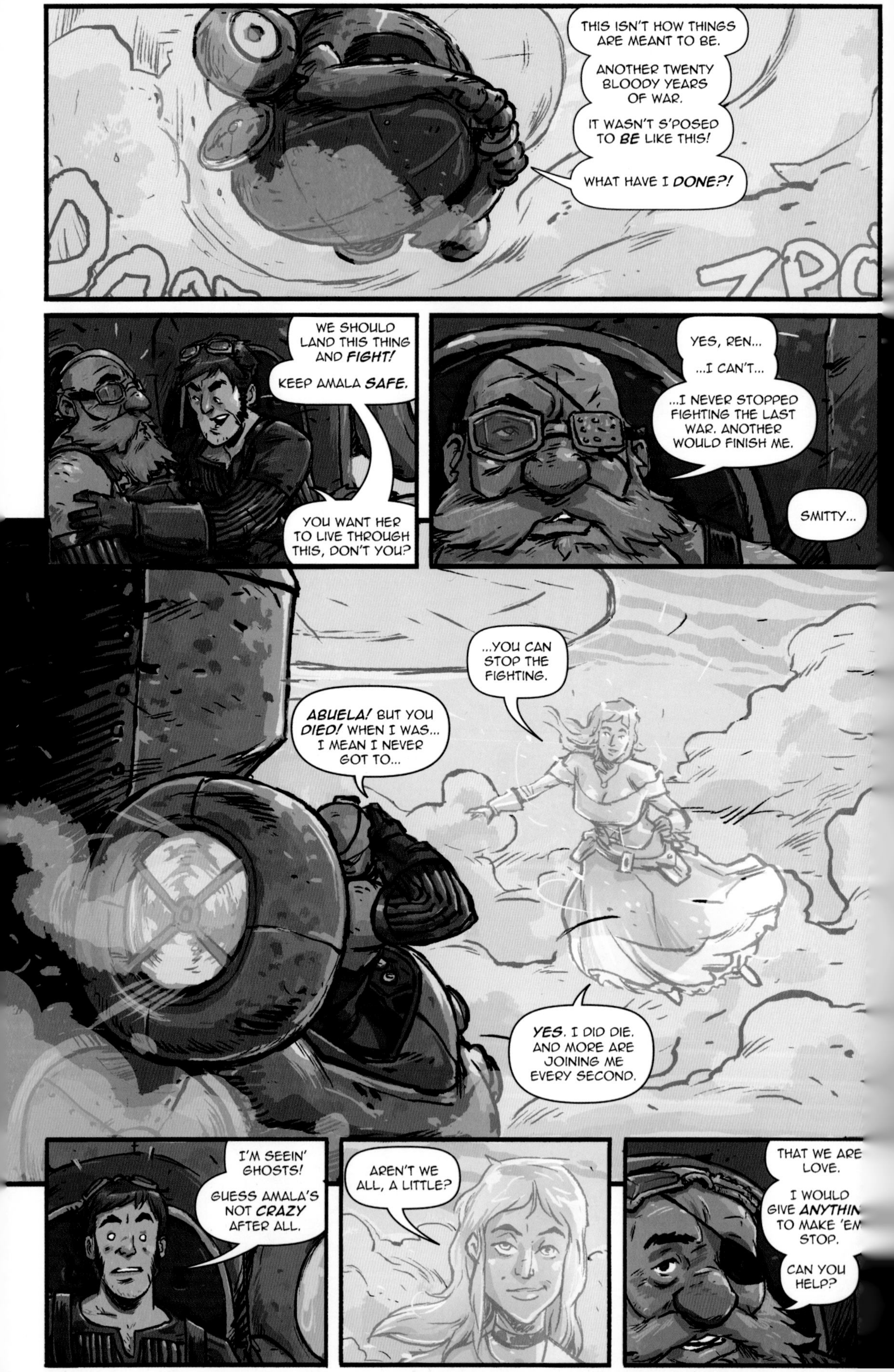
THIS ISN'T HOW THINGS ARE MEANT TO BE.
ANOTHER TWENTY BLOODY YEARS OF WAR.
IT WASN'T S'POSED TO *BE* LIKE THIS!
WHAT HAVE I *DONE?!*
WE SHOULD LAND THIS THING AND *FIGHT!*
KEEP AMALA *SAFE.*
YOU WANT HER TO LIVE THROUGH THIS, DON'T YOU?
YES, REN...
...I CAN'T...
...I NEVER STOPPED FIGHTING THE LAST WAR. ANOTHER WOULD FINISH ME.
SMITTY...
...YOU CAN STOP THE FIGHTING.
ABUELA! BUT YOU *DIED!* WHEN I WAS... I MEAN I NEVER GOT TO...
YES. I DID DIE. AND MORE ARE JOINING ME EVERY SECOND.
I'M SEEIN' GHOSTS!
GUESS AMALA'S NOT *CRAZY* AFTER ALL.
AREN'T WE ALL, A LITTLE?
THAT WE ARE LOVE.
CAN YOU HELP?

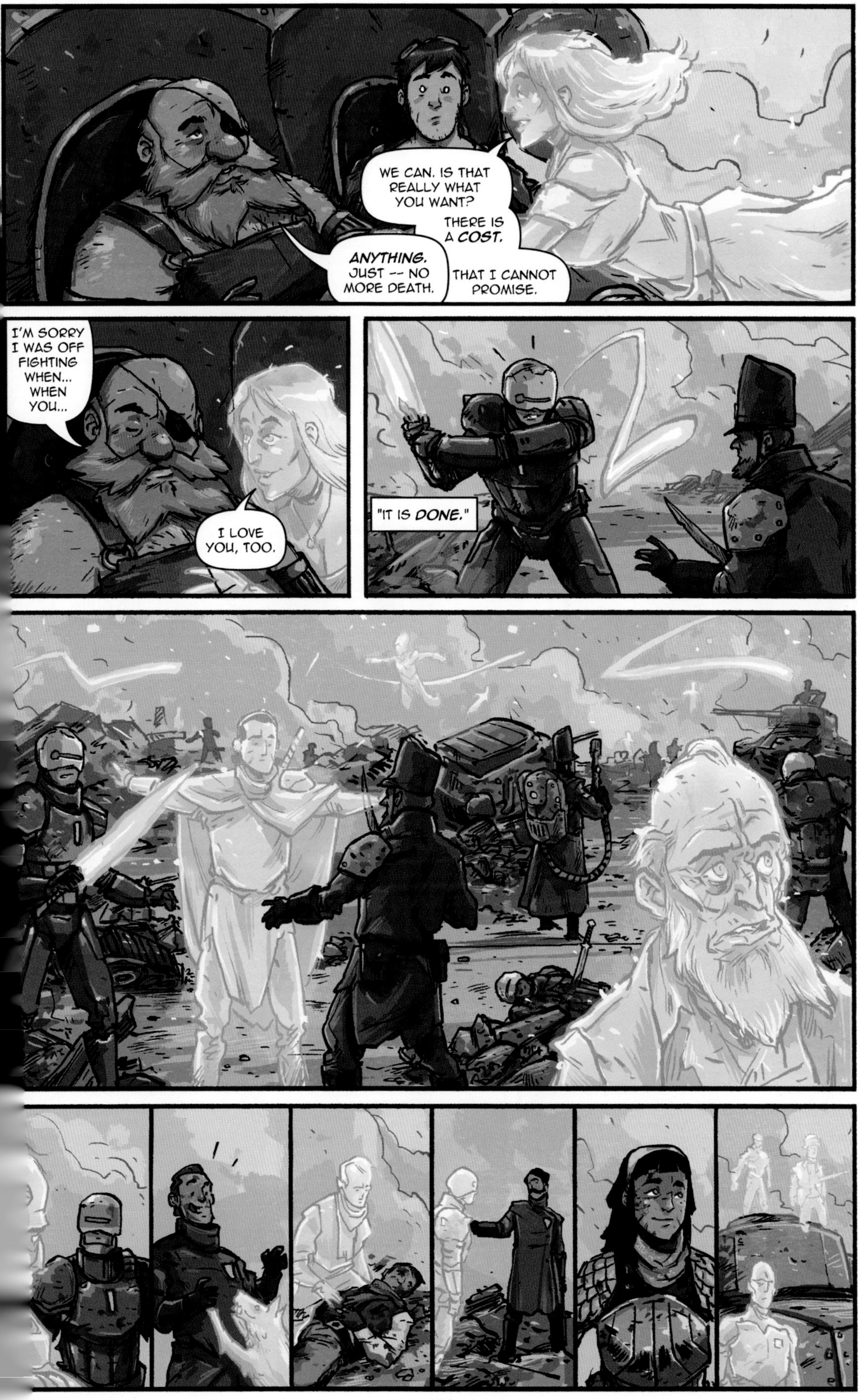
WE CAN. IS THAT REALLY WHAT YOU WANT?
THERE IS A COST.
ANYTHING. JUST -- NO MORE DEATH.
THAT I CANNOT PROMISE.
I'M SORRY I WAS OFF FIGHTING WHEN... WHEN YOU...
I LOVE YOU, TOO.
"IT IS DONE."

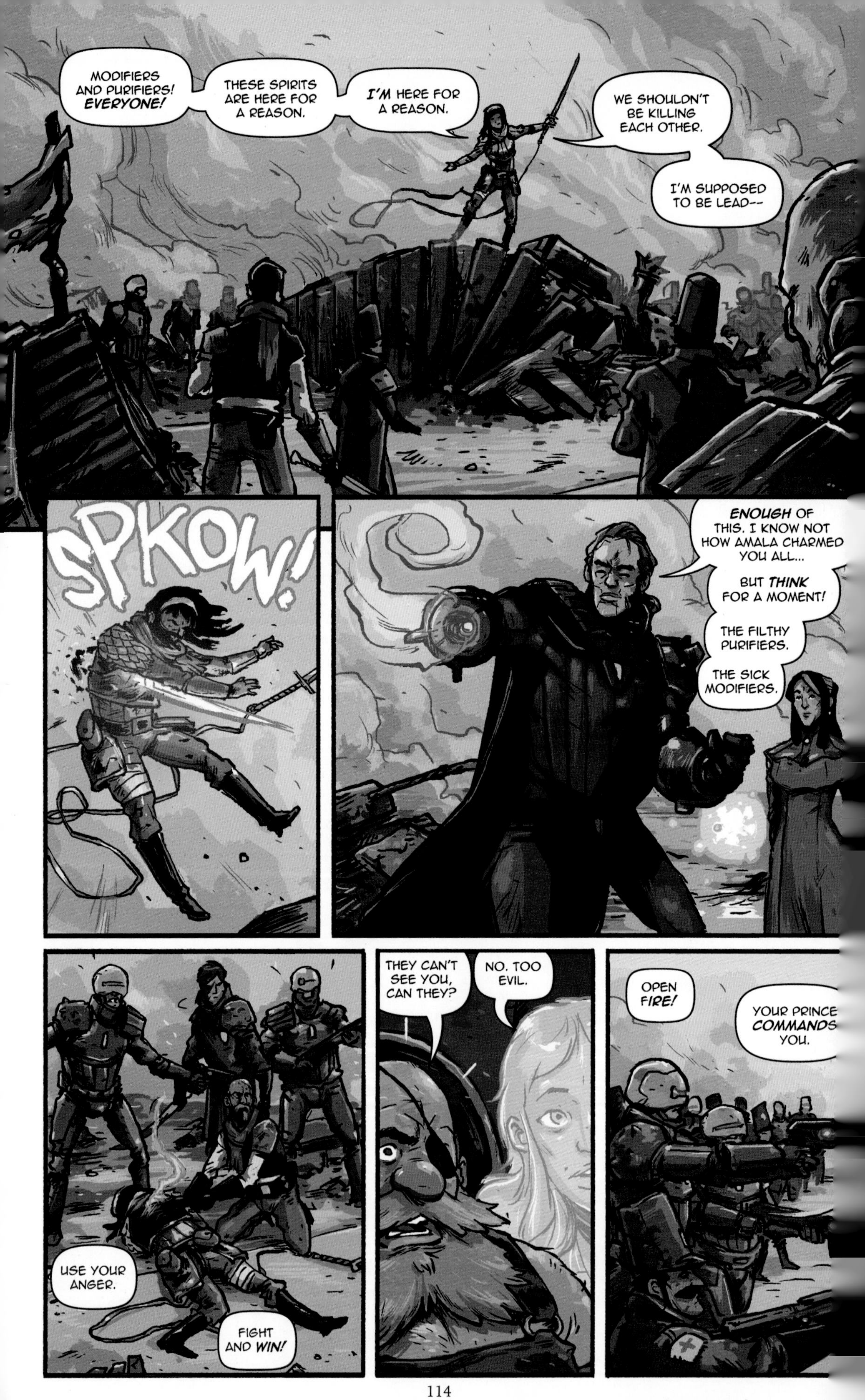
MODIFIERS AND PURIFIERS! EVERYONE!
THESE SPIRITS ARE HERE FOR A REASON.
I'M HERE FOR A REASON.
WE SHOULDN'T BE KILLING EACH OTHER.
I'M SUPPOSED TO BE LEAD--
SPKOW!
ENOUGH OF THIS. I KNOW NOT HOW AMALA CHARMED YOU ALL...
BUT THINK FOR A MOMENT!
THE FILTHY PURIFIERS.
THE SICK MODIFIERS.
USE YOUR ANGER.
FIGHT AND WIN!
THEY CAN'T SEE YOU, CAN THEY?
NO. TOO EVIL.
OPEN FIRE!
YOUR PRINCE COMMANDS YOU.

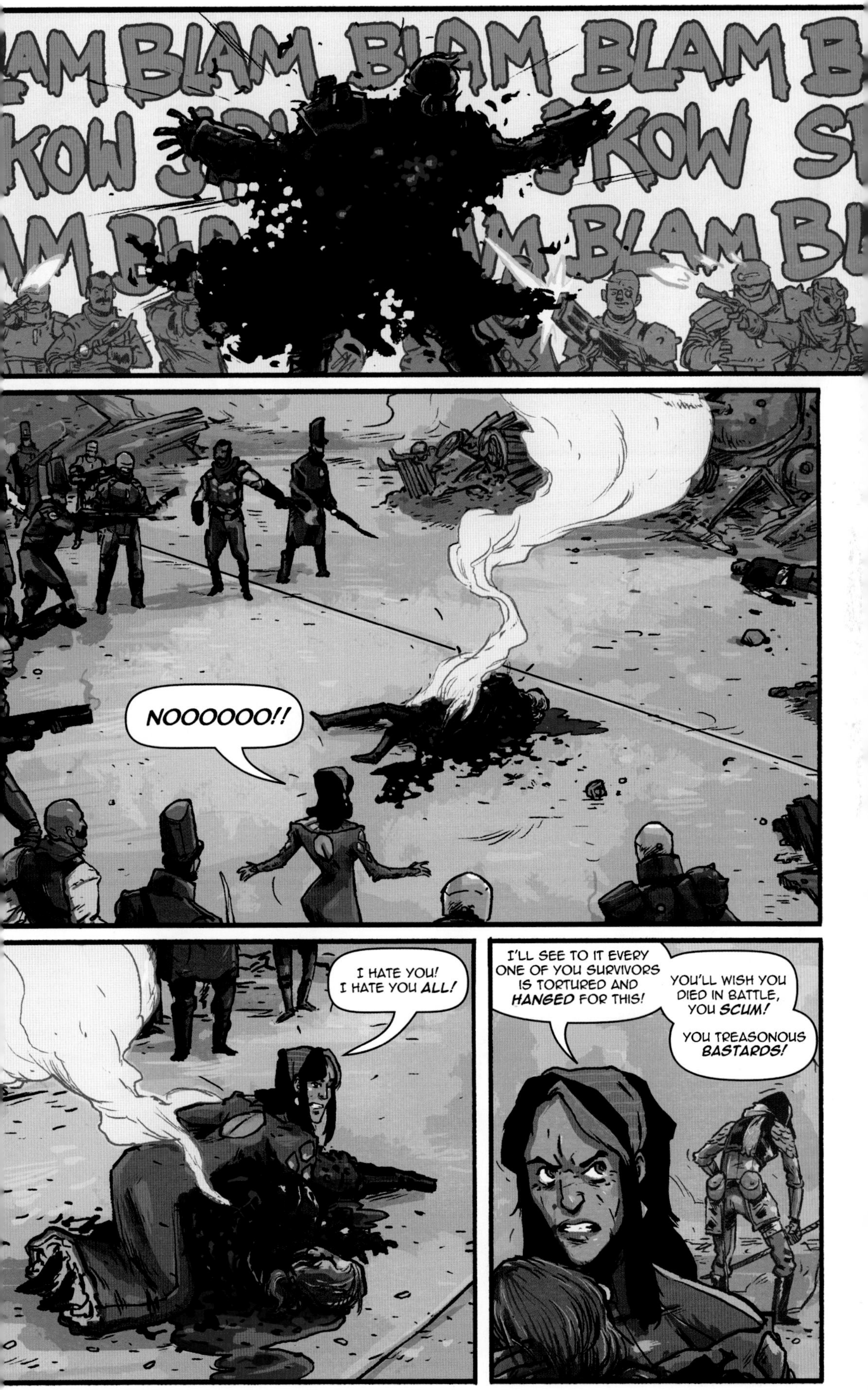
BLAM BLAM BLAM BLAM B
KOW KOW S
BLAM BLAM BL
NOOOOOO!!
I HATE YOU! I HATE YOU ALL!
I'LL SEE TO IT EVERY ONE OF YOU SURVIVORS IS TORTURED AND HANGED FOR THIS!
YOU'LL WISH YOU DIED IN BATTLE, YOU SCUM!
YOU TREASONOUS BASTARDS!

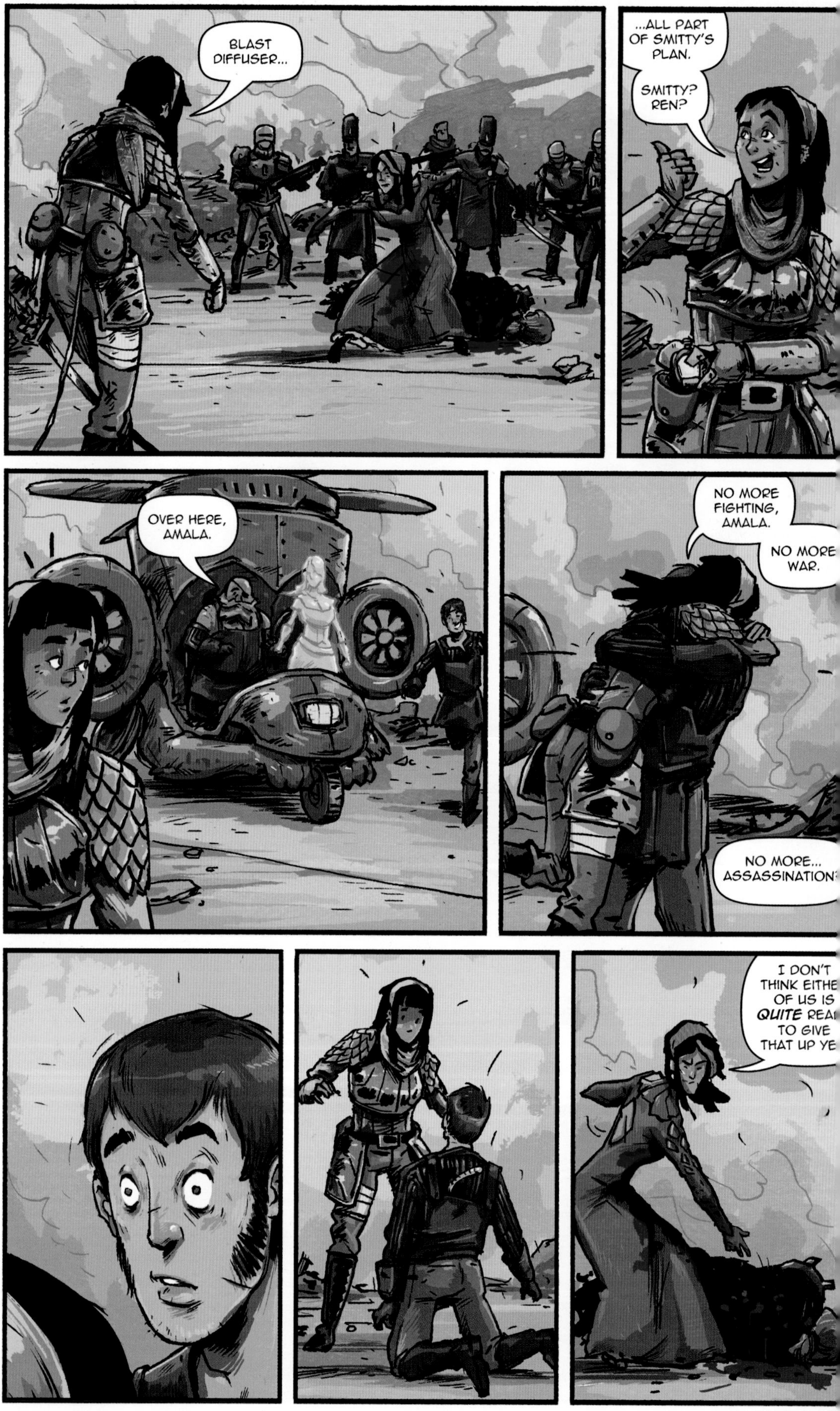
BLAST DIFFUSER...
...ALL PART OF SMITTY'S PLAN.
SMITTY? REN?
OVER HERE, AMALA.
NO MORE FIGHTING, AMALA.
NO MORE WAR.
NO MORE... ASSASSINATION?
I DON'T THINK EITHE OF US IS *QUITE* REA TO GIVE THAT UP YE

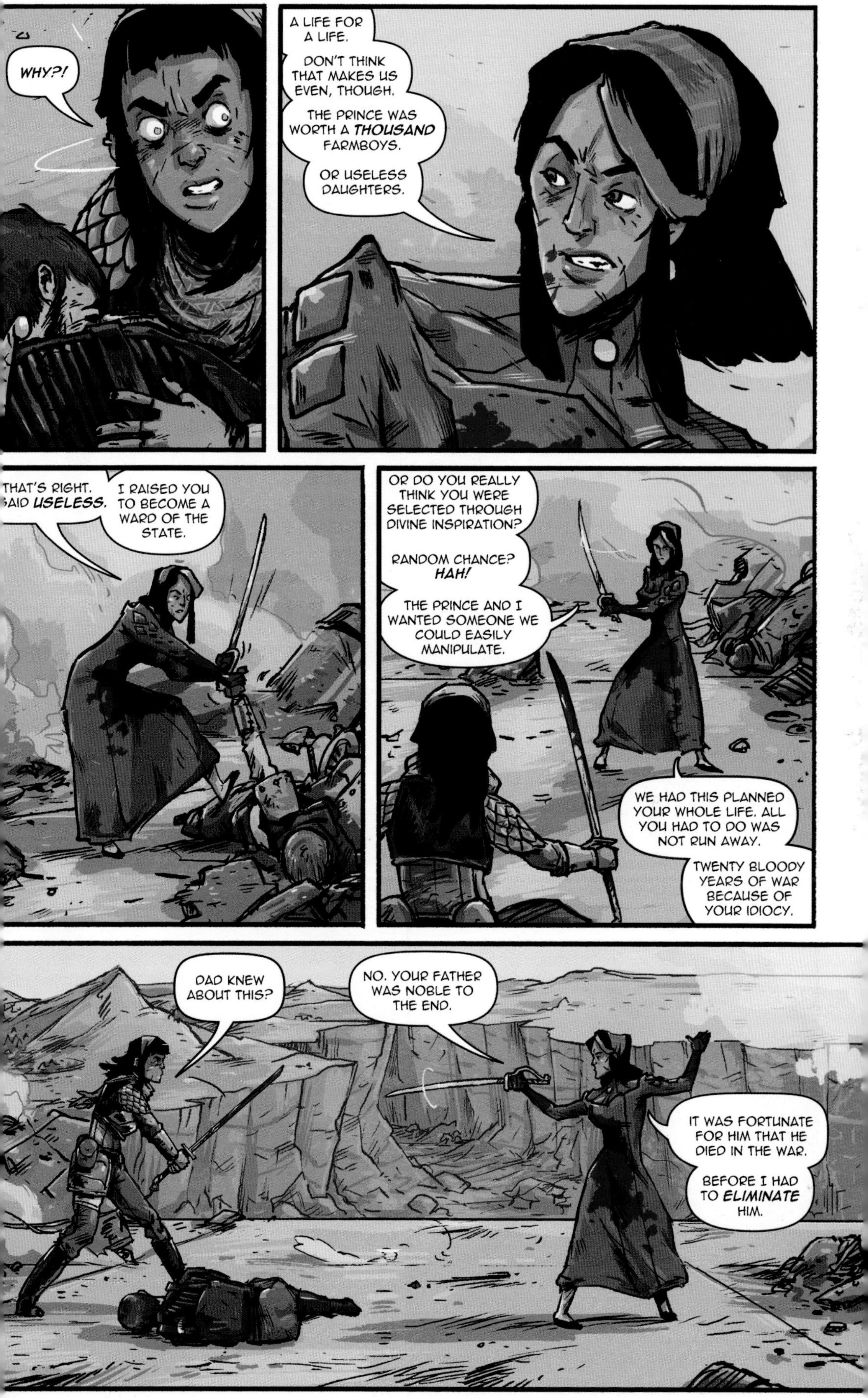
WHY?!
A LIFE FOR A LIFE.
DON'T THINK THAT MAKES US EVEN, THOUGH.
THE PRINCE WAS WORTH A ***THOUSAND*** FARMBOYS.
OR USELESS DAUGHTERS.
THAT'S RIGHT. AID ***USELESS.***
I RAISED YOU TO BECOME A WARD OF THE STATE.
OR DO YOU REALLY THINK YOU WERE SELECTED THROUGH DIVINE INSPIRATION?
RANDOM CHANCE? ***HAH!***
THE PRINCE AND I WANTED SOMEONE WE COULD EASILY MANIPULATE.
WE HAD THIS PLANNED YOUR WHOLE LIFE. ALL YOU HAD TO DO WAS NOT RUN AWAY.
TWENTY BLOODY YEARS OF WAR BECAUSE OF YOUR IDIOCY.
DAD KNEW ABOUT THIS?
NO. YOUR FATHER WAS NOBLE TO THE END.
IT WAS FORTUNATE FOR HIM THAT HE DIED IN THE WAR.
BEFORE I HAD TO ***ELIMINATE*** HIM.

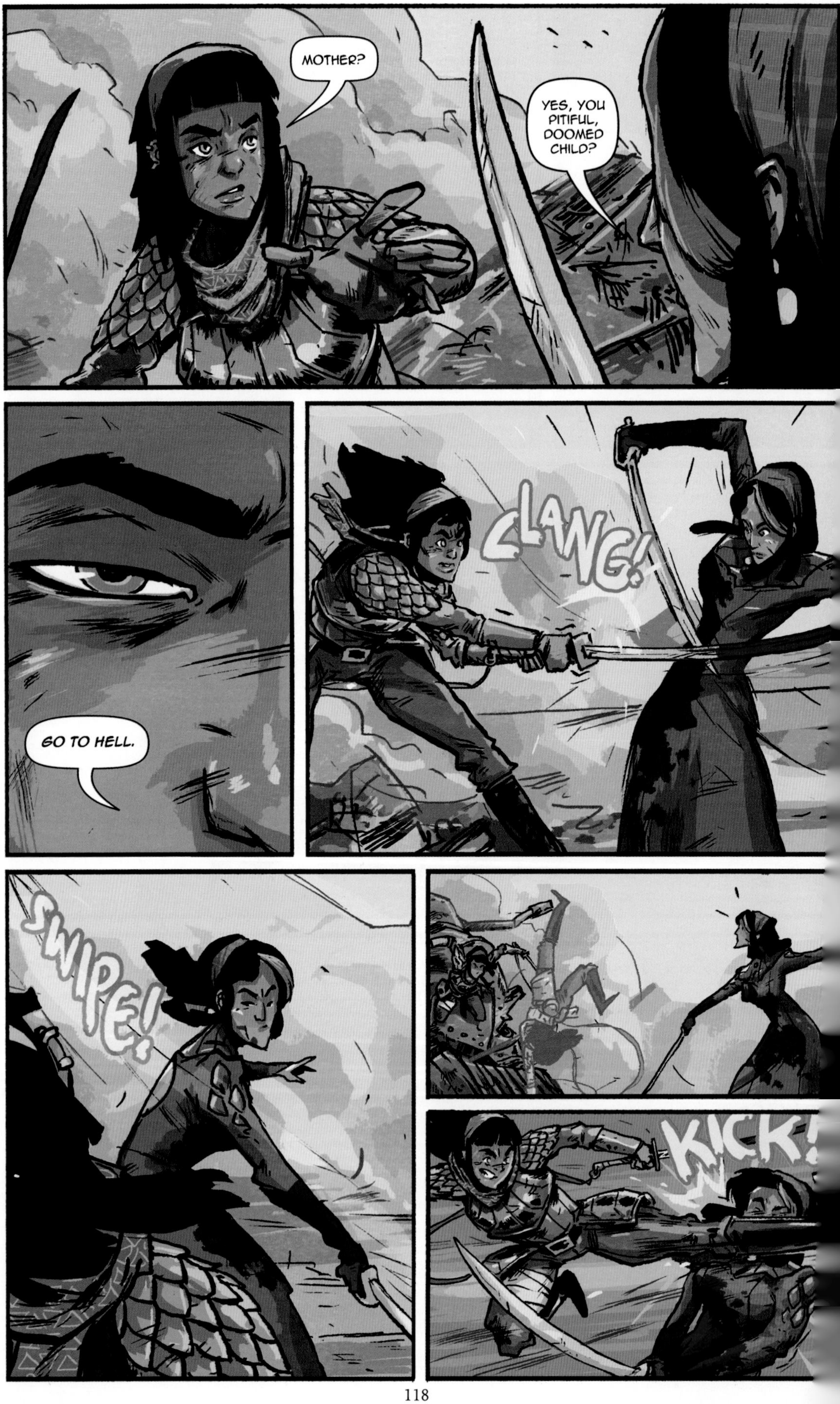
MOTHER?
YES, YOU PITIFUL, DOOMED CHILD?
GO TO HELL.
CLANG!
SWIPE!
KICK!

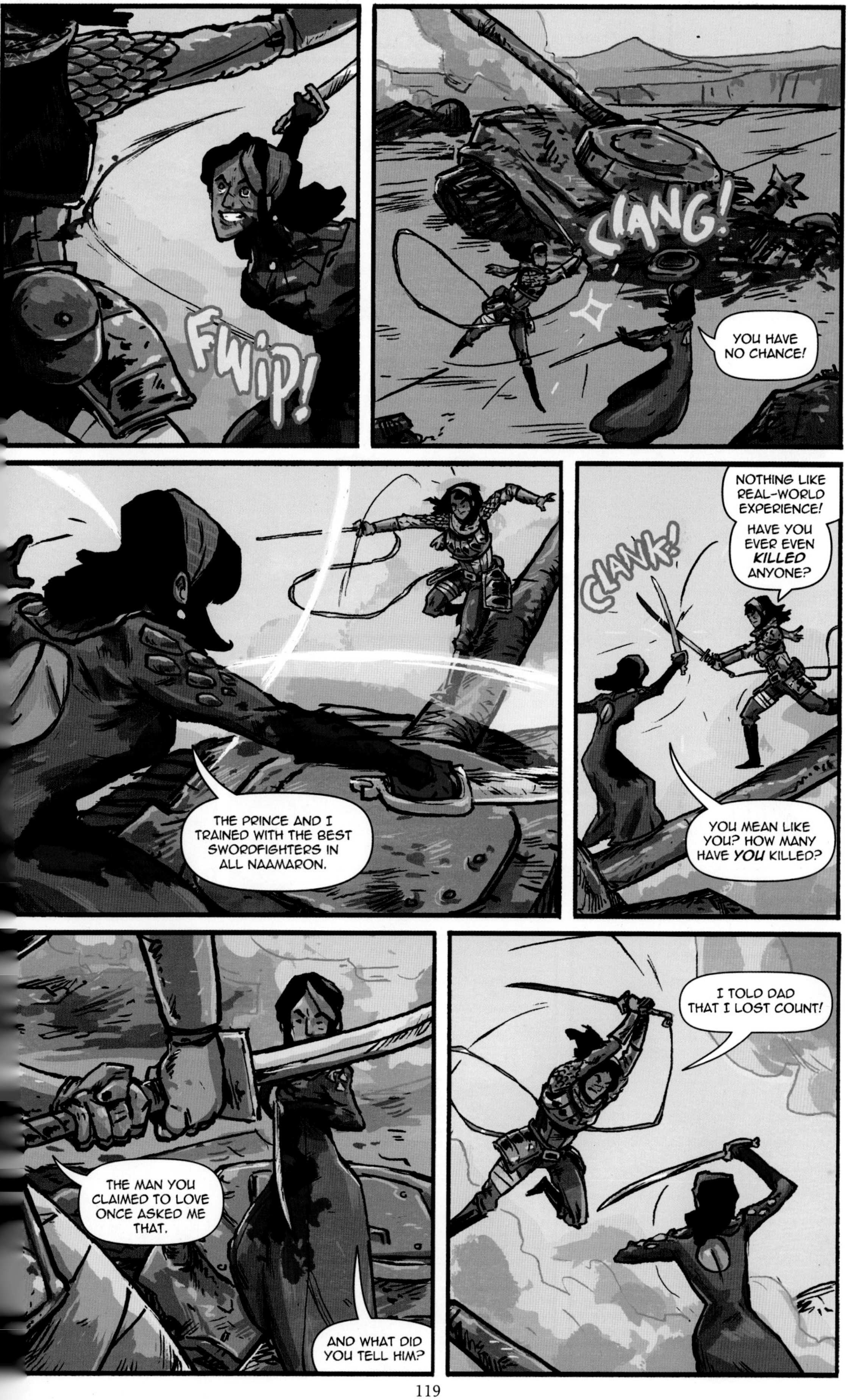
FWIP!
CLANG!
YOU HAVE NO CHANCE!
THE PRINCE AND I TRAINED WITH THE BEST SWORDFIGHTERS IN ALL NAAMARON.
CLANK!
NOTHING LIKE REAL-WORLD EXPERIENCE!
HAVE YOU EVER EVEN KILLED ANYONE?
YOU MEAN LIKE YOU? HOW MANY HAVE YOU KILLED?
THE MAN YOU CLAIMED TO LOVE ONCE ASKED ME THAT.
AND WHAT DID YOU TELL HIM?
I TOLD DAD THAT I LOST COUNT!

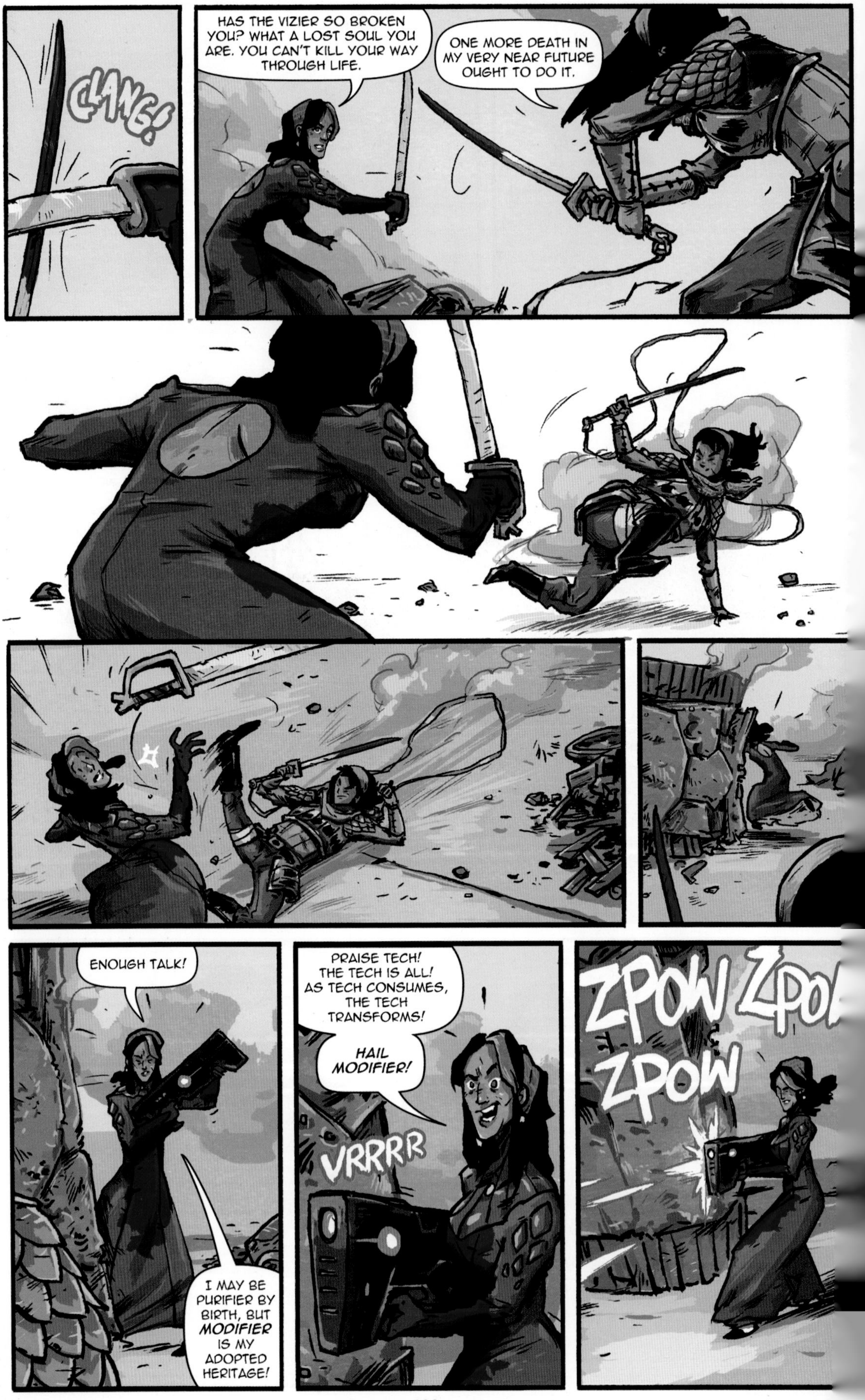
CLANG!
HAS THE VIZIER SO BROKEN YOU? WHAT A LOST SOUL YOU ARE. YOU CAN'T KILL YOUR WAY THROUGH LIFE.
ONE MORE DEATH IN MY VERY NEAR FUTURE OUGHT TO DO IT.
ENOUGH TALK!
I MAY BE PURIFIER BY BIRTH, BUT *MODIFIER* IS MY ADOPTED HERITAGE!
PRAISE TECH! THE TECH IS ALL! AS TECH CONSUMES, THE TECH TRANSFORMS!
HAIL MODIFIER!
VRRRR
ZPOW ZPOW
ZPOW

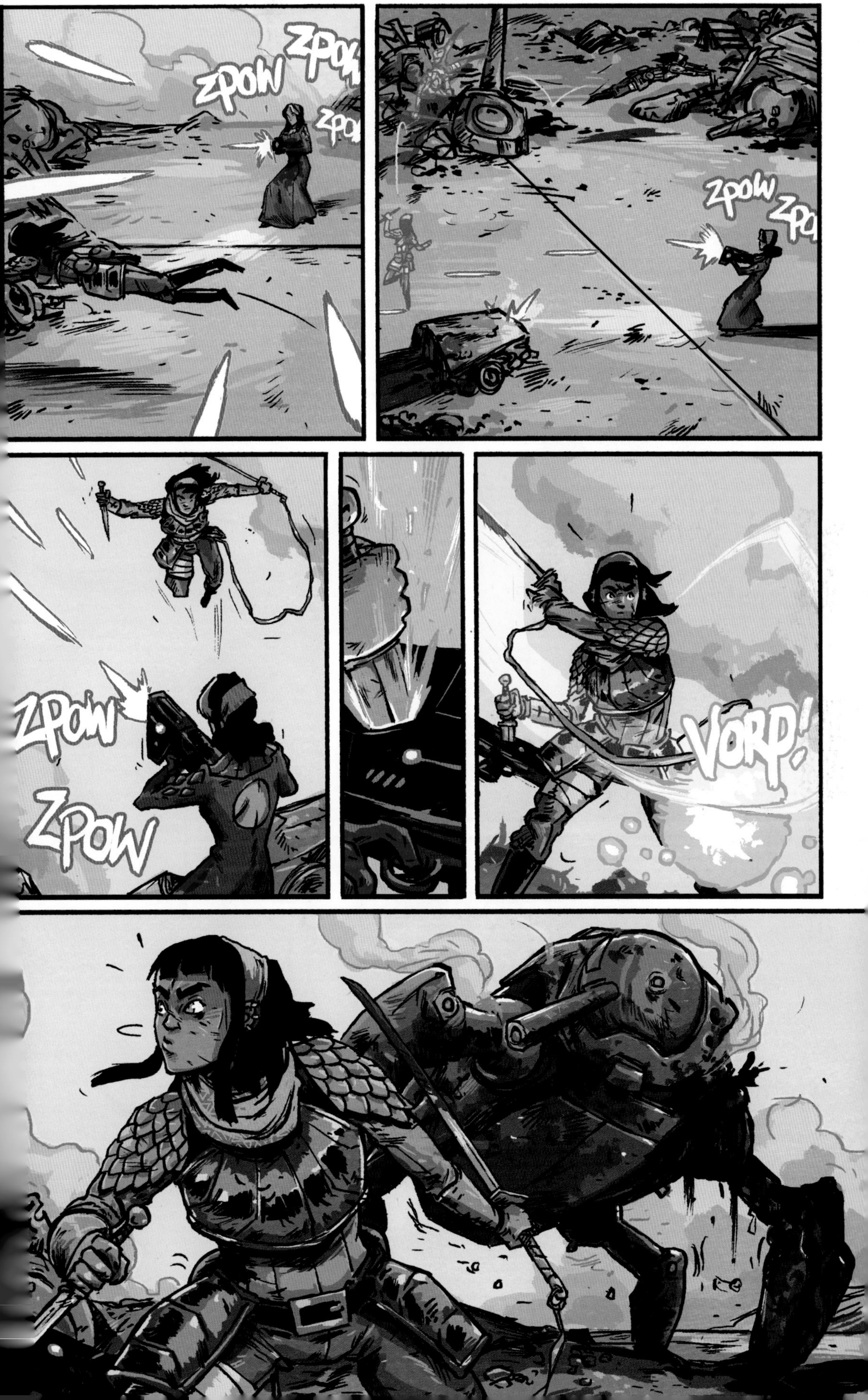
ZPOW
ZPOW
ZPOW
ZPOW
ZPOW
ZPOW
ZPOW
VORP!

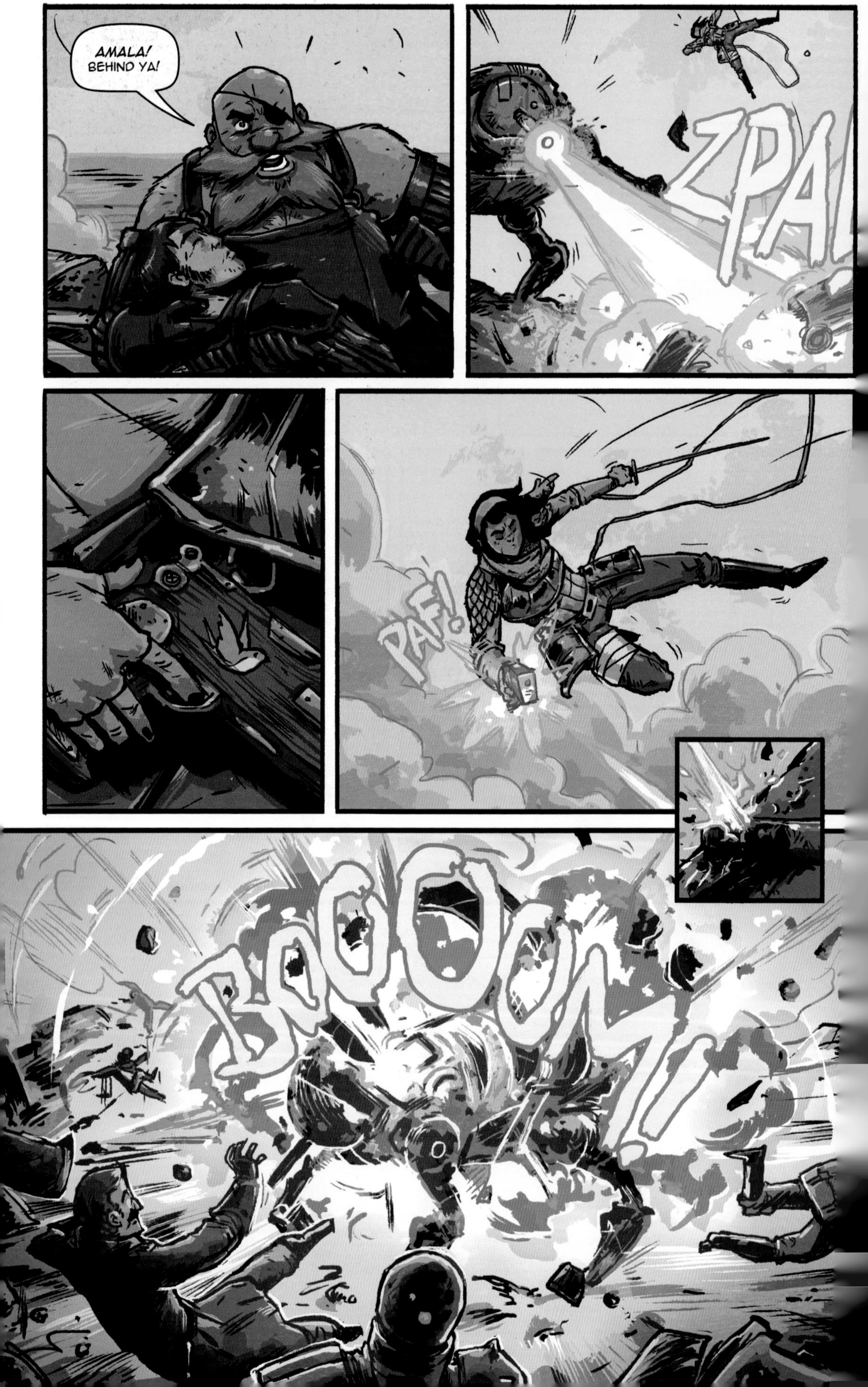
AMALA! BEHIND YA!
ZPA
PAF!
BOOOOM!!

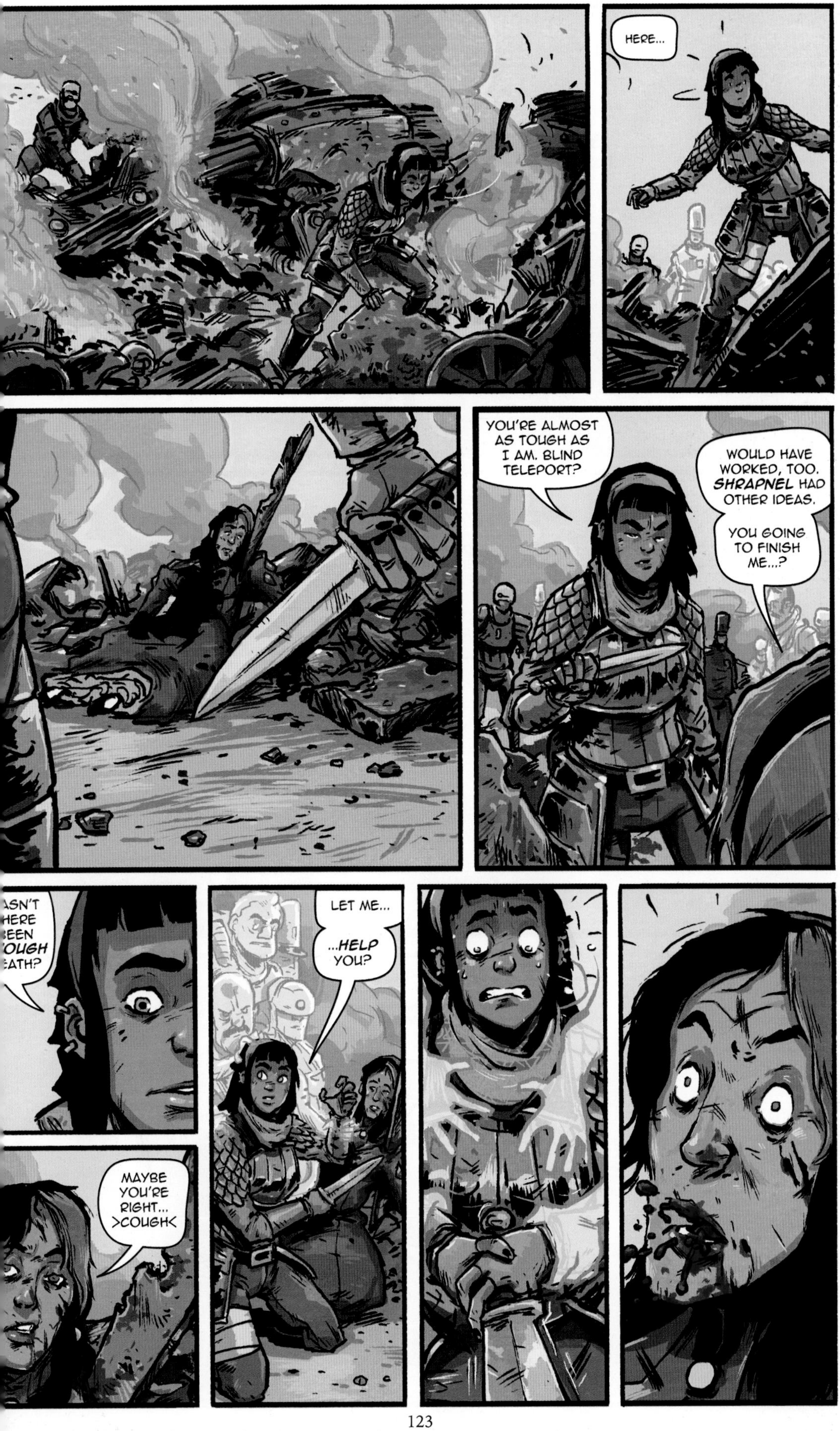
HERE...
YOU'RE ALMOST AS TOUGH AS I AM. BLIND TELEPORT?
WOULD HAVE WORKED, TOO. **SHRAPNEL** HAD OTHER IDEAS.
YOU GOING TO FINISH ME...?
ASN'T HERE EEN OUGH EATH?
MAYBE YOU'RE RIGHT... >COUGH<
LET ME...
...**HELP** YOU?

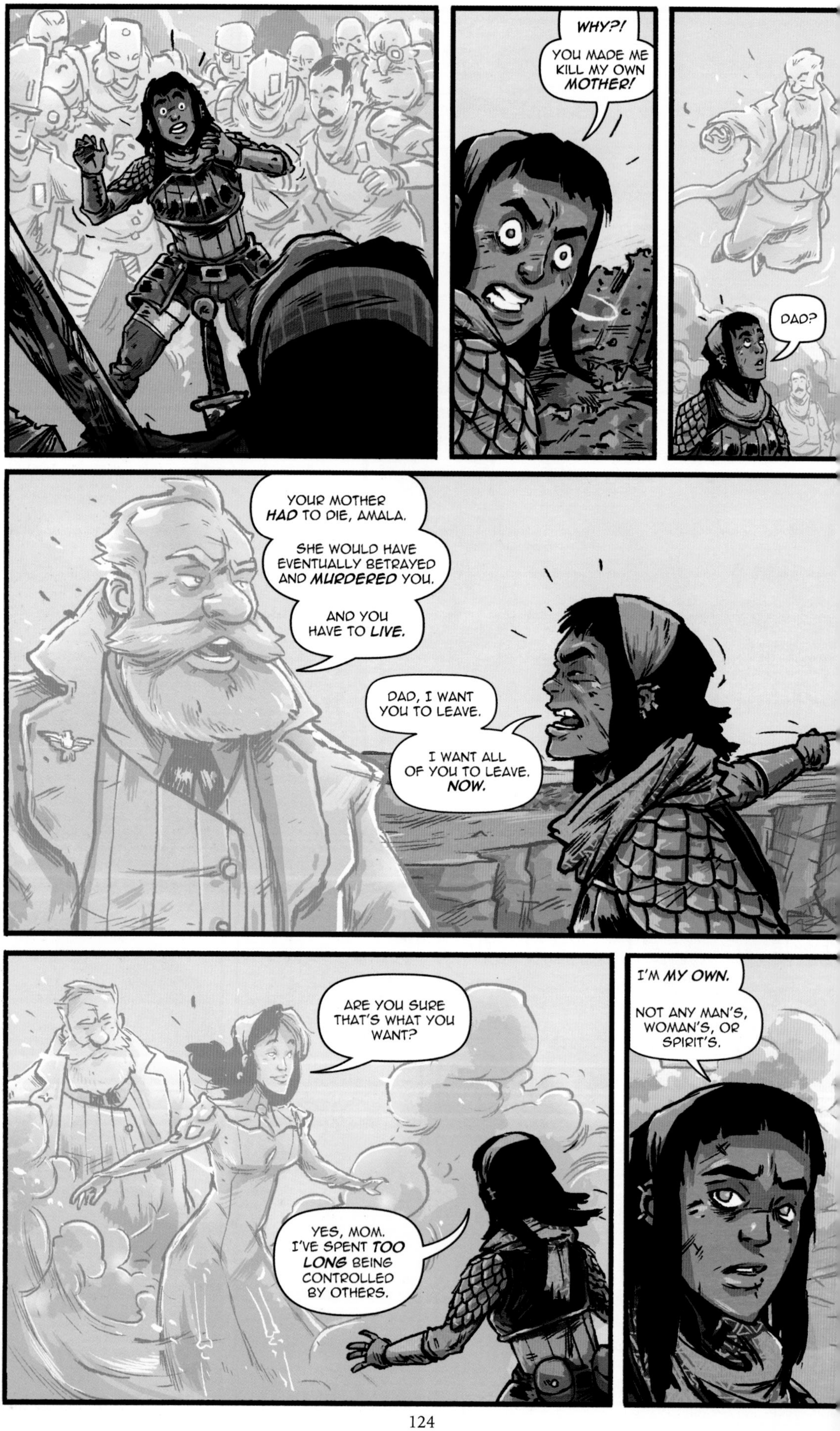
WHY?!
YOU MADE ME KILL MY OWN MOTHER!
DAD?
YOUR MOTHER HAD TO DIE, AMALA.
SHE WOULD HAVE EVENTUALLY BETRAYED AND MURDERED YOU.
AND YOU HAVE TO LIVE.
DAD, I WANT YOU TO LEAVE.
I WANT ALL OF YOU TO LEAVE. NOW.
ARE YOU SURE THAT'S WHAT YOU WANT?
YES, MOM. I'VE SPENT TOO LONG BEING CONTROLLED BY OTHERS.
I'M MY OWN.
NOT ANY MAN'S, WOMAN'S, OR SPIRIT'S.

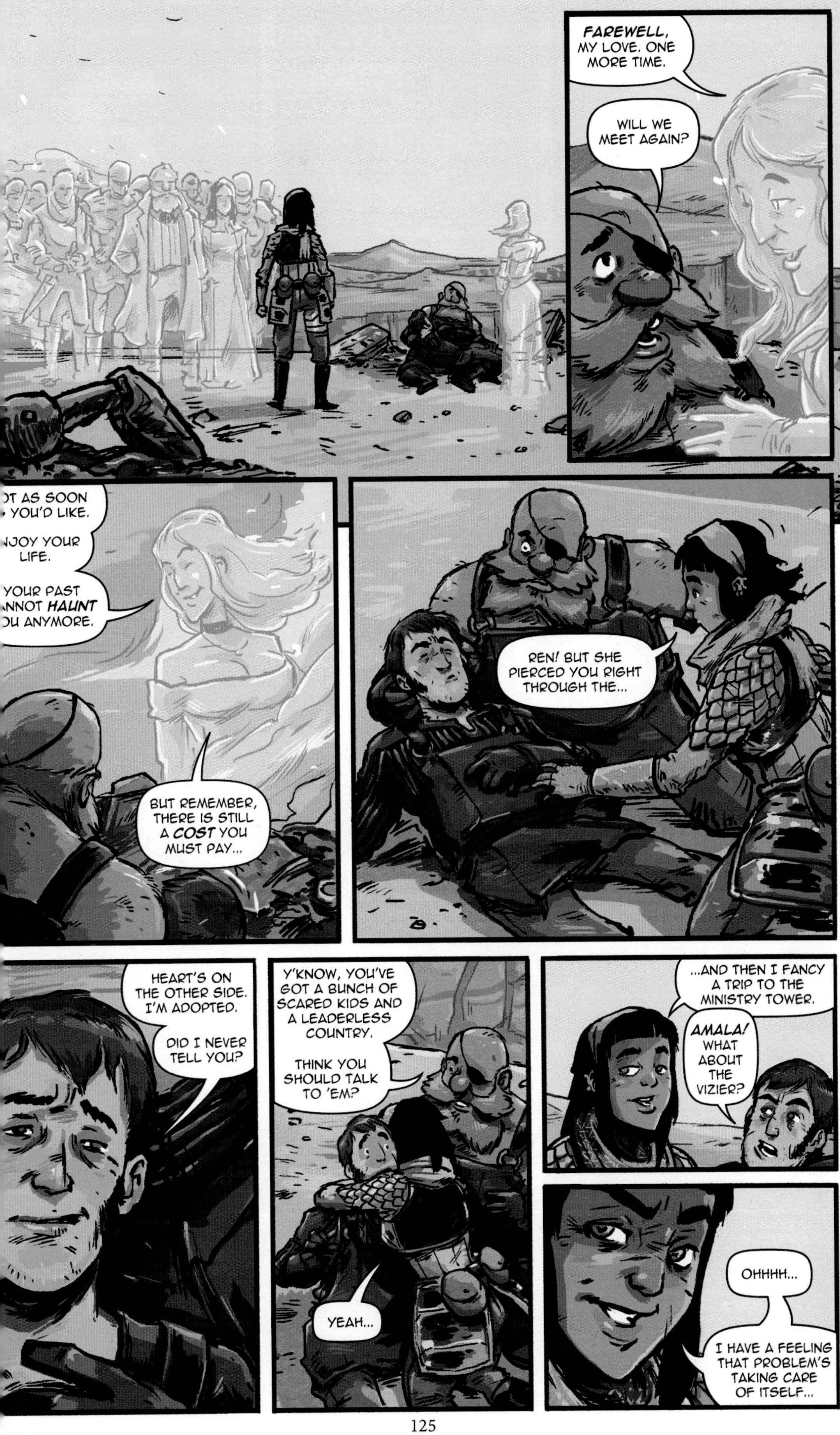

FAREWELL, MY LOVE. ONE MORE TIME.
WILL WE MEET AGAIN?
OT AS SOON YOU'D LIKE.
NJOY YOUR LIFE.
YOUR PAST ANNOT HAUNT OU ANYMORE.
BUT REMEMBER, THERE IS STILL A COST YOU MUST PAY...
REN! BUT SHE PIERCED YOU RIGHT THROUGH THE...
HEART'S ON THE OTHER SIDE. I'M ADOPTED.
DID I NEVER TELL YOU?
Y'KNOW, YOU'VE GOT A BUNCH OF SCARED KIDS AND A LEADERLESS COUNTRY.
THINK YOU SHOULD TALK TO 'EM?
YEAH...
...AND THEN I FANCY A TRIP TO THE MINISTRY TOWER.
AMALA! WHAT ABOUT THE VIZIER?
OHHHH...
I HAVE A FEELING THAT PROBLEM'S TAKING CARE OF ITSELF...

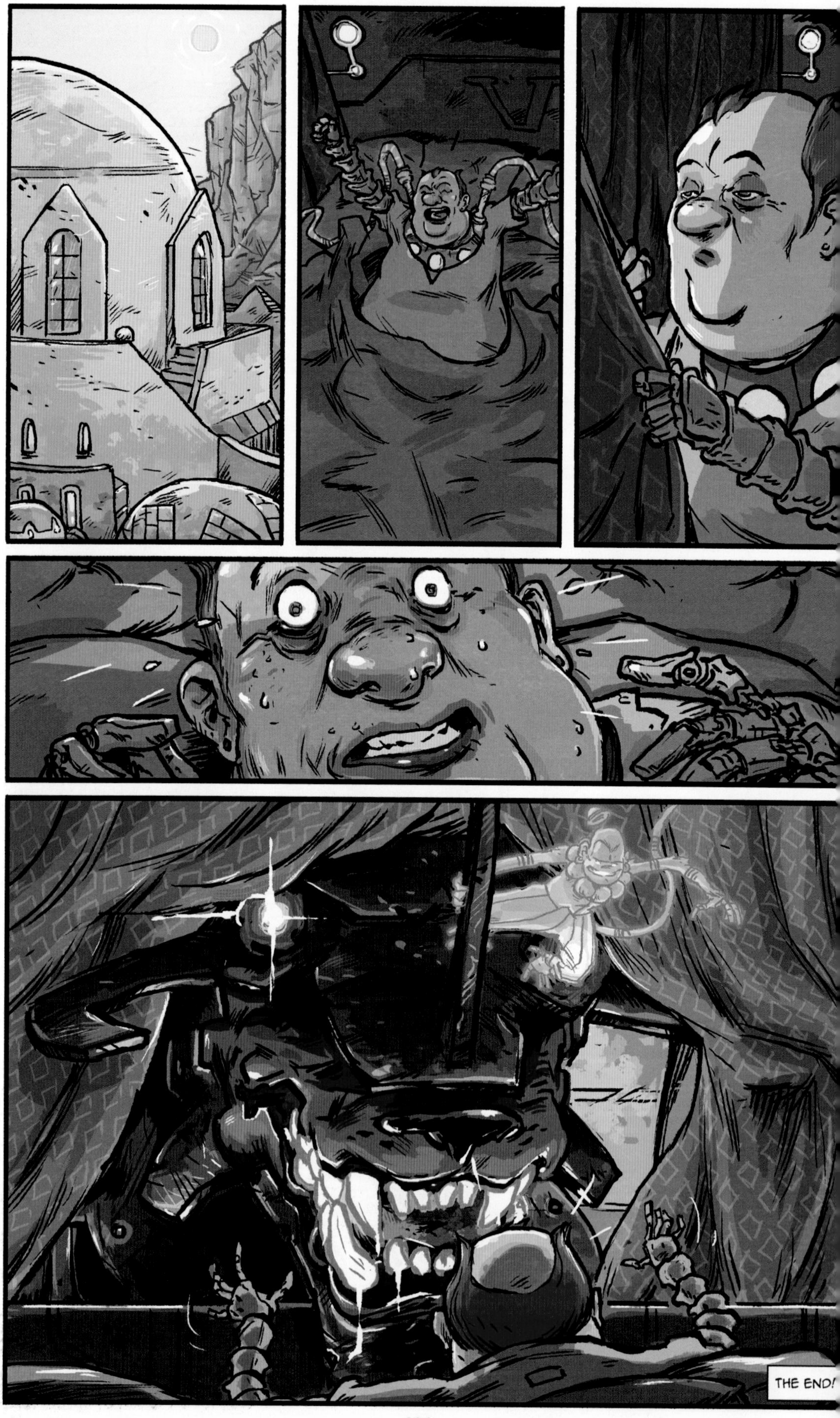
THE END!

AMALA'S EXTRAS
WITH CREATORS' NOTES

DEVELOPMENT

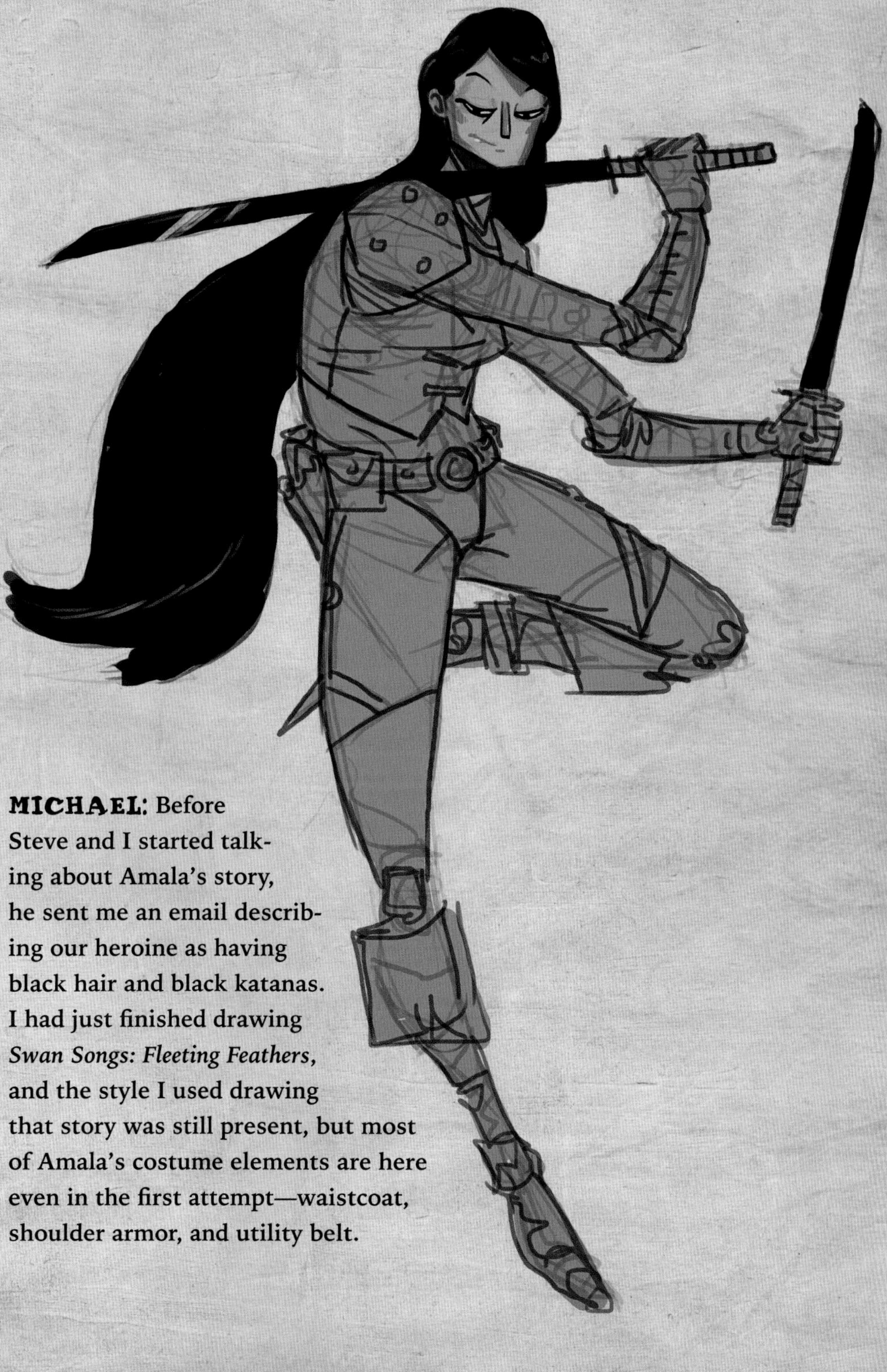

MICHAEL: Before Steve and I started talking about Amala's story, he sent me an email describing our heroine as having black hair and black katanas. I had just finished drawing *Swan Songs: Fleeting Feathers*, and the style I used drawing that story was still present, but most of Amala's costume elements are here even in the first attempt—waistcoat, shoulder armor, and utility belt.

CONCEPT ART

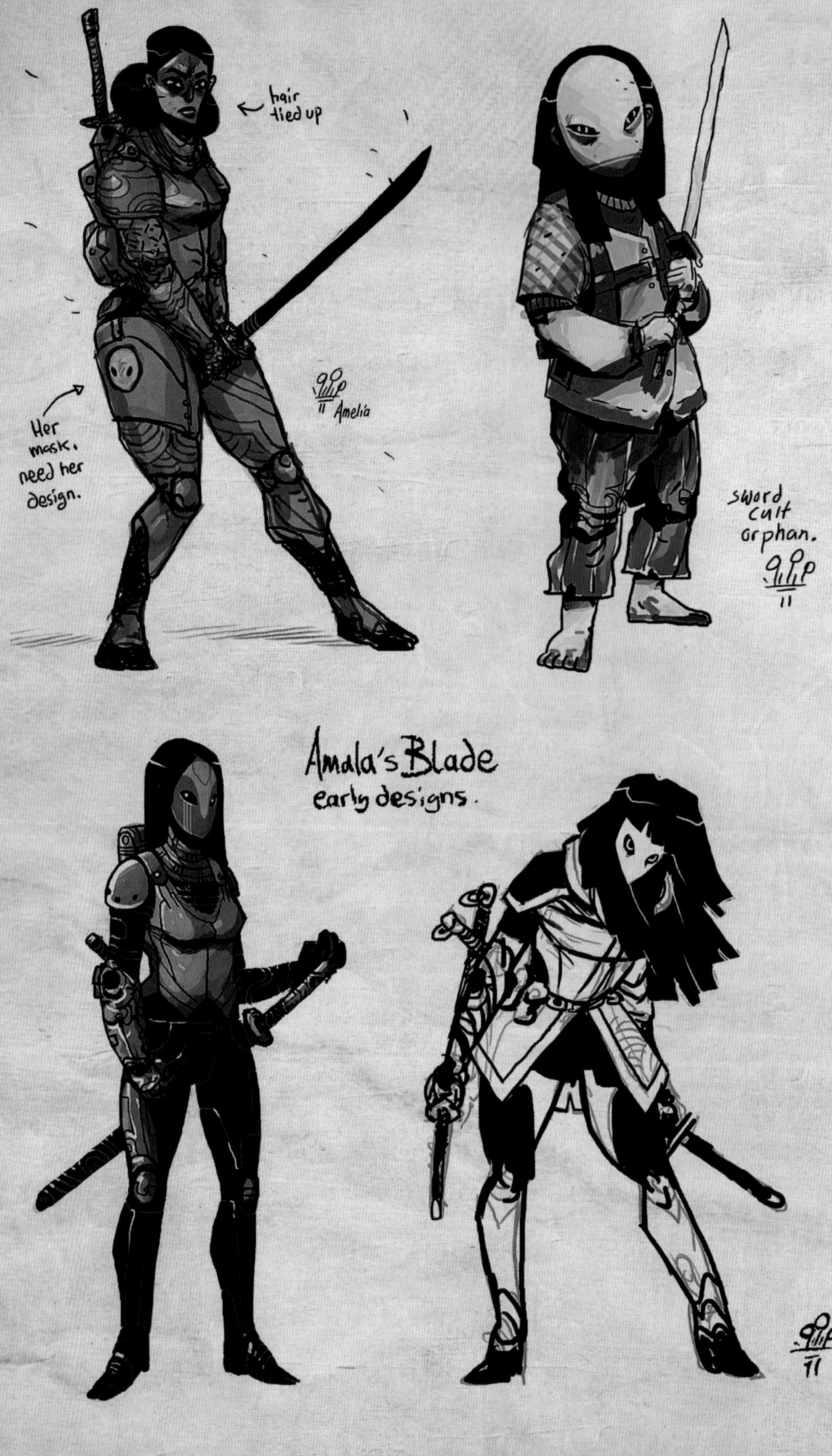
hair tied up
Her mask, need her design.
Amelia
sword cult orphan.
Amala's Blade
early designs.

Assassin
Amala

THE
DANCE
OF
DEATH

the messengers

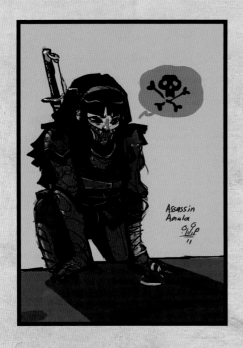

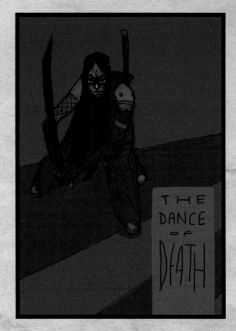

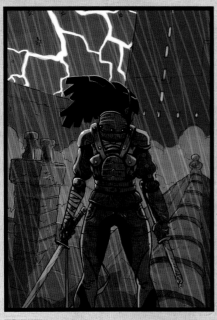

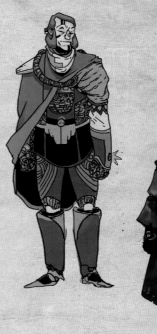

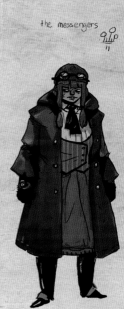

MICHAEL: After playing around with various designs, we started to head in the right direction, and as you can see here, I had thought of the possibility of Amala having some "Modifications" of her own before we went to a "Purer" version.

STEVE: Maybe Amala gets modified in a later story? Possibilities!

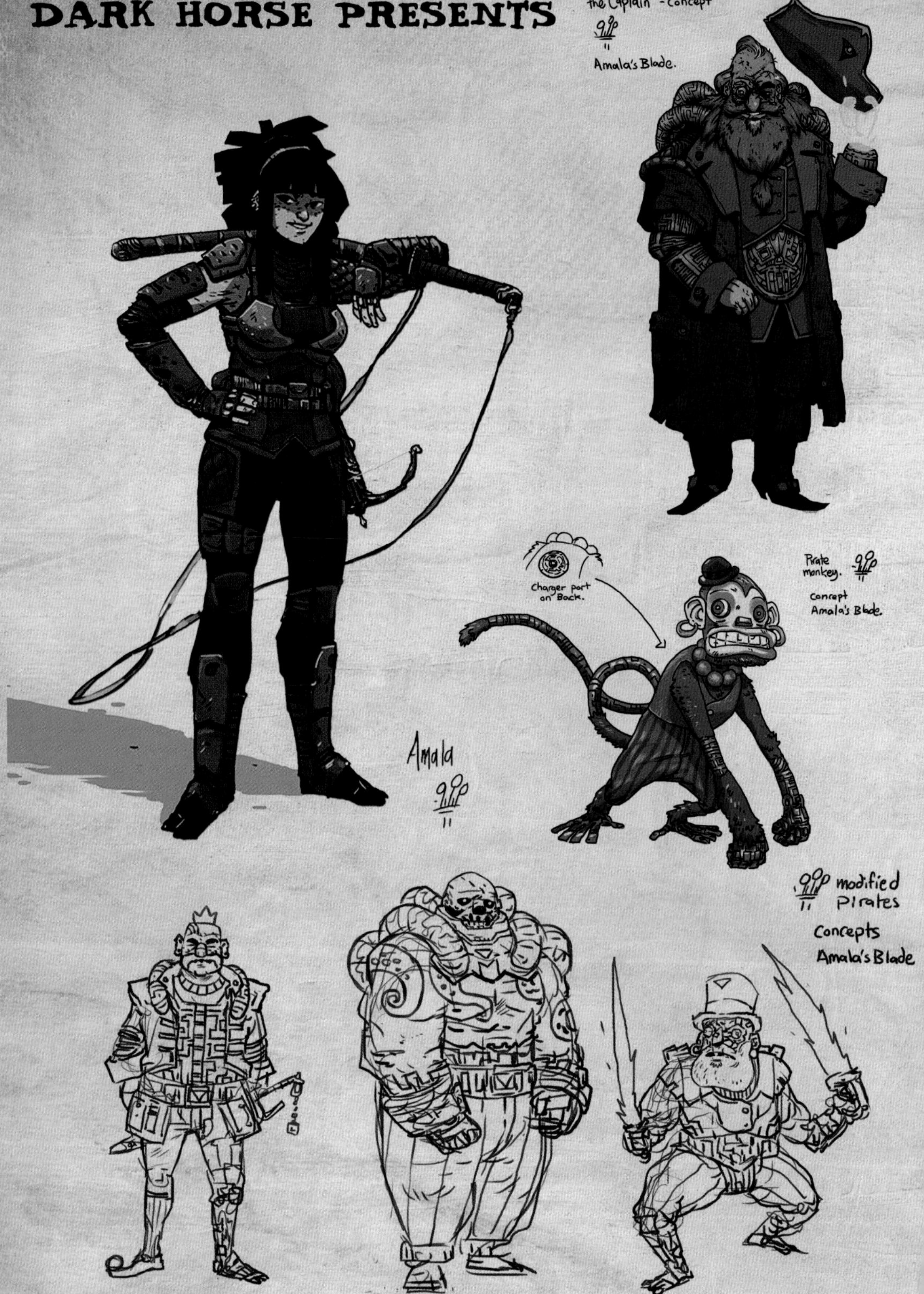
the Captain - concept
Amala's Blade.
Charger port on Back.
Pirate monkey.
concept
Amala's Blade.
Amala
modified Pirates
Concepts
Amala's Blade

MICHAEL: I think it's pretty obvious, looking at these designs again, that the pirate scum here are a reference to *Zero Wing*, heh, heh. Steve, we should do more pirate stories!

STEVE: All your pirates are belong to us.

MINISERIES

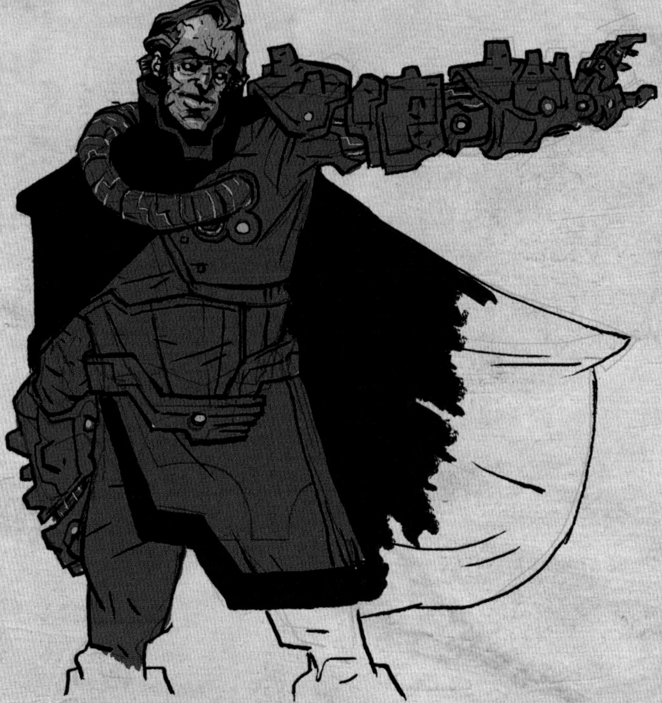

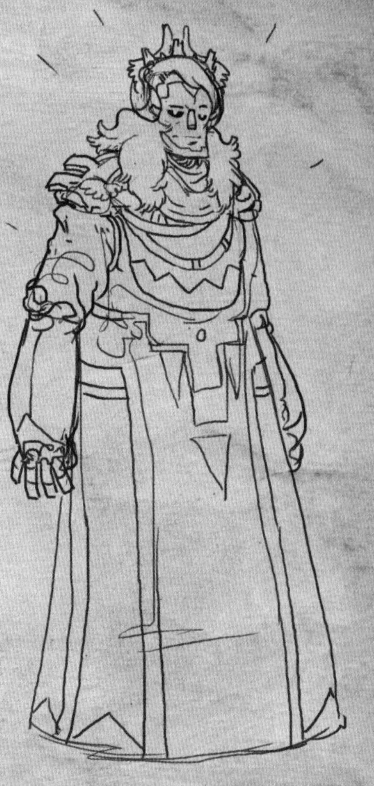

MICHAEL: This, like Amala's first sketch, was drawn before we had nailed down what the prince was, and I was just playing around with what the Modifiers would look like. I imagined this version of him would glow!

MICHAEL: After the dust had settled from Amala's debut in *DHP*, I decided to find a slightly grittier look for the miniseries. This sketch was where I found all the elements I wanted to keep and gave her a different look from her pirate adventure—a more day-to-day, battle-ready outfit.

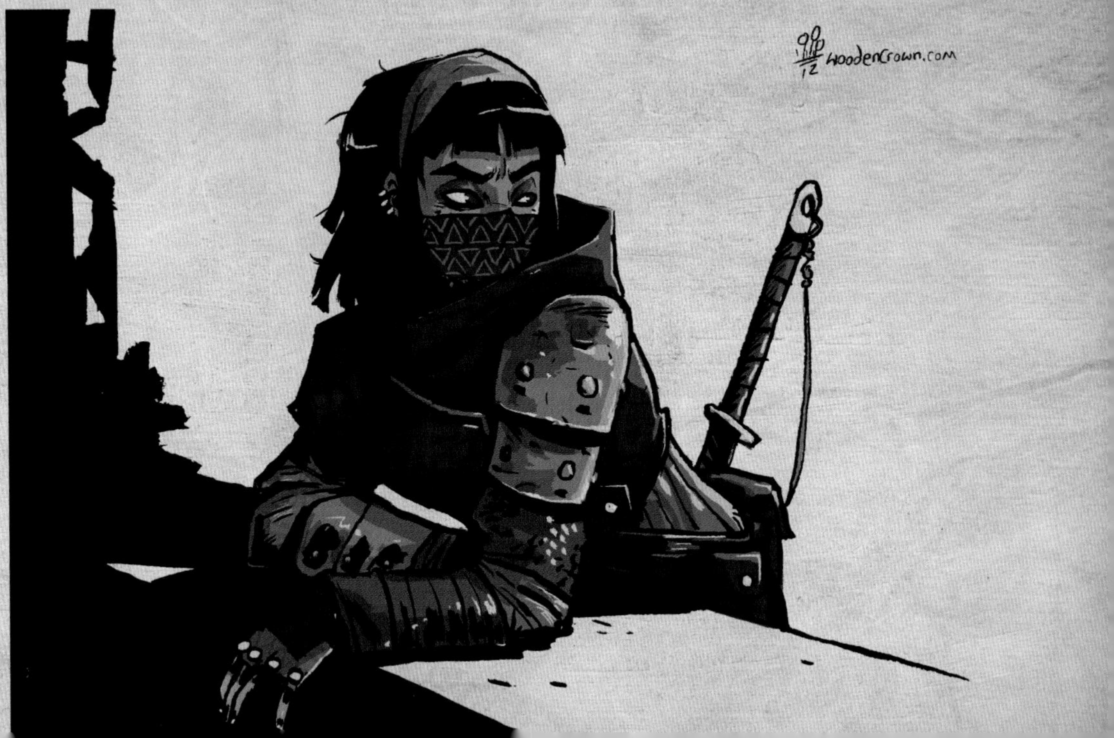
WoodenCrown.com

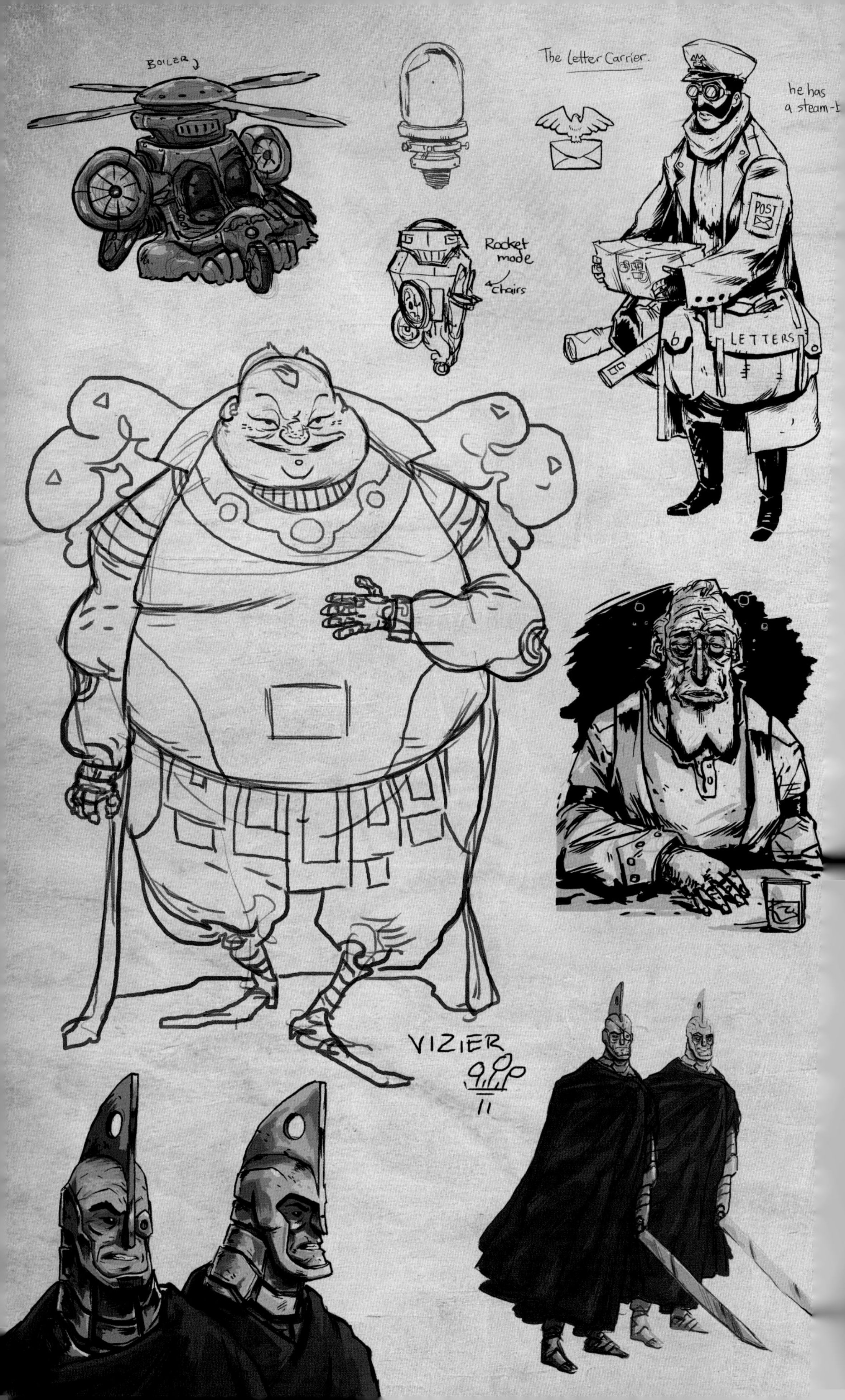

BOILER
The Letter Carrier.
he has
a steam-t
Rocket
mode
chairs
POST
LETTERS
VIZIER

FIGHT THE EVILS OF MODIFICATION!
We are purifiers! We will overcome!

KNOW YOUR ENEMY!

THEIR HEARTS ARE ON THE OTHER SIDE!

If the war resumes tomorrow...!

MICHAEL: We really wanted to put references to the land's history in the background of the story. These posters are a great example of that. I think I was designing these for a few days to have them ready for the tavern scene, and when the time came to draw layouts, I noticed that we didn't really have much space for them! But that's the fun part about sketchbooks—I knew they would have a home here.

STEVE: We took inspiration from a Russian anti-Nazi propaganda poster for this series of posters that appear in the background of the bar in issue #1. I liked Michael's design for the wurm creature so much that I immediately wrote the wurm —now called Stormscale, the Skolynx— into the story of issues #3 and #4.

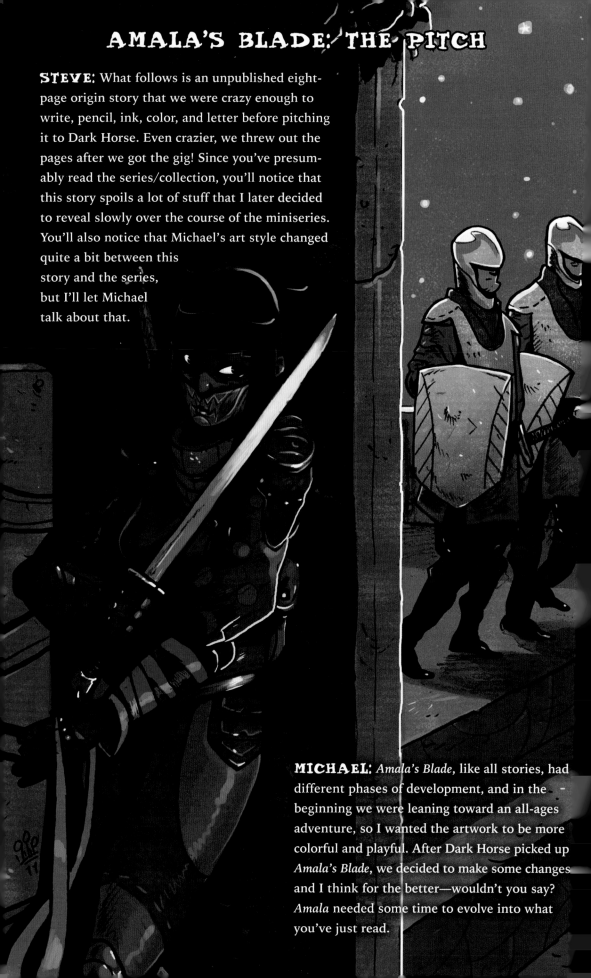

AMALA'S BLADE: THE PITCH

STEVE: What follows is an unpublished eight-page origin story that we were crazy enough to write, pencil, ink, color, and letter before pitching it to Dark Horse. Even crazier, we threw out the pages after we got the gig! Since you've presumably read the series/collection, you'll notice that this story spoils a lot of stuff that I later decided to reveal slowly over the course of the miniseries. You'll also notice that Michael's art style changed quite a bit between this story and the series, but I'll let Michael talk about that.

MICHAEL: *Amala's Blade*, like all stories, had different phases of development, and in the beginning we were leaning toward an all-ages adventure, so I wanted the artwork to be more colorful and playful. After Dark Horse picked up *Amala's Blade*, we decided to make some changes and I think for the better—wouldn't you say? *Amala* needed some time to evolve into what you've just read.

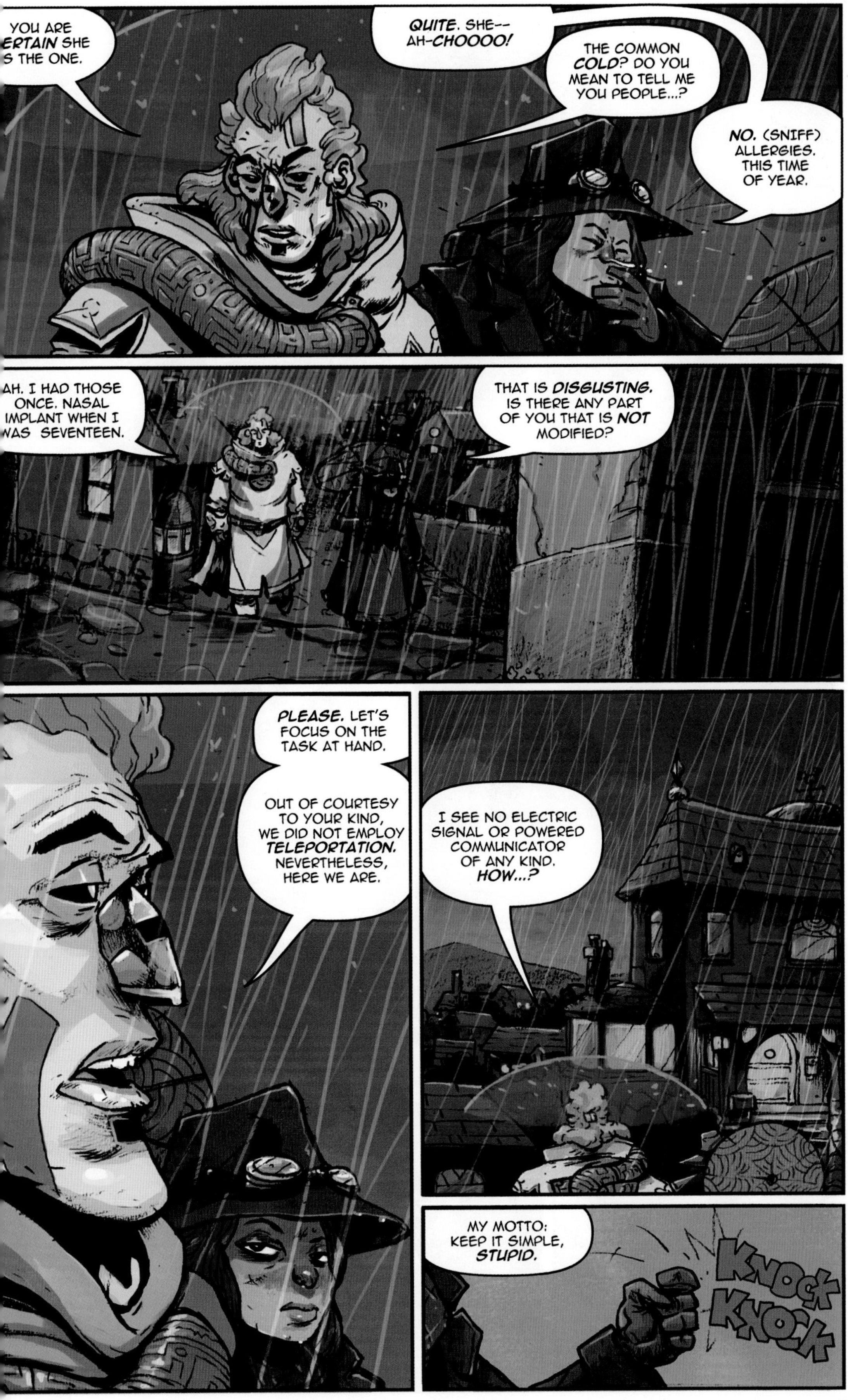
YOU ARE ERTAIN SHE S THE ONE.
QUITE. SHE-- AH-CHOOOO!
THE COMMON COLD? DO YOU MEAN TO TELL ME YOU PEOPLE...?
NO. (SNIFF) ALLERGIES. THIS TIME OF YEAR.
AH. I HAD THOSE ONCE. NASAL IMPLANT WHEN I WAS SEVENTEEN.
THAT IS DISGUSTING. IS THERE ANY PART OF YOU THAT IS NOT MODIFIED?
PLEASE. LET'S FOCUS ON THE TASK AT HAND.
OUT OF COURTESY TO YOUR KIND, WE DID NOT EMPLOY TELEPORTATION. NEVERTHELESS, HERE WE ARE.
I SEE NO ELECTRIC SIGNAL OR POWERED COMMUNICATOR OF ANY KIND. HOW...?
MY MOTTO: KEEP IT SIMPLE, STUPID.
KNOCK KNOCK

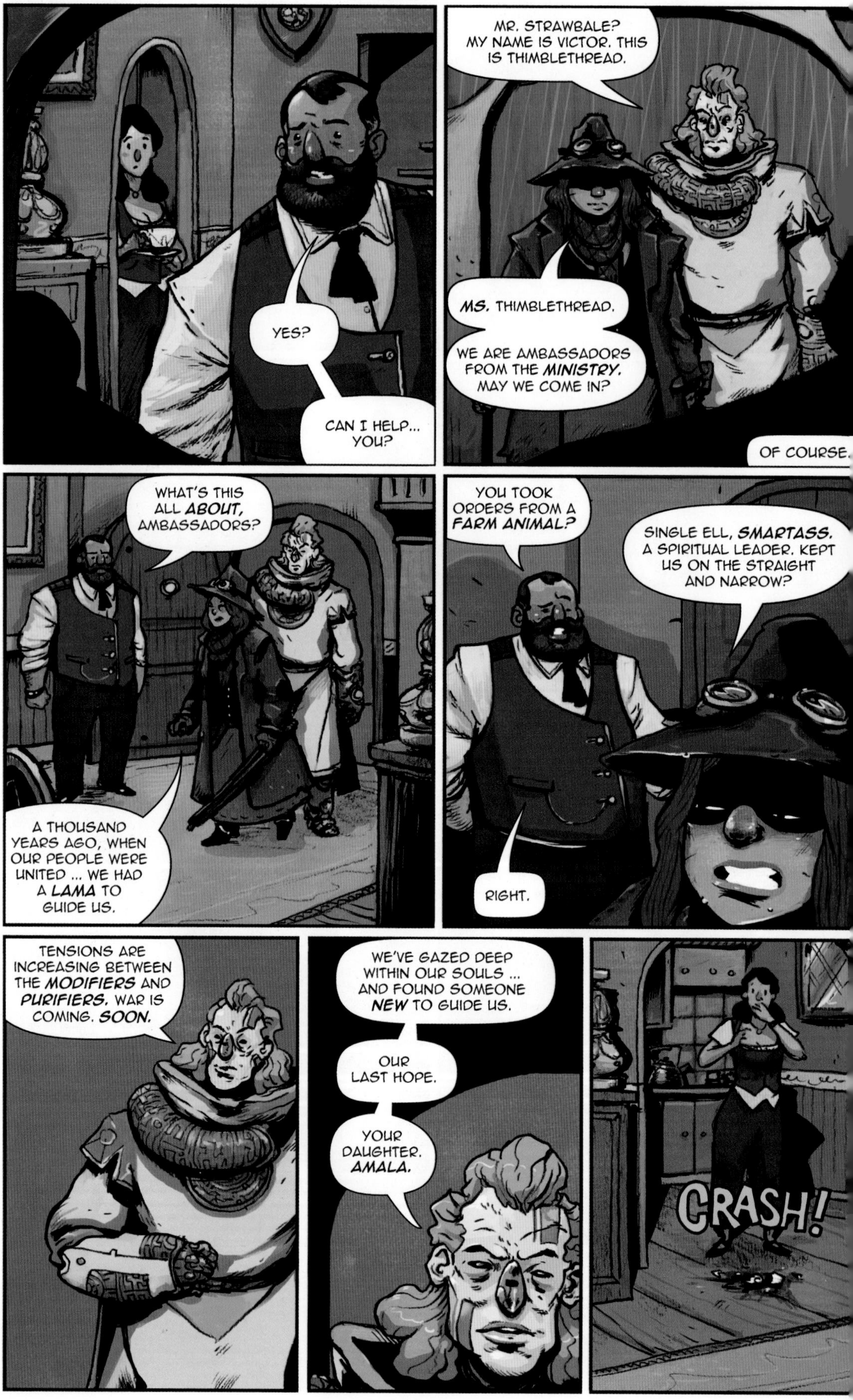
YES?
CAN I HELP... YOU?
MR. STRAWBALE? MY NAME IS VICTOR. THIS IS THIMBLETHREAD.
MS. THIMBLETHREAD.
WE ARE AMBASSADORS FROM THE MINISTRY. MAY WE COME IN?
OF COURSE.
WHAT'S THIS ALL ABOUT, AMBASSADORS?
A THOUSAND YEARS AGO, WHEN OUR PEOPLE WERE UNITED ... WE HAD A LAMA TO GUIDE US.
YOU TOOK ORDERS FROM A FARM ANIMAL?
SINGLE ELL, SMARTASS. A SPIRITUAL LEADER. KEPT US ON THE STRAIGHT AND NARROW?
RIGHT.
TENSIONS ARE INCREASING BETWEEN THE MODIFIERS AND PURIFIERS. WAR IS COMING. SOON.
WE'VE GAZED DEEP WITHIN OUR SOULS ... AND FOUND SOMEONE NEW TO GUIDE US.
OUR LAST HOPE.
YOUR DAUGHTER. AMALA.
CRASH!

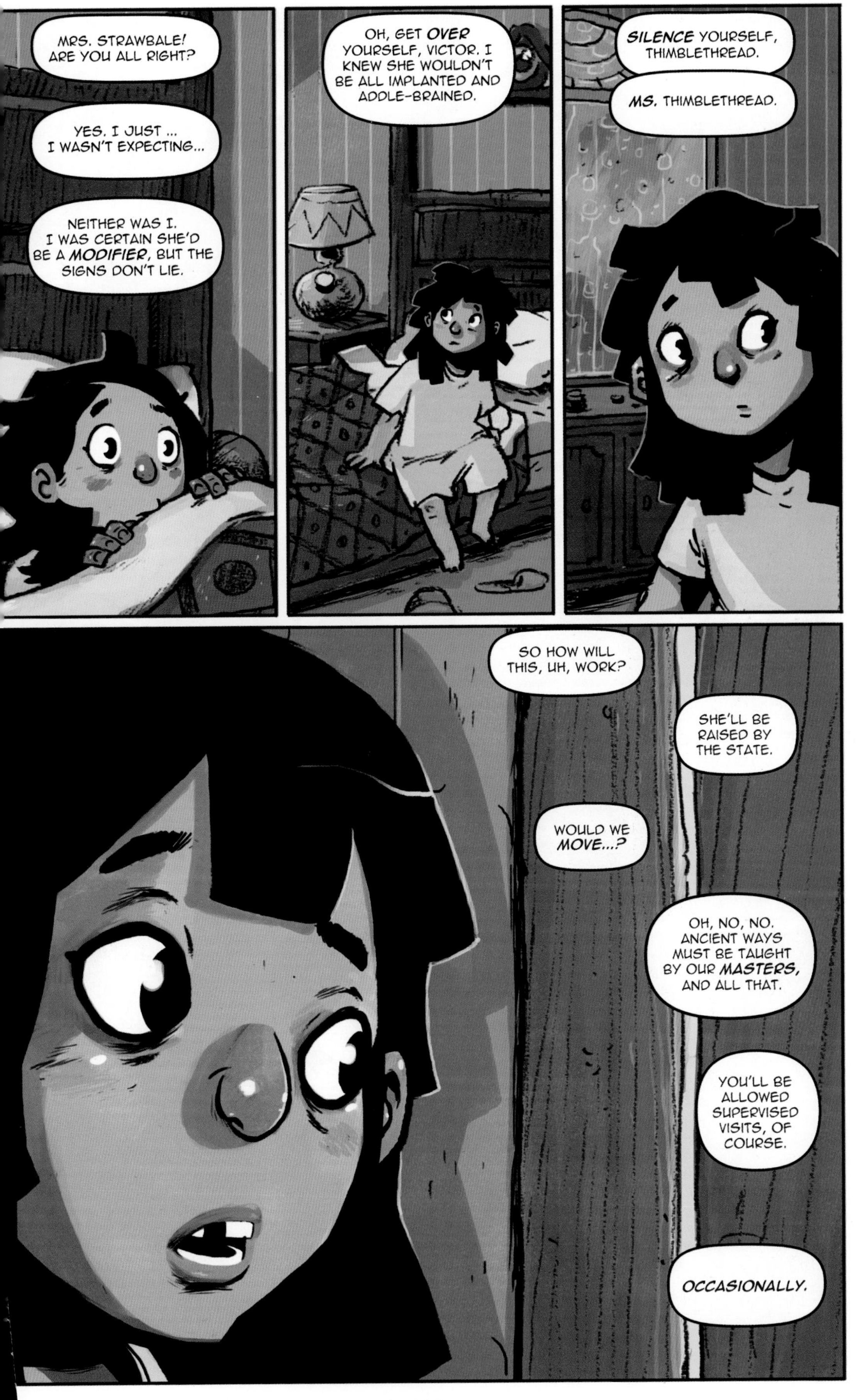
MRS. STRAWBALE! ARE YOU ALL RIGHT?
YES. I JUST ... I WASN'T EXPECTING...
NEITHER WAS I. I WAS CERTAIN SHE'D BE A *MODIFIER*, BUT THE SIGNS DON'T LIE.
OH, GET *OVER* YOURSELF, VICTOR. I KNEW SHE WOULDN'T BE ALL IMPLANTED AND ADDLE-BRAINED.
SILENCE YOURSELF, THIMBLETHREAD.
MS. THIMBLETHREAD.
SO HOW WILL THIS, UH, WORK?
SHE'LL BE RAISED BY THE STATE.
WOULD WE *MOVE...?*
OH, NO, NO. ANCIENT WAYS MUST BE TAUGHT BY OUR *MASTERS,* AND ALL THAT.
YOU'LL BE ALLOWED SUPERVISED VISITS, OF COURSE.
OCCASIONALLY.

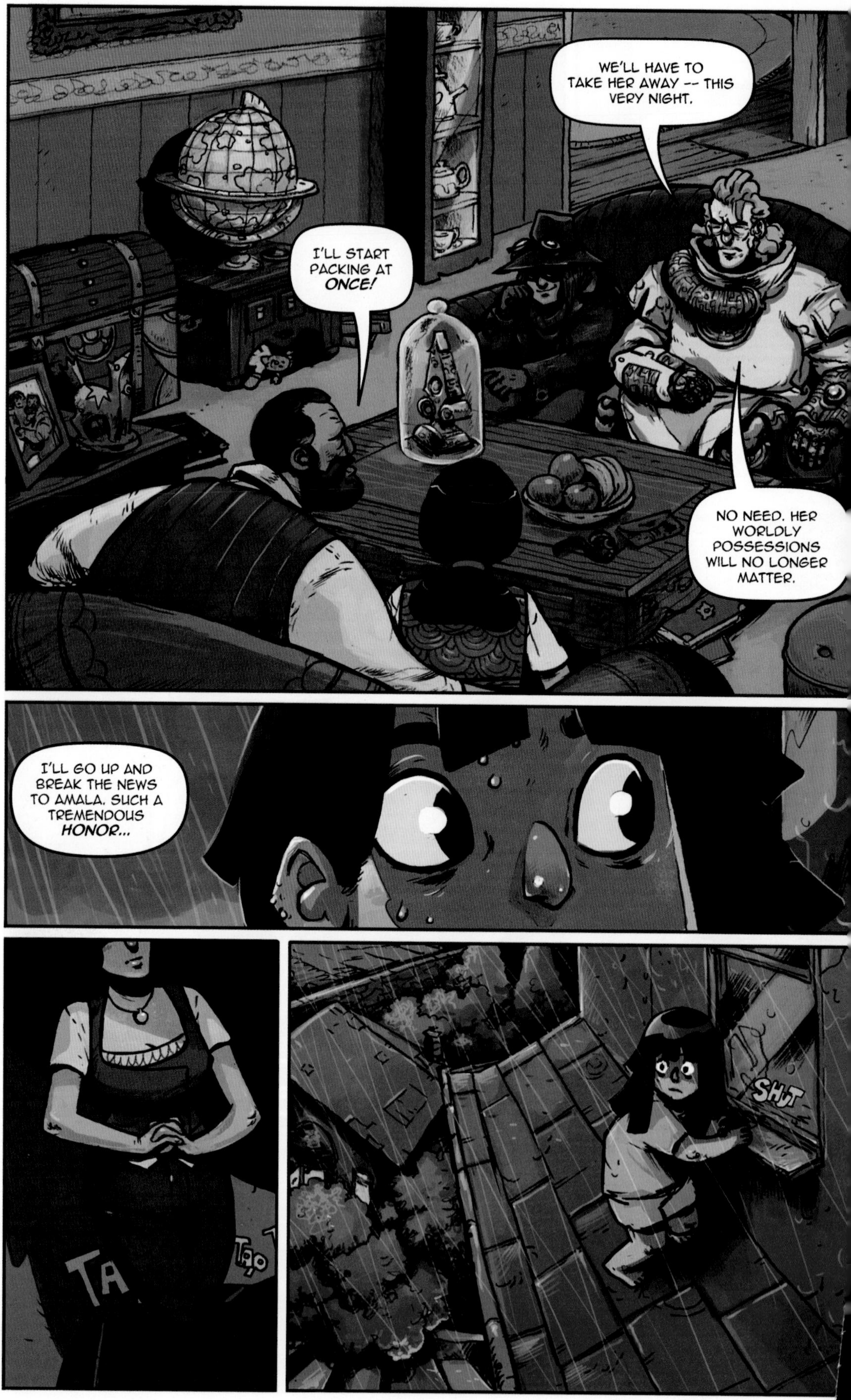
WE'LL HAVE TO TAKE HER AWAY -- THIS VERY NIGHT.
I'LL START PACKING AT *ONCE!*
NO NEED. HER WORLDLY POSSESSIONS WILL NO LONGER MATTER.
I'LL GO UP AND BREAK THE NEWS TO AMALA. SUCH A TREMENDOUS *HONOR...*
TA
SHUT

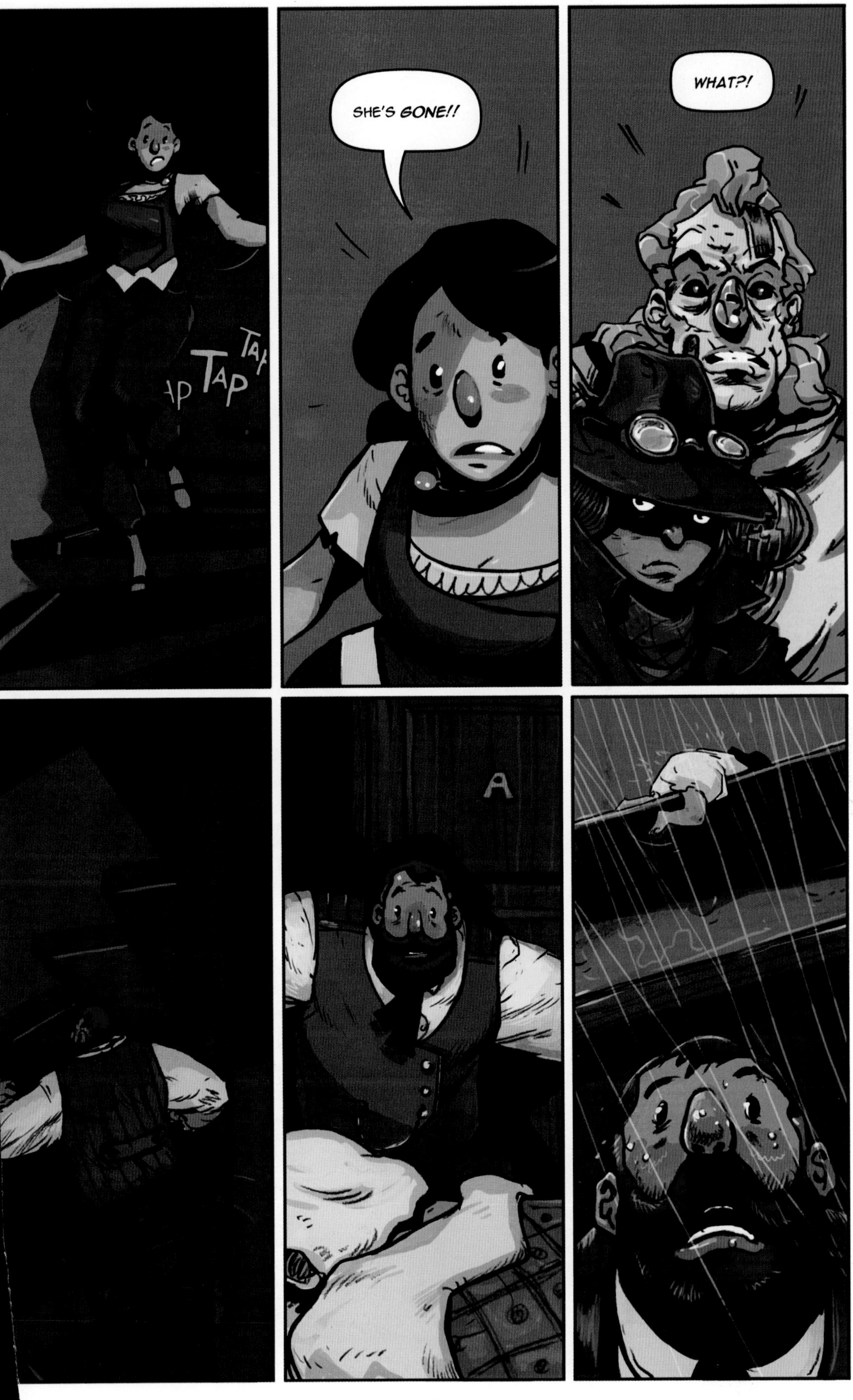

TAP TAP TAP
SHE'S GONE!!
WHAT?!

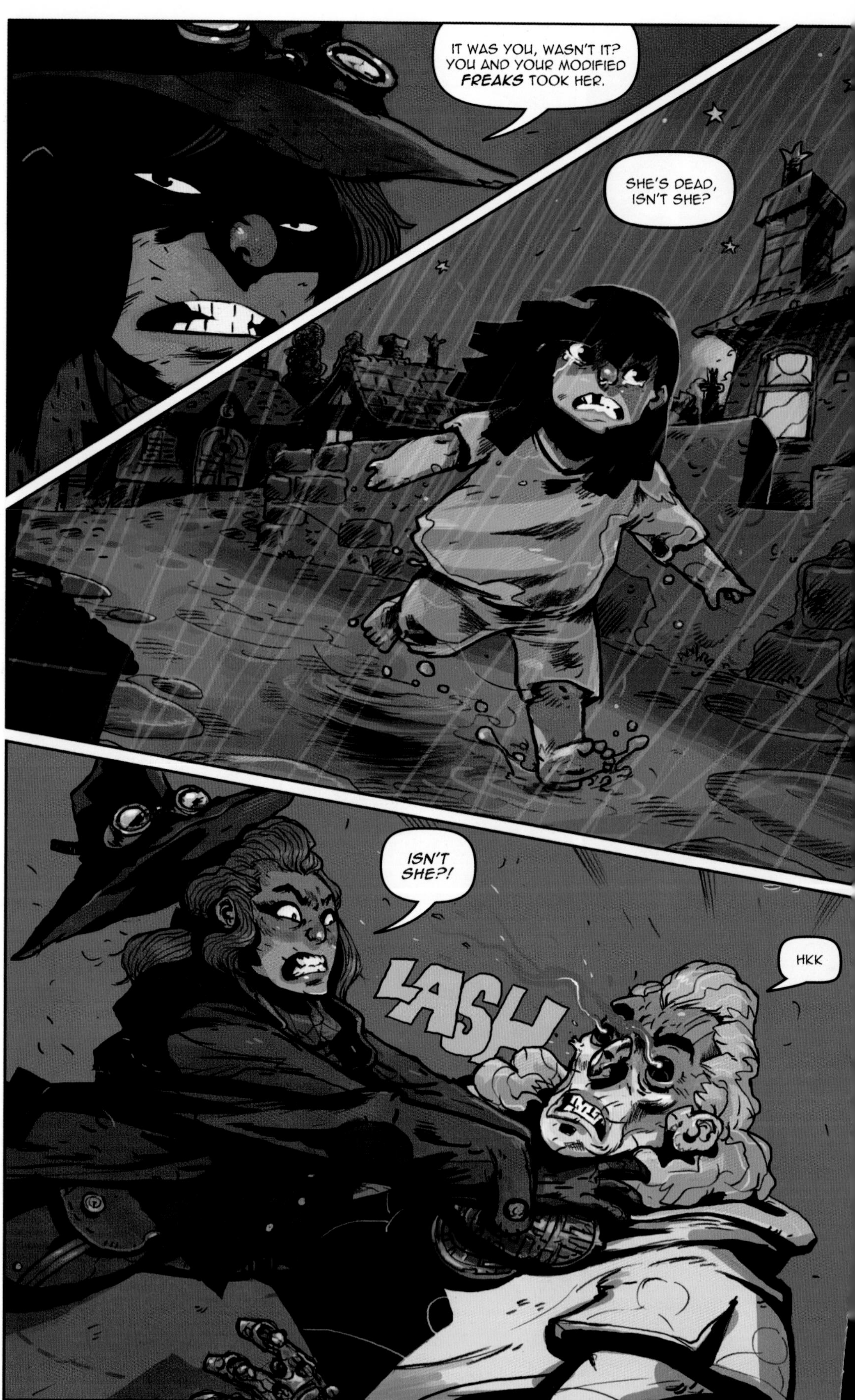
IT WAS YOU, WASN'T IT? YOU AND YOUR MODIFIED FREAKS TOOK HER.
SHE'S DEAD, ISN'T SHE?
ISN'T SHE?!
LASH
HKK

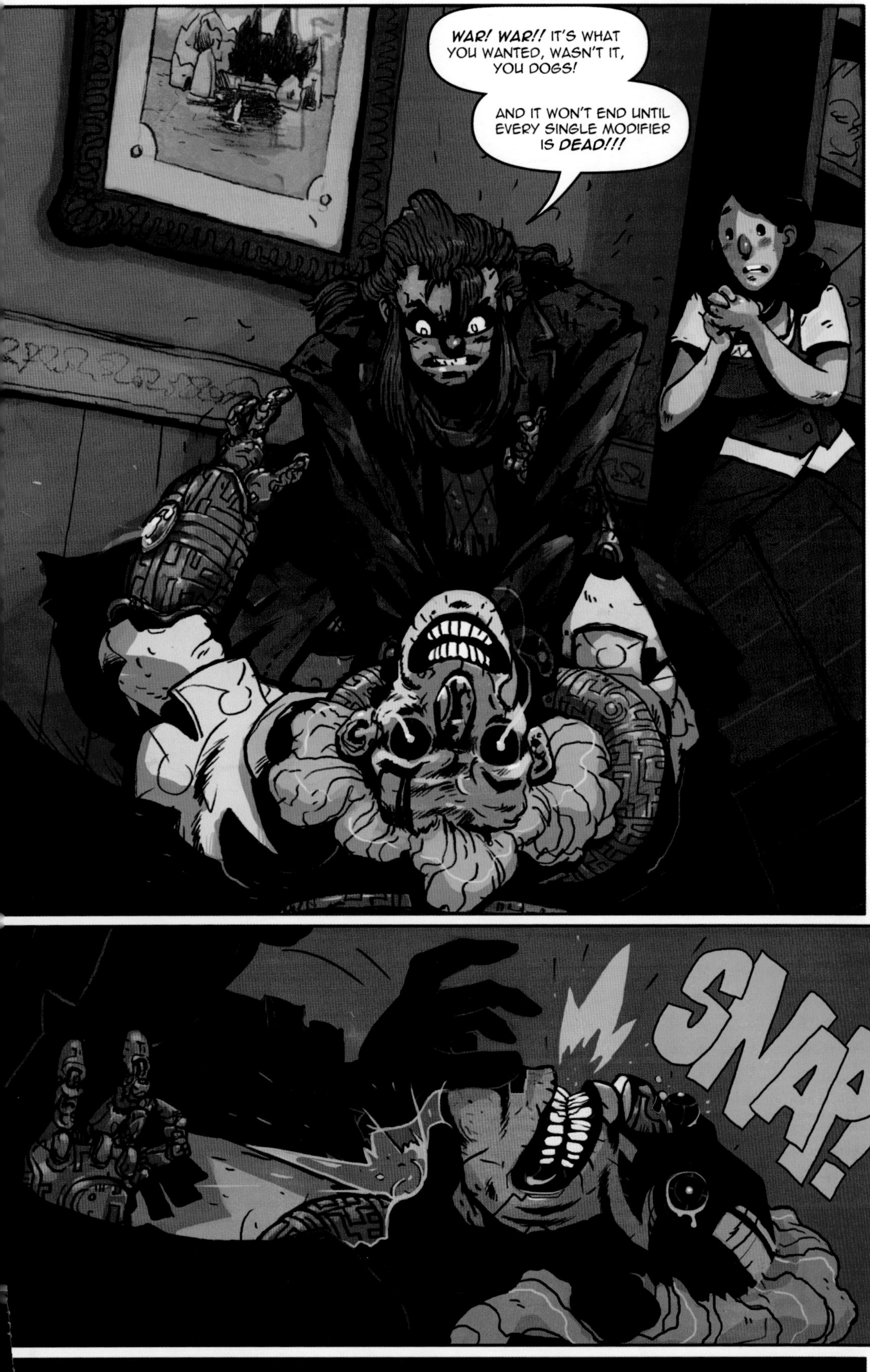
WAR! WAR!! IT'S WHAT YOU WANTED, WASN'T IT, YOU DOGS!
AND IT WON'T END UNTIL EVERY SINGLE MODIFIER IS DEAD!!!
SNAP!

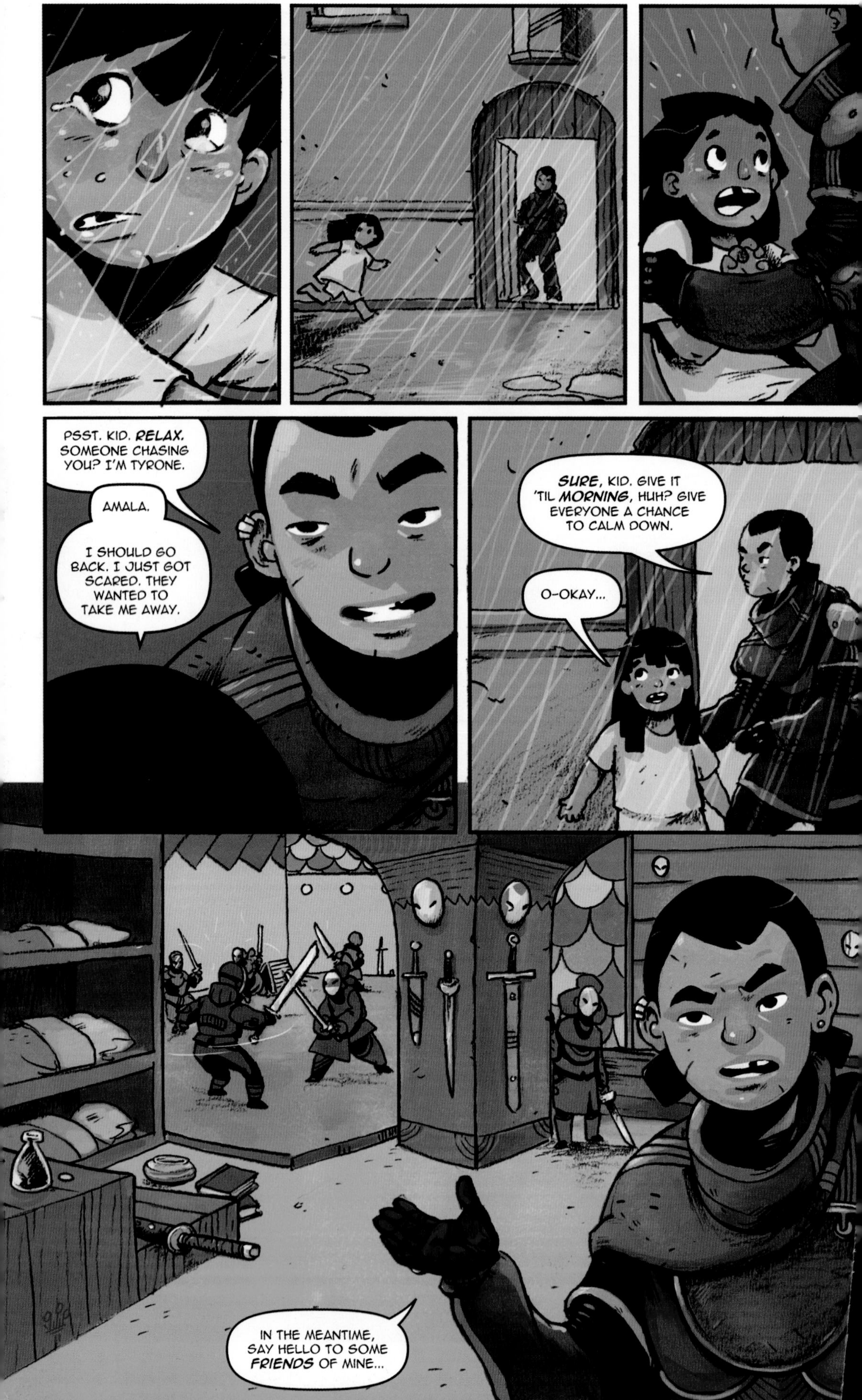
PSST. KID. **RELAX.** SOMEONE CHASING YOU? I'M TYRONE.
AMALA.
I SHOULD GO BACK. I JUST GOT SCARED. THEY WANTED TO TAKE ME AWAY.
SURE, KID. GIVE IT 'TIL **MORNING**, HUH? GIVE EVERYONE A CHANCE TO CALM DOWN.
O-OKAY...
IN THE MEANTIME, SAY HELLO TO SOME **FRIENDS** OF MINE...

STEVE HORTON is the cocreator, writer, and letterer of *Amala's Blade*. He's also all of the above for *Monstrous*, appearing in *Dark Horse Presents*. Steve has done a couple of short projects for DC Comics and has a whole lot of other comics in development. He spends his spare time with his wife, three kids, and impatient beagle.

Find more about Steve at About.Me/TropicalSteve.

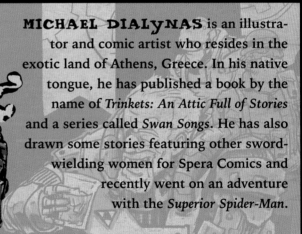

MICHAEL DIALYNAS is an illustrator and comic artist who resides in the exotic land of Athens, Greece. In his native tongue, he has published a book by the name of *Trinkets: An Attic Full of Stories* and a series called *Swan Songs*. He has also drawn some stories featuring other sword-wielding women for Spera Comics and recently went on an adventure with the *Superior Spider-Man*.

Find more about Michael at WoodenCrown.com.

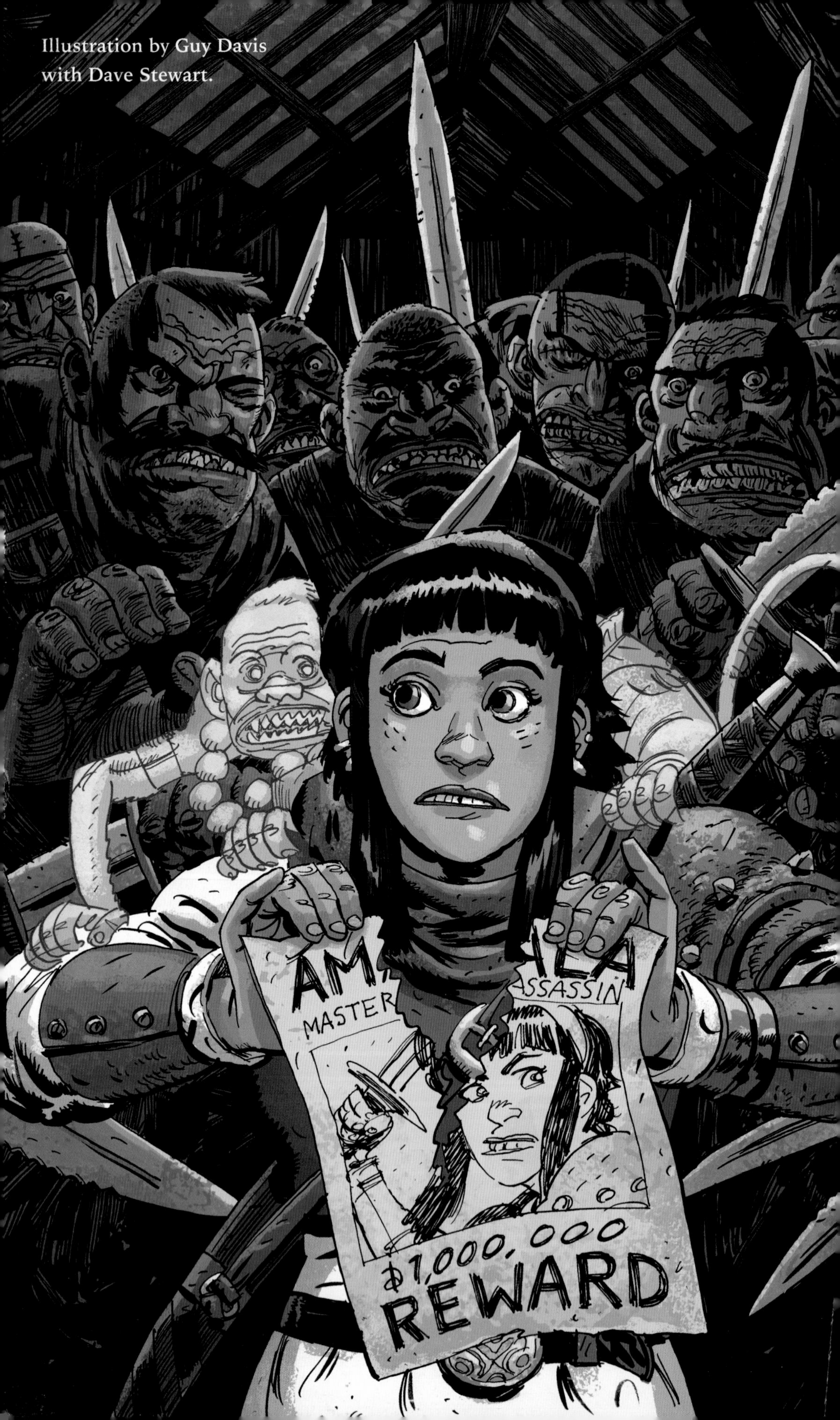
AM
LA
MASTER
ASSASSIN
1,000,000
REWARD

Illustration by Guy Davis
with Dave Stewart.